HNC HND BUSINESS

Core Unit 7:

Management Information Systems

Course Book

BPP

PUBLISHING

EDEXCEL HNC & HND BUSINESS

First edition August 2000

Second edition August 2002

ISBN 0 7517 7064 7 (previous edition 0 7517 7037 X)

British Library Cataloguing-in Publication Data

A catalogue record for this book is available from the British Library

Printed in Great Britain

Published by

BPP Publishing Limited

Aldine House, Aldine Place

London W12 8AW

www.bpp.com

We are grateful to Edexcel for permission to reproduce the Guidelines in this Text.

CONTENTS

Introduction		(v)
Edexcel Guidelines		(vii)
Study Guide		(ix)
1	Information and information systems	3
2	Information management	28
3	System design	54
4	System implementation, maintenance and review	82
5	Selecting and managing Information Technology	113
6	Using software: word processing and spreadsheets	150
7	Using software: more spreadsheets, databases and e-mail	196
8	Security and privacy	220
9	The impact of the IT revolution	234
Answers to assignments		251
Glossary		265
Index		269
Order form		
Review form		

INTRODUCTION

The HNC and HND qualifications in Business are very demanding. The suggested content, set out by Edexcel in guidelines for each unit, includes topics which are normally covered at degree level. Students therefore need books which get straight to the core of these topics, and which build upon the student's existing knowledge and experience. BPP's series of Course Books have been designed to meet that need.

This is the second edition of the Course Book for Unit 7: *Management Information Systems*. It covers the Edexcel guidelines and includes the following features.

- The Edexcel guidelines

- A study guide explaining the key features of the book and how to get the most from your studies

- A glossary and index

Unit 7 is a practical unit and your study should also include practical 'hands-on' exercises and real world case studies.

Each chapter contains:

- An introduction and study objectives

- Summary diagrams and signposts, to guide you through the chapter

- Numerous activities, topics for discussion, definitions and examples

- A chapter roundup, a quick quiz, answers to activities and an assignment

BPP Publishing are the leading providers of targeted texts for professional qualifications. Our customers need to study effectively. They cannot afford to waste time. They expect clear, concise and highly-focused study material. This series of Course Books for HNC and HND Business has been designed and produced to fulfil those needs.

BPP Publishing
August 2002

Titles in this series:

Core Unit 1	Marketing (8/00)
Core Unit 2	Managing Financial Resources (8/02)
Core Unit 3	Organisations and Behaviour (8/00)
Core Unit 4	Organisations, Competition and Environment (8/02)
Core Unit 5	Quantitative Techniques for Business (8/02)
Core Unit 6	Legal and Regulatory Framework (8/02)
Core Unit 7	Management Information Systems (8/02)
Core Unit 8	Business Strategy (8/00)
Option Units 9-12	Business & Finance (8/02)
Option Units 13-16	Business & Management (1/01)
Option Units 17-20	Business & Marketing (1/01)
Option Units 21-24	Business & Personnel (1/01)

For more information, or to place an order, please call 020 8740 2211, or fill in the order form at the back of this book.

If you would like to send in your comments on this book, please turn to the review form on the last page.

EDEXCEL GUIDELINES FOR CORE UNIT 7: MANAGEMENT INFORMATION SYSTEMS

Description of the Unit

The aim of this unit is to introduce the student to the role and function of management information systems in business operations. It will develop the students' ability to identify sources of management information and how these can be used in the decision-making process via electronic and paper-based communication. It will require the students to develop practical applications ability and knowledge as well as the ability to recommend how MIS should be used in business.

Outcomes and assessment criteria

The learning outcomes and the criteria used to assess them are shown in the table below.

Outcomes	Assessment criteria To achieve each outcome a student must demonstrate the ability to:
1 Explain the purpose and scope of MIS	• Evaluate the need for and use of internal and external business information in organisations • Discuss the contribution and limitations of MIS as an aid to improving business information • Evaluate the future impact of IT on MIS and improvement in organisational performance
2 Evaluate the use of MIS as a business management function	• Compare and contrast MIS in two differing organisations • Propose an MIS solution and implementation process for a given organisation • Recommend training requirements to support MIS implementation in a given situation
3 Identify and assess differing systems applications to store, retrieve and analyse data	• Use integrated packages to produce management information data which synthesises text, spreadsheet and database information • Identify and discuss the benefits and limitations of at least two different systems for improving business performance

Generating evidence

The evidence of outcomes can be in the form of written or oral assignments or tests. The assignments may be on real problems or case studies. Learning and assessment can be across units, at unit level or outcome level. Evidence could be at outcome level although opportunities exist for covering more than one outcome in an assignment.

Links

Opportunities exist for linking work in this unit with *Marketing* (Unit 1), *Quantitative Techniques for Business* (Unit 5) and *Business Strategy* (Unit 8).

This unit offers opportunities for demonstrating common skills in managing and developing self, communicating, managing tasks and solving problems and applying technology.

Resources

Library should provide the key texts. Access should be made available to computers which have the capacity to run integrated programmes. The use of text should be supported by use of broadsheet newspapers and information technology journals. Case studies, videos and documented examples of current practice and the dynamic use of MIS in organisations should illustrate the dynamic nature of this unit.

Websites can be useful in providing information and case studies (eg *www.bized.ac.uk* which provides business case studies appropriate for educational purposes).

Delivery

Wherever possible a link should be made between the academic underpinning and its practical application. Students should be given time to develop skills and analyse the benefits and limitations of the use of MIS in organisations. A 'hands on' approach should ensure that students can use integrated programmes and have a wide range of knowledge of different applications. The practical knowledge should be used to develop an awareness of how MIS can be adopted by organisations to improve business efficiency. This could be achieved via a tutor-developed case study or an evaluation of a local organisation. The use of outside speakers and visits of how organisations are using MIS to enhance business performance.

STUDY GUIDE

This text gives full coverage of the Edexcel guidelines. This text also includes features designed specifically to make learning effective and efficient.

(a)   Each chapter begins with a summary diagram which maps out the areas covered by the chapter. There are detailed summary diagrams at the start of each main section of the chapter. You can use the diagrams during revision as a basis for your notes.

(b)   After the main summary diagram there is an introduction, which sets the chapter in context. This is followed by learning objectives, which show you what you will learn as you work through the chapter.

(c)   Throughout the text, there are special aids to learning. These are indicated by symbols in the margin,

Signposts guide you through the text, showing how each section connects with the next.

Definitions give the meanings of key terms. The *glossary* at the end of the text summarises these.

Activities help you to test how much you have learnt. An indication of the time you should take on each is given. Answers are given at the end of each chapter.

Topics for discussion are for use in seminars. They give you a chance to share you views with your fellow students. They allow you to highlight holes in your knowledge and to see how others understand concepts. If you have time, try "teaching" someone the concepts you have learnt in a session. This helps you to remember key points and answering their questions will consolidate your knowledge.

Examples relate what you have learnt to the outside world. Try to think up your own examples as you work through the text.

Chapter roundups present the key information from the chapter in a concise format. Useful for revision.

(d) The wide **margin** on each page is for your notes. You will get the best out of this book if you interact with it. Write down your thoughts and ideas. Record examples, question theories, add references to other pages in the text and rephrase key points in your own words.

(e) At the end of each chapter, there is a **chapter roundup**, a **quick quiz** with answers and an **assignment**. Use these to revise and consolidate your knowledge. The chapter roundup summarises the chapter. The quick quiz tests what you have learnt (the answers often refer you back to the chapter so you can look over subjects again). The assignment (with a time guide) allows you to put your knowledge into practice. Answer guidelines for the assignments are at the end of the text.

(f) At the end of the text, there is a glossary of key terms and an index.

Management Information Systems

Chapter 1 :
INFORMATION AND INFORMATION SYSTEMS

Introduction

Welcome to Unit 7 Management Information Systems. In this Chapter we introduce the concept of an information system, and in particular a management information system.

We start with the information requirements of the modern organisation.

Your objectives

After completing this chapter you should:

(a)   Understand systems theory and its relevance to Management Information Systems (MIS).

(b)   Appreciate the information requirements of a range of organisations.

(c)   Know the main features of different types of MIS.

(d)   Be aware of a range of data collection methods.

NOTES

1 SYSTEMS THEORY

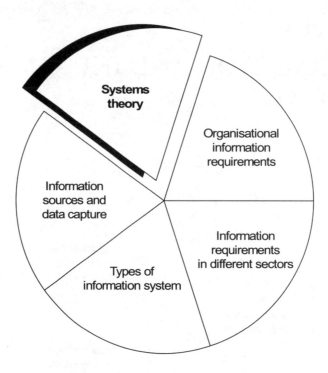

The term 'system' is hard to define because it is so widely used. One definition of a system is given below, followed by a definition relevant in a business context.

Definition

A **system** is a set of interacting components that operate together to accomplish a purpose.

A **business system** is a collection of people, machines and methods organised to accomplish a set of specific functions.

1.1 Why study systems theory?

An understanding of the concepts of systems theory is relevant to the design of Management Information Systems and it presents a particularly useful way of describing and analysing computer systems. The application of systems theory may:

(a) Create an awareness of subsystems (the different parts of an organisation), each with potentially conflicting goals which must be brought into line with each other.

(b) Help in the design and development of information systems to help decision makers ensure that decisions are made for the benefit of the organisation as a whole.

(c) Help identify the effect of the environment on systems. The external factors that affect an organisation may be wide ranging. For example, the government (in all its forms), competitors, trade unions, creditors and shareholders all have an interactive link with an organisation.

(d)   Highlight the dynamic aspects of the business organisation, and the factors which influence the growth and development of all its subsystems.

1.2   The component parts of a system

A system has three component parts: inputs, processes and outputs.

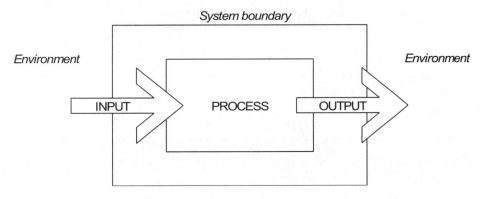

Inputs

Inputs provide the system with what it needs to be able to operate. Input may vary from matter, energy or human actions, to information.

(a)   Matter might include, in a manufacturing operation, adhesives or rivets.

(b)   Human input might consist of typing an instruction booklet or starting up a piece of machinery.

Inputs may be outputs from other systems. For example, output from a transactions processing system may be input to an executive support system.

Processes

A process transforms an input into an output. Processes may involve tasks performed by people, machines, computers, chemicals and a wide range of other actions.

Outputs

Outputs are the results of the processing. They could be said to represent the purpose for which the system exists. Many outputs are used as inputs to other systems.

1.3   The system boundary

Every system has a boundary that separates it from its environment. For example, an accounting department's boundary can be expressed in terms of who works in it and what work it does. This boundary will separate it from other departments, such as the marketing department.

1.4 The environment

Anything which is outside the system boundary belongs to the system's environment. A system accepts inputs from the environment and provides outputs into the environment.

Often, whether something is a system or a subsystem is a matter of definition, and depends on the context of the observer. For example, an organisation is a social system, and its 'environment' may be seen as society as a whole. Another way of looking at an organisation would be to regard it as a subsystem of the entire social system. Information links up the different systems and subsystems in an organisation.

1.5 Open systems and closed systems

In systems theory a distinction is made between open systems and closed systems.

Definitions

> A **closed system** is a system which is isolated from its environment and independent of it.
>
> An **open system** is a system connected to an interacting with its environment.

All business organisations, have some interaction with their environment, and so are open systems.

Open and closed systems can be described by diagram as follows.

Closed system

```
┌─────────────────────┐
│  ┌───────────────┐  │
│  │  Shut off from │  │
│  │ its environment│  │
│  └───────────────┘  │
└─────────────────────┘
```

Open system

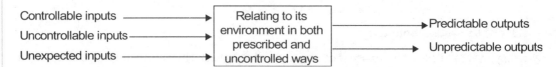

Controllable inputs ───────▶
Uncontrollable inputs ─────▶   Relating to its environment in both prescribed and uncontrolled ways   ───▶ Predictable outputs
Unexpected inputs ─────────▶   ───▶ Unpredictable outputs

A business is an open system where management decisions are influenced by or have an influence on suppliers, customers, competitors, society as a whole and the government.

1.6 Control systems

A system must be controlled to keep it steady or enable it to change safely, in other words each system must have its control system. Control is required because unpredictable disturbances arise and enter the system, so that actual results (outputs of the system) deviate from the expected results.

Examples of disturbances in a business system would be the entry of a powerful new competitor into the market, an unexpected rise in labour costs, the failure of a supplier to deliver promised raw materials, or the tendency of employees to stop working in order to chatter or gossip.

A control system must ensure that the business is capable of surviving these disturbances by dealing with them in an appropriate manner.

To have a control system, there has to be a plan, standard, budget, rule book or some other guideline towards which the system as a whole should be aiming. The standard is defined by the objectives of the system.

1.7   Feedback

Feedback is the return of part of the output of a system to the input as a means towards improved quality or correction of errors. In a business organisation, feedback is information produced from within the organisation (for example management control reports) with the purpose of helping management and other employees and triggering control decisions.

Definition

> **Feedback** may be defined as modification or control of a process or system by its results or effects, by measuring differences between desired and actual results.

In a control system part of the output is fed back, so that the output can initiate control action to change either the activities of the system or the system's input.

You might like to think of a budgetary control system in a company, by which results are monitored, deviations from plan are identified and control (corrective) action taken as appropriate.

1.8   Filtering

Definition

> **Filtering** means removing 'impurities' such as excessive detail from data as it is passed up the organisation hierarchy.

Operational staff may need all the detail to do their jobs, but when they report to higher and higher subsystems the data can be progressively summarised. Unnecessary detail is filtered out leaving only the important points.

A possible problem with this is that sometimes the 'filter' may let through unimportant information and/or remove important information, with the result that the message is distorted at the next level.

2   ORGANISATIONAL INFORMATION REQUIREMENTS

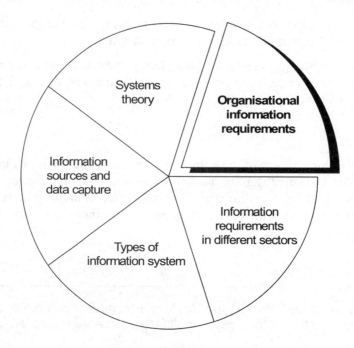

Definitions

Data is the raw material for data processing. Data consists of numbers, letters and symbols and relates to facts, events, and transactions.

Information is data that has been processed in such a way as to be meaningful to the person who receives it.

2.1   What is information used for?

All organisations require information for a range of purposes. These can be categorised as follows.

- Information for planning
- Information for controlling
- Information for recording transactions
- Information for performance measurement
- Information for decision making

Planning

Planning requires a knowledge of the available resources, possible time-scales and the likely outcome under alternative scenarios. Information is required that helps decision making, and how to implement decisions taken.

Controlling

Once a plan is implemented, its actual performance must be controlled. Information is required to assess whether it is proceeding as planned or whether there is some unexpected deviation from plan. It may consequently be necessary to take some form of corrective action.

Recording transactions

Information about each transaction or event is required. Reasons include:

(a)   Documentation of transactions can be used as evidence in a case of dispute.

(b)   There may be a legal requirement to record transactions, for example for accounting and audit purposes.

(c)   Operational information can be built up, allowing control action to be taken.

Performance measurement

Just as individual operations need to be controlled, so overall performance must be measured. Comparisons against budget or plan are able to be made. This may involve the collection of information on, for example, costs, revenues, volumes, time-scale and profitability.

Decision making

Good quality information should lead to better informed decisions.

2.2   Types of information

Strategic information

Strategic information is used to plan the objectives of the organisation, and to assess whether the objectives are being met in practice. Such information includes overall profitability, the profitability of different segments of the business, future market prospects, the availability and cost of raising new funds, total cash needs, total manning levels and capital equipment needs.

Strategic information is:

- Derived from both internal and external sources
- Summarised at a high level
- Relevant to the long term
- Concerned with the whole organisation
- Often prepared on an 'ad hoc' basis
- Both quantitative and qualitative
- Uncertain, as the future cannot be predicted

Tactical information

Tactical information is used to decide how the resources of the business should be employed, and to monitor how they are being and have been employed. Such information includes productivity measurements (output per man hour or per machine hour) budgetary control or variance analysis reports, and cash flow forecasts, manning levels and profit results within a particular department of the organisation, labour turnover statistics within a department and short-term purchasing requirements.

Tactical information is:

- Primarily generated internally (but may have a limited external component)
- Summarised at a lower level
- Relevant to the short and medium term
- Concerned with activities or departments
- Prepared routinely and regularly
- Based on quantitative measures

NOTES

Operational information

Operational information is used to ensure that specific tasks are planned and carried out properly within a factory or office.

In the payroll office, for example, operational information relating to day-rate labour will include the hours worked each week by each employee, his rate of pay per hour, details of his deductions, and for the purpose of wages analysis, details of the time each man spent on individual jobs during the week. In this example, the information is required weekly, but more urgent operational information, such as the amount of raw materials being input to a production process, may be required daily, hourly, or in the case of automated production, second by second.

Operational information is:

- Derived from internal sources
- Detailed, being the processing of raw data
- Relevant to the immediate term
- Task-specific
- Prepared very frequently
- Largely quantitative

2.3 The qualities of good information

'Good' information is information that adds to the understanding of a situation. The qualities of good information are outlined in the following table.

Quality		Example
A	currate	Figures should add up, the degree of rounding should be appropriate, there should be no typos, items should be allocated to the correct category, assumptions should be stated for uncertain information.
C	omplete	Information should includes everything that it needs to include, for example external data if relevant, or comparative information.
C	ost-beneficial	It should not cost more to obtain the information than the benefit derived from having it. Providers or information should be given efficient means of collecting and analysing it. Presentation should be such that users do not waste time working out what it means.
U	ser-targeted	The needs of the user should be borne in mind, for instance senior managers need summaries, junior ones need detail.
R	elevant	Information that is not needed for a decision should be omitted, no matter how 'interesting' it may be.
A	uthoritative	The source of the information should be a reliable one (not, for instance, 'Joe Bloggs Predictions Page' on the Internet unless Joe Bloggs is known to be a reliable source for that type of information).
T	imely	The information should be available when it is needed.
E	asy to use	Information should be clearly presented, not excessively long, and sent using the right medium and communication channel (e-mail, telephone, hard-copy report etc).

Perfect information

Obtaining more information first about what is likely to happen can sometimes reduce the uncertainty about the future outcome from taking a decision. We can categorise information depending upon how reliable it is likely to be for predicting what will happen in the future and hence for helping managers to make better decisions.

Definitions

> **Perfect information** is information that is guaranteed to predict the future with 100% accuracy.
>
> **Imperfect information** is information which cannot be guaranteed to be completely accurate. Almost all information is therefore imperfect - but may still be very useful.

Improvements to information

The table on the following page contains suggestions as to how poor information can be improved.

Feature	Example of possible improvements
Accurate	Use computerised systems with automatic input checks rather than manual systems.
	Allow sufficient time for collation and analysis of data if pinpoint accuracy is crucial.
	Incorporate elements of probability within projections so that the required response to different future scenarios can be assessed.
Complete	Include past data as a reference point for future projections.
	Include any planned developments, such as new products.
	Information about future demand would be more useful than information about past demand.
	Include external data.
Cost-beneficial	Always bear in mind whether the benefit of having the information is greater than the cost of obtaining it.
User-targeted	Information should be summarised and presented together with relevant ratios or percentages.
Relevant	The purpose of the report should be defined. It may be trying to fulfil too many purposes at once. Perhaps several shorter reports would be more effective.
	Information should include exception reporting, where only those items that are worthy of note - and the control actions taken by more junior managers to deal with them - are reported.

Feature	Example of possible improvements
Authoritative	Use reliable sources and experienced personnel.
	If some figures are derived from other figures the method of derivation should be explained.
Timely	Information collection and analysis by production managers needs to be speeded up considerably, probably by the introduction of better information systems.
Easy-to-use	Graphical presentation, allowing trends to be quickly assimilated and relevant action decided upon.
	Alternative methods of presentation should be considered, such as graphs or charts, to make it easier to review the information at a glance. Numerical information is sometimes best summarised in narrative form or vice versa.
	A 'house style' for reports should be devised and adhered to by all. This would cover such matters as number of decimal places to use, table headings and labels, paragraph numbering and so on.

3   INFORMATION REQUIREMENTS IN DIFFERENT SECTORS

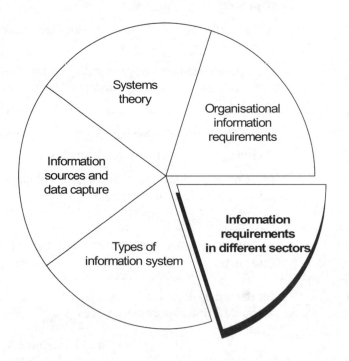

The following table provides examples of the typical information requirements of organisations operating in different sectors.

Sector	Information type	Example(s)	General comment
Manufacturing	Strategic	Future demand estimates New product development plans Competitor analysis	The information requirements of commercial organisations are influenced by the need to make and monitor profit. Information that contributes to the following measures is important: • Changeover times • Number of common parts • Level of product diversity • Product and process quality
	Tactical	Variance analysis Departmental accounts Stock turnover	
	Operational	Production reject rate Materials and labour used Stock levels	
Service	Strategic	Forecast sales growth and market share Profitability, capital structure	Organisations have become more customer and results-oriented over the last decade. As a consequence, the difference between service and other organisations information requirements has decreased. Businesses have realised that most of their activities can be measured, and many can be measured in similar ways regardless of the business sector.
	Tactical	Resource utilisation such as average staff time charged out, number of customers per hairdresser, number of staff per account Customer satisfaction rating	
	Operational	Staff timesheets Customer waiting time Individual customer feedback	

NOTES

Sector	Information type	Example(s)	General comment
Public	Strategic	Population demographics	Public sector (and non-profit making) organisations often don't have one overriding objective. Their information requirements depend on the objectives chosen. The information provided often requires interpretation (eg student exam results are not affected by the quality of teaching alone).
		Expected government policy	
	Tactical	Hospital occupancy rates	
		Average class sizes	
		Percent of reported crimes solved	
	Operational	Staff timesheets	
		Vehicles available	
		Student daily attendance records	Information may compare actual performance with:
			• Standards
			• Targets
			• Similar activities
			• Indices
			• Activities over time as trends
Non-Profit / charities	Strategic	Activities of other charities	Many of the comments regarding Public Sector organisations can be applied to not- for- profit organisations.
		Government (and in some cases overseas government) policy	
		Public attitudes	Information to judge performance usually aims to assess economy, efficiency and effectiveness.
	Tactical	Percent of revenue spent on admin	
		Average donation	
		'Customer' satisfaction statistics	A key measure of efficiency for charities is the percentage of revenue that is spent on the publicised cause. (eg rather than on advertising or administration).
	Operational	Households collected from / approached	
		Banking documentation	
		Donations	

PUBLISHING

4 TYPES OF INFORMATION SYSTEM

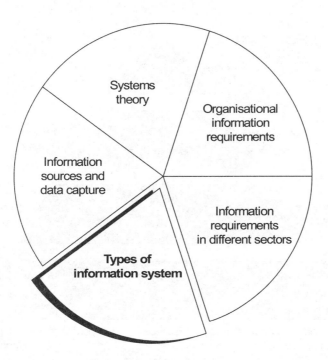

4.1 What is a Management Information System?

Definition

Two definitions of the term Management Information System (MIS) are shown below.

A **Management Information System (MIS)** converts data from internal and external sources into information, and communicates that information in an appropriate form to managers at all levels. This enables them to make timely and effective decisions for planning, directing and controlling the activities for which they are responsible.

(Lucey, *Management Information Systems*)

A computer system or related group of systems which collects and presents management information to a business in order to facilitate control.

(CIMA, *Computing Terminology*)

A modern organisation requires a **wide range of systems** to hold, process and analyse information. We will now examine the various information systems used to serve organisational information requirements.

Organisations require different **types of information system** to provide different **levels of information** in a range of **functional areas**. One way of portraying this concept is shown on the following diagram (taken from *Laudon* and *Laudon*, *Management Information Systems*).

Types of information systems

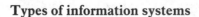
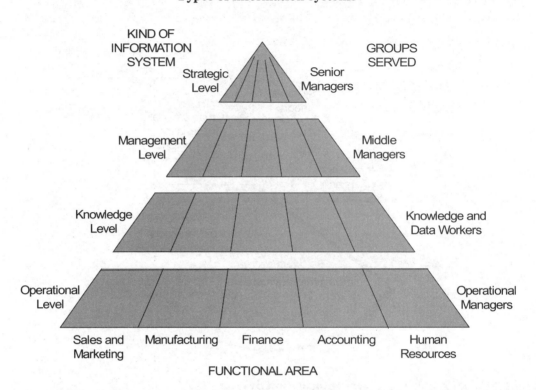

System level	System purpose
Strategic	To help senior managers with long-term planning. Their main function is to ensure changes in the external environment are matched by the organisation's capabilities.
Management	To help middle managers monitor and control. These systems check if things are working well or not. Some management- level systems support non-routine decision making such as 'what if?' analyses.
Knowledge	To help knowledge and data workers design products, distribute information and perform administrative tasks. These systems help the organisation integrate new and existing knowledge into the business and to reduce the reliance on paper documents.
Operational	To help operational managers track the organisation's day-to-day operational activities. These systems enable routine queries to be answered, and transactions to be processed and tracked.

4.2 Executive Support Systems (ESS)

Definition

> An **Executive Support System (ESS)** pools data from internal and external sources and makes information available to senior managers in an easy-to-use form. ESS help senior managers make strategic, unstructured decisions.

An ESS should provide senior managers with easy access to key **internal and external** information. The system summarises and tracks strategically critical information, possibly drawn from internal MIS and DSS, but also including data from external sources eg competitors, legislation, external databases such as Reuters.

An ESS is likely to have the following **features**.

- Flexibility
- Quick response time
- Sophisticated data analysis and modelling tools

A model of a typical ESS is shown below.

An Executive Support System (ESS)

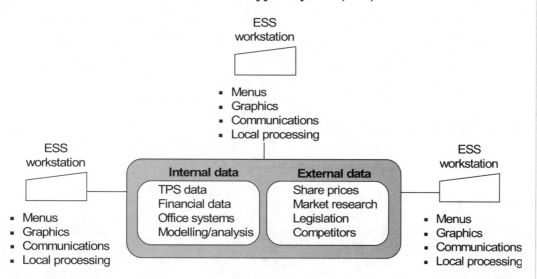

4.3   Decision Support Systems (DSS)

Definition

> **Decision Support Systems (DSS)** combine data and analytical models or data analysis tools to support semi-structured and unstructured decision making.

DSS are used by management to assist in making decisions on issues which are subject to high levels of uncertainty about the problem, the various **responses** which management could undertake or the likely **impact** of those actions.

Decision support systems are intended to provide a wide range of alternative information gathering and analytical tools with a major emphasis upon **flexibility** and **user-friendliness**.

DSS have more analytical power than other systems enabling them to analyse and condense large volumes of data into a form that aids managers make decisions. The objective is to allow the manager to consider a number of **alternatives** and evaluate them under a variety of potential conditions.

4.4 Knowledge Work Systems (KWS)

Definition

> **Knowledge Work Systems (KWS)** are information systems that facilitate the creation and integration of new knowledge into an organisation.
>
> **Knowledge Workers** are people whose jobs consist of primarily creating new information and knowledge. They are often members of a profession such as doctors, engineers, lawyers and scientists.

KWS help knowledge workers create new knowledge and expertise. Examples include:

- Computer Aided Design (CAD)
- Computer Aided Manufacturing (CAM)
- Specialised financial software that analyses trading situations

We look at KWS in greater detail in Chapter 2.

4.5 Office Automation Systems (OAS)

Definition

> **Office Automation Systems (OAS)** are computer systems designed to increase the productivity of data and information workers.

OAS support the major activities performed in a typical office such as document management, facilitating communication and managing data. Examples include:

- Word processing, desktop publishing, and digital filing systems
- E-mail, voice mail, videoconferencing, groupware, intranets, schedulers
- Spreadsheets, desktop databases

4.6 Transaction Processing Systems (TPS)

Definition

> A **Transaction Processing System (TPS)** performs and records routine transactions.

TPS are used for **routine tasks** in which data items or transactions must be processed so that operations can continue. TPS support most business functions in most types of organisations. The following table shows a range of TPS applications.

Transaction processing systems					
	Sales/marketing systems	**Manufacturing/ production systems**	**Finance/ accounting systems**	**Human resources systems**	**Other types (eg university)**
Major functions of system	• Sales management • Market research • Promotion • Pricing • New products	• Scheduling • Purchasing Shipping/ receiving • Engineering • Operations	• Budgeting • General ledger • Billing • Management accounting	• Personnel records • Benefits • Salaries • Labour relations • Training	• Admissions • Student academic records • Course records • Graduates
Major application systems	• Sales order information system • Market research system • Pricing system	• Materials resource planning • Purchase order control • Engineering • Quality control	• General ledge • Accounts receivable/ payable • Budgeting • Funds management	• Payroll • Employee records • Employee benefits • Career path systems	• Registration • Student record • Curriculum/ class control systems • Benefactor information system

Batch processing and On-line processing

A TPS will process transactions using either **batch** processing or **on-line** processing.

Batch processing involves transactions being **grouped** and **stored** before being processed at regular intervals, such as daily, weekly or monthly. Because data is not input as soon as it is received the system will not always be up-to-date.

The lack of up-to-date information means batch processing is usually not suitable for systems involving customer contact. Batch processing is suitable for internal, regular tasks such as payroll.

On-line processing involves transactions being input and processed immediately. An airline ticket sales and reservation system is an example.

The workings of both processing methods are shown in the following diagram.

Batch processing and on-line processing

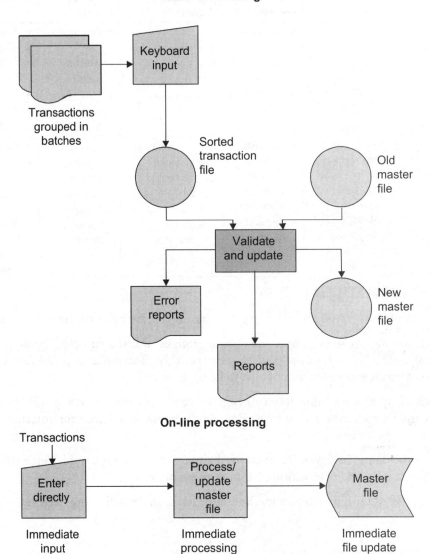

4.7 System dependencies and integration

The types of system we have identified exchange data with each other. The ease with which data flows from one system to another depends on the extent of **integration** between systems.

The level of automated integration will depend on the nature of the organisation and the systems involved. The cost of integrating systems (eg programmer time) should be considered against benefits of integration (quicker availability of information, less time spent inputting information).

Interrelationships between systems are shown in the following diagram from *Loudon and Loudon*.

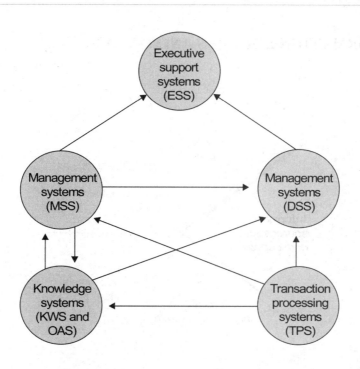

4.8 Information systems: levels, types and functions

Examples of the levels and types of information system we have discussed in this section are shown in the following diagram.

TYPES OF SYSTEMS	Strategic-Level Systems				
Executive Support Systems (ESS)	5-year sales trend forecasting	5-year operating plan	5-year budget forecasting	Profit planning	Human resource planning

	Management-Level Systems				
Management Support Systems (MSS)	Sales management	Inventory control	Annual budgeting	Capital investment analysis	Relocation analysis
Decision Support Systems (DSS)	Sales region analysis	Production scheduling	Cost analysis	Pricing/profit ability analysis	Contract cost analysis

	Knowledge-Level System		
Knowledge Work Systems (KWS)	Engineering workstations	Graphics workstations	Managerial workstations
Office Automation Systems (OAS)	Word processing	Document imaging	Electronic calendars

	Operational-Level Systems				
		Machine control	Securities trading	Payroll	Compensation
Transaction Processing Systems (TPS)	Order tracking	Plant scheduling		Accounts payable	Training & development
	Order processing	Material movement control	Cash management	Accounts receivable	Employee record keeping
	Sales and Marketing	**Manufacturing**	**Finance**	**Accounting**	**Human Resources**

5 INFORMATION SOURCES AND DATA CAPTURE

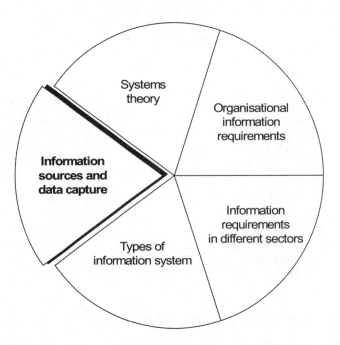

Data and information come from sources both inside and outside an organisation. An information system should be designed so as to obtain - or capture - all relevant data and information.

5.1 Internal information

Capturing data/information from inside the organisation involves the following.

(a) A system for collecting or measuring transactions data - for example sales, purchases, stock turnover etc which sets out procedures for what data is collected, how frequently, by whom, and by what methods, and how it is processed, and filed or communicated.

(b) Communication between managers and staff (for example, by word-of-mouth, meetings, e-mail or via an intranet).

(c) Managing knowledge and information to ensure it is available to those who need it.

5.2 Internal data sources

The accounting records

You should be familiar with various accounting ledgers such as sales ledgers and purchase ledgers, general ledgers, cash books and so on. Some of this information is of value outside the accounts department, for example, sales information for the marketing function.

These ledgers hold valuable information. A stock control system is a good example: besides actually recording the monetary value of purchases and stock in hand for financial reporting purposes, the system will include purchase orders, goods received notes, goods returned notes and so on, and these can be analysed to provide management information about speed of delivery, say, or the quality of supplies.

Other internal sources

Much information that is not strictly part of the accounting records nevertheless is closely tied in to the accounting system.

(a) Information about personnel will be linked to the payroll system. Additional information may be obtained from this source if, say, a project is being costed and it is necessary to ascertain the availability and rate of pay of different levels of staff, or the need for and cost of recruiting staff from outside the organisation.

(b) Much information will be produced by a production department about machine capacity, fuel consumption, movement of people, materials, and work in progress, set up times, maintenance requirements and so on. A large part of the traditional work of cost accounting involves ascribing costs to the physical information produced by this source.

(c) Many service businesses, notably accountants and solicitors, need to keep detailed records of the time spent on various activities, both to justify fees to clients and to assess the efficiency and profitability of operations.

(d) Staff themselves are one of the primary sources of internal information. Information may be obtained either informally in the course of day-to-day business or through meetings, interviews or questionnaires.

5.3 External information

Capturing information from outside the organisation might be entrusted to particular individuals, or might be 'informal'.

Formal collection of data from outside sources includes the following.

(a) A company's tax specialists will be expected to gather information about changes in tax law and how this will affect the company.

(b) Obtaining information about any new legislation on health and safety at work, or employment regulations, must be the responsibility of a particular person - for example the company's legal expert or company secretary - who must then pass on the information to other managers affected by it.

(c) Research and development (R & D) work often relies on information about other R & D work being done by another company or by government institutions. An R & D official might be made responsible for finding out about R & D work in the company.

(d) Marketing managers need to know about the opinions and buying attitudes of potential customers. To obtain this information, they might carry out market research exercises.

Informal gathering of information from the environment goes on all the time, consciously or unconsciously, because the employees of an organisation learn what is going on in the world around them - perhaps from newspapers, television reports, meetings with business associates or the trade press.

5.4 External data sources

An organisation's files are full of external information such as invoices, letters, advertisements and so on received from customers and suppliers. But there are many occasions when an active search outside the organisation is necessary.

Definition

> The phrase **environmental scanning** is often used to describe the process of gathering external information, which is available from a wide range of sources.

(a) The government.

(b) Advice or information bureaux.

(c) Consultancies of all sorts.

(d) Newspaper and magazine publishers.

(e) There may be specific reference works which are used in a particular line of work.

(f) Libraries and information services.

(g) Increasingly businesses can use each other's systems as sources of information, for instance via electronic data interchange (EDI).

(h) Electronic sources of information are becoming increasingly important.

   (i) For some time there have been 'viewdata' services such as Prestel offering a very large bank of information gathered from organisations such as the Office for National Statistics, newspapers and the British Library. Topic offers information on the stock market. Companies like Reuters operate primarily in the field of provision of information.

   (ii) **The Internet** is a vast network linking up millions of computers across the world via telecommunications links. We look at the Internet in detail in Chapter 5.

Activity 1   (20 minutes)

Drawing on personal experience (if possible), give five examples of the inefficient use of information.

FOR DISCUSSION

Discuss your examples from Activity 1 with others in your group.

With organisations able to collect and store ever-increasing amounts of information, the importance of managing information effectively can not be over-stated. We look at how information can be managed in the next chapter.

Chapter roundup

- General system principles apply to any type of system, including management information systems.

- Any system can be thought of in terms of inputs, processing and outputs.

- An environment surrounds the system but is not part of it. A systems boundary separates the system from its environment.

- An open system has a relationship with its environment which has both prescribed and uncontrolled elements.

- A closed system is shut off from its environment and has no relationship with it.

- Control in a system is needed to ensure that the system's operations go according to plan. Control cannot be applied unless there is information about the operations of the system

- Feedback is control information generated by the system itself, and involves a comparison of actual results against the target or plan.

- Organisations require information for recording transactions, measuring performance, making decisions, planning and controlling.

- 'Good' information aids understanding. ACCURATE is a handy mnemonic for the qualities of good information.

- An organisation's information requirements will be influenced by the sector they operate in.

- Information may be strategic, tactical or operational.

- A wide range of systems are available to hold, process and analyse information. Examples include ESS, DSS, KWS, OAS and TPS.

- An information system should be designed to obtain information from all relevant sources - both internal and external.

Quick quiz

1   List the three component parts of a system. (See section 1.2)

2   Distinguish between strategic, tactical and operational information. (See section 2.2)

3   List five qualities of 'good' information. (See section 2.3)

4   Give an example of strategic, tactical and operational information relevant to an organisation operating in the service sector. (See section 3)

5   Decision support systems are used for routine decisions. TRUE or FALSE? (See section 4.3)

6   Distinguish between batch processing and on-line processing. (See section 4.6)

7   What does 'environmental scanning' mean? (See section 5.4)

Answers to Activities

1   There are many possible suggestions, including those given below.

The organisation's bankers take decisions affecting the amount of money they are prepared to lend.

The public might have an interest in information relating to an organisation's products or services.

The media (press, television etc) use information generated by organisations in news stories, and such information can adversely or favourably affect an organisation's relationship with its environment.

The government (for example the Department of Trade and Industry) regularly requires organisational information.

The Inland Revenue and HM Customs and Excise authorities require information for taxation and VAT assessments.

An organisation's suppliers and customers take decisions whether or not to trade with the organisation.

Assignment 1 (30 minutes)

Cheap 'n' Cheerful is a nationwide chain of supermarkets. The main retail areas are food and drink. Currently the chain is attempting to diversify into other lines such as clothing and electrical goods like refrigerators and dishwashers.

The company plan to introduce a customer loyalty card, called Privilege, to retain existing customers and to attract new customers by offering discounts on selected purchases. Cardholders who are very frequent shoppers will also receive a discount of 5% on all cash purchases. It is envisaged that lapsed customers who have owned a Privilege card will be targeted with special offers in an attempt to entice them back to Cheap 'n' Cheerful stores.

The management of Cheap 'n' Cheerful believes that their information system will be able to gather significant amounts of data on their customers' behaviour that will allow the chain to predict shopping patterns and lifestyle aspirations. This data will be sold to other retail organisations who pose no competitive threat to Cheap 'n' Cheerful.

Tasks

(a) Explain the differences between data and information. Illustrate your answer with examples from the case study and your experience.

(b) Explain how the information gathered can be used as an aid to decision making by Cheap 'n' Cheerful.

Chapter 2 :
INFORMATION MANAGEMENT

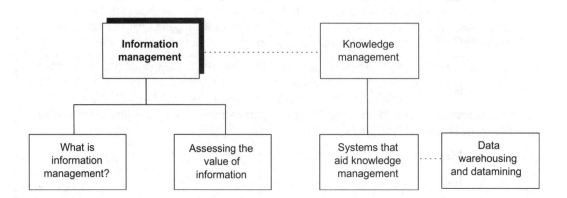

Introduction

The modern business environment can be volatile. Businesses are increasingly reliant on good quality information and knowledge to anticipate and respond to change. As the importance of information and knowledge has increased, organisations have come to realise that, like any other valuable resource, **information and knowledge should be managed effectively.**

Your objectives

After completing this chapter you should:

    (a)   Understand the importance of information to modern organisations.

    (b)   Understand the concepts of information management and knowledge management.

    (c)   Be able to describe some widely used information management tools and techniques.

1 WHAT IS INFORMATION MANAGEMENT?

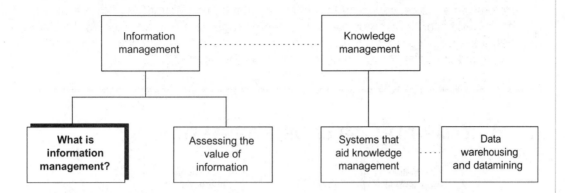

1.1 What is information management?

Information must be managed just like any other organisational resource. Information management entails the following tasks.

(a) Identifying current and future information **needs**.

(b) Identifying information **sources**.

(c) **Collecting** the information.

(d) **Storing** the information.

(e) Facilitating existing methods of **using** information and identifying new ways of using it.

(f) Ensuring that information is **communicated** to those who need it, and is **not communicated** to those who are **not** entitled to see it.

Technology has provided new sources of information, new ways of collecting it, storing it and processing it, and new methods of communicating and sharing it. This in turn has meant that information needs have **changed** and will continue to change as new technologies become available.

Although computing and telecommunications technology provide fabulous tools for carrying out the information management tasks listed above, they are **not always the best tools**; nor are they always even available.

1.2 Users of information

The information generated by an organisation may be used internally or externally. **Internal** users of information include (by status) the following.

- The board (or equivalent)
- Directors with functional responsibilities
- Divisional general managers
- Divisional heads
- Departmental heads
- Section leaders, forepeople or supervisors
- Employees

Activity 1 **(20 minutes)**

It is important to bear in mind that information may be relevant to people outside the organisation as well as to its internal management and employees. In fact, decisions relating to an organisation can be taken by outsiders. Give four examples of decisions which may be taken by outsiders.

---

2 ASSESSING THE VALUE OF INFORMATION

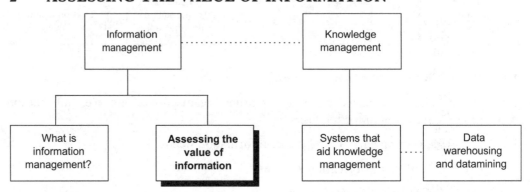

2.1 Factors that make information a valuable commodity

Information is now recognised as a valuable resource that can enable an organisation to establish an advantage over their competitors; a **competitive advantage**. Easy **access** to information, the **quality** of that information and **speedy methods of exchanging** the information have become essential elements of business success.

Organisations that make **good use of information** in decision-making, and which use new technologies to access, process and exchange information are likely to be **best placed to survive** in increasingly competitive world markets.

The **factors which make information valuable** are as follows.

(a) The **source** of the information

If the information comes from a source that is widely known and respected for quality, thoroughness and accuracy (Reuters, say, or the BBC) it will be more valuable to users than information from an unknown or untested source, because it can be relied upon with confidence.

(b) The ease of assimilation

Modern methods of presentation can use not only words and figures but also **colour graphics, sound and movement**. This makes the receipt of information a richer (and so more valuable) experience, and it means that information can be more easily, and therefore more quickly, understood: again a feature that people will be willing to pay for.

(c) Accessibility

If information can be made available in an easily accessible place (such as the **Internet**) users do not have to commit too much time and effort to retrieve it. If just a few sentences of information is required, and they can find these (for instance using an Internet search engine) without having to buy a whole book or newspaper, then they should be willing to pay for this convenience.

Information which is **obtained but not used** has no value to the person that obtains it. Also, an item of information which leads to savings of £90 is not worth having if it costs £100 to collect.

Activity 2 **(20 minutes)**

The value of information lies in the action taken as a result of receiving it. What questions might you ask in order to make an assessment of the value of information?

An assessment of the value of information can be derived in this way, and the cost of obtaining it should then be compared against this value. On the basis of this comparison, it can be decided whether certain items of information are worth having. It should be remembered that there may also be intangible benefits which may be harder to quantify.

Deciding whether it is worthwhile having more information should depend on the **benefits** expected from getting it and the **extra costs** of obtaining it. The benefits of more information should be measured in terms of the difference it would make to management decisions if the information were made available.

2.2 Assessing cost and value

The information system is used to produce a wide variety of information. The **cost** of an individual item of information is **not always easy to quantify**. For example, if a manager uses a MIS to obtain the sales history of a customer what is the cost of this enquiry? The cost is difficult to calculate because:

(a) The information **already exists**, as it is used for a number of different purposes. It might be impossible to predict how often it will be used, and hence the economic benefits to be derived from it.

(b) The information system which is used to process these requests has also been purchased..

Just as the costs of an item of information are hard to assess, so too the **benefits are often hard to quantify**. While nobody doubts that information is vital, it is not always easy to construct an economic assessment of the value of information. For example a monthly variance analysis report may lead to operational decisions being made but the economic consequences of this decision may not be easy to predict or **measure**.

Traditional methods

Traditional **investment appraisal methods** can be applied with varying degrees of success to problems of this kind. There are three principal methods of evaluating a capital project: the payback method, the accounting rate of return and discounted cashflow methods.

These methods are explained in HND Unit 2. You may need to revise this material before attempting the following activity.

Activity 3 (Revision from HND Unit 2) **(30 minutes)**

Draw up a table which identifies, for each of the four methods of evaluating a project (payback, ARR, NPV, IRR), two advantages and two disadvantages.

2.3 The benefits of a proposed information system

The benefits from a proposed information system should be evaluated against the costs. To quantify the benefits several factors need to be considered.

(a) **Savings** generated because the old system will no longer be operated. The savings may include **staff costs** and **other operating costs**.

(b) **Extra savings** or **revenue benefits** because of the improvements or enhancements that the new system should bring:

(i) Possibly more **sales revenue** and so additional contribution.

(ii) Better **stock control** (with a new stock control system) and so fewer stock losses from obsolescence and deterioration.

(iii) Savings in **staff time**, resulting perhaps in reduced future staff growth.

Some benefits might be **intangible**, or impossible to give a money value to. Even if they cannot be quantified, they must be identified and fully explained. It is arguable that the larger proportion of all computerised information systems benefits is intangible.

(a) Greater **customer satisfaction**, arising from a more prompt service (eg because of a computerised sales and delivery service).

(b) Improved **staff morale** from working with a 'better' system.

(c) **Better decision making** is hard to quantify, but may result from a better MIS, DSS or EIS.

3 KNOWLEDGE MANAGEMENT

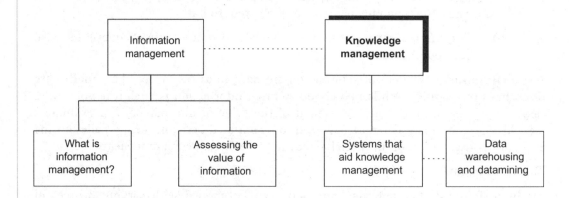

3.1 What is knowledge management?

Studies have indicated that 20 to 30 percent of company resources are wasted because organisations are not aware of what **knowledge they already possess**. Lew Platt, Chief executive of Hewlett Packard, has articulated this in the phrase 'If only HP knew what HP knows, we would be three times as profitable'.

Definitions

Knowledge is information within people's minds.

Knowledge management describes the process of collecting, storing and using the knowledge held within an organisation.

Knowledge is now commonly viewed as a sustainable source of **competitive advantage,** and one that it is essential f or companies to tap. In an era of rapid change and uncertainty, companies need to **create new knowledge, nurture it and disseminate it** throughout the organisation, and **embody it in technologies, products and services.** Several sectors – for example, the financial services industries - depend on knowledge as their principal means of value creation.

Knowledge is valuable because humans use it to create new ideas, insights and interpretations and apply these to information use and decision making. However knowledge, like information, is of no value unless it is applied to decisions and actions in a purposeful business context.

People in organisations are constantly **converting knowledge into various forms of information** (memos, reports, e-mails, briefings) and **acquiring information for others to improve their knowledge.**

Knowledge management programmes are attempts at:

(a) Designing and installing techniques and processes to create, protect and use **explicit knowledge** (that is knowledge that the company knows that it has). Explicit knowledge includes facts, transactions and events that can be clearly stated and **stored in management information systems.**

(b) Designing and creating environments and activities to discover and release **tacit knowledge** (that is, knowledge that the company does not know it has). Tacit knowledge is implied or inferred, it concerns the feelings and experiences **stored in peoples minds.**

Organisations should encourage people to share their knowledge. This can be done through **improved management of information** about **where knowledge resides,** how it can be **deployed and reused** and when it can create greater business value through **new ideas and innovations.**

A range of **technology** is available to support KM. The three main threads are information retrieval, document management and workflow processing.

3.2 Organisational learning

The process by which an organisation develops its store of knowledge is sometimes called organisational learning. A learning organisation is centred on the **people** that make up the organisation and the **knowledge** they hold. The organisation and employees feed off and into the central pool of knowledge. The organisation uses the knowledge pool as a tool to teach itself and its employees.

3.3 Knowledge management or information management?

There are dozens of **different approaches** to KM, including document management, information management, business intelligence, competence management, information systems management, intellectual asset management, innovation, business process design, and so on.

You might be forgiven for thinking, therefore, that 'knowledge management' is just a different, more up-market **label** for information management?

(a) It is true that many KM projects have a significant element of information management. After all, people need information about where knowledge resides, and to share knowledge they need to transform it into more or less transient forms of information.

(b)   But beyond that, KM does have two distinctive tasks: to facilitate the **creation** of knowledge and to **manage the way people share and apply it**. Companies that prosper with KM will be those that realise that it is as much about **managing people** as about information and technology.

EXAMPLE: HOW TO FACILITATE KNOWLEDGE SHARING

The business trend for the new millennium might well be summed up as, 'Tradition is out, innovation is in.' World-class companies now realise that the best ideas do not necessarily come from the executive boardroom but from all levels of the company; from line workers all the way through top management.

Companies that have cultures that **encourage best practice sharing** can unlock the rich stores of knowledge within each employee: sharing promotes overall knowledge, and facilitates further creativity. World-class companies are innovatively implementing best practice sharing to shake them of out of the rut of 'the way it's always been done.' Programs such as General Electric's Work-Out sessions or Wal-Mart's Saturday meetings help employees challenge conventions and suggest creative new ideas that drive process improvement, increased efficiency, and overall, **a stronger bottom line.**

The fundamental goal of **knowledge management** is to capture and disseminate knowledge across an increasingly global enterprise, enabling individuals to avoid repeating mistakes and to operate more intelligently - striving to create an entire **learning organisation** that work as efficiently as its most seasoned experts.

Best Practices recently updated report, '*Knowledge Management of Internal Best Practices*', profiles innovative methods used by world-class companies to communicate best practices internally. The study provides recommendations for how to create a best practice-sharing culture through all levels of the organisation, how to use both external and internal sources to find best practices and how to capture that knowledge and communicate it to all employees.

Best Practices, LLC contacted over fifty leading companies at the vanguard of knowledge management to compile its report. Some of the vital issues these thought leaders addressed include **measurement and management of intellectual assets**, best practice identification and recognition systems, best practice prioritisation systems, communication of best practices, and **knowledge sharing through technology**. For example, in the area of best practice **communications, the report examines how General Electric spreads best practices with regular** job rotations.

Adapted from Chapel Hill, N.C. (Business Wire) Feb 2000 via News Edge Corporation

4 SYSTEMS THAT AID KNOWLEDGE MANAGEMENT

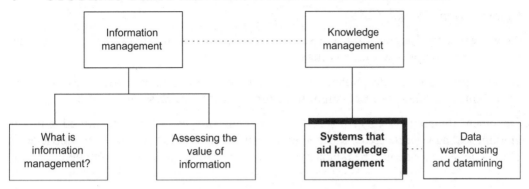

4.1 What type of systems aid knowledge management?

Information systems play an important role in knowledge management, helping with **information flows** and helping formally **capture** the knowledge held within the organisation.

Any system that encourages people to work together and share information and knowledge will aid knowledge management. Examples are shown in the following table.

What the systems facilitate	Examples
Knowledge distribution	**Office automation systems**
	• Word processing
	• Electronic schedulers
	• Desktop databases
	• Web publishing
	• Voice mail
	• E-mail
Knowledge sharing	**Group collaboration systems**
	• Groupware
	• Intranets
	• Extranets
Knowledge creation	**Knowledge work systems**
	• CAD
	• Virtual Reality
	• Investment workstations
Knowledge capture and codification	**Artificial intelligence systems**
	• Expert systems
	• Neural Nets
	• Fuzzy logic
	• Intelligent agents

4.2 Distributing knowledge

Office automation systems (OAS)

As we learnt in Chapter 1, an OAS is any application of information technology that increases productivity within an office.

Knowledge work is dependant on the efficient production and distribution of documents and other forms of communication such as voice messaging systems.

Document imaging systems convert documents and images to digital form, reducing the amount of paper required. Electronic information should be easier to retrieve as electronic searches should be quicker than hunting through a mountain of paper.

4.3 Knowledge sharing

Groupware

Definition

> **Groupware** is a term used to describe software that provides functions for the use of collaborative work groups.

Typically, groups utilising groupware are small project-oriented teams that have important tasks and tight deadlines Perhaps the best-known groupware product at present is **Lotus Notes**. However, there are many related products and technologies.

Features might include the following.

(a) A **scheduler** (or diary or calendar), allowing users to keep track of their schedule and plan meetings with others.

(b) An electronic **address book** to keep personal and business contact information up-to-date and easy to find. Contacts can be sorted and filed in any way.

(c) **To do** lists. Personal and business to-do lists can be kept in one easy-to-manage place, and tasks can quickly be prioritised.

(d) A **journal**, which is used to record interactions with important contacts, record items (such as e-mail messages) and files that are significant to the user, and record activities of all types and track them all without having to remember where each one was saved.

(e) A **jotter** for jotting down notes as quick reminders of questions, ideas, and so on.

There are clearly advantages in having information such as this available from the desktop at the touch of a button, rather than relying on scraps of paper, address books, and corporate telephone directories. However, it is when groupware is used to **share information** with colleagues that it comes into its own. Here are some of the features that may be found.

(a) **Messaging**, comprising an **e-mail** in-box which is used to send and receive messages from the office, home, or the road and **routing** facilities, enabling users to send a message to a single person, send it sequentially to a number of people (who may add to it or comment on it before passing it on), or sending it to every one at once.

(b) Access to an **information database**, and customisable 'views' of the information held on it, which can be used to standardise the way information is viewed in a workgroup.

(c) **Group scheduling**, to keep track of colleagues' itineraries. Microsoft Exchange Server, for instance offers a 'Meeting Wizard', which can consult the diaries of everyone needed to attend a meeting and automatically work out when they will be available, which venues are free, and what resources are required.

(d) **Public folders**. These collect, organise, and share files with others on the team or across the organisation.

(e) One person (for instance a secretary or a stand-in during holidays or sickness) can be given 'delegate access' to another's groupware folders and send mail on their behalf, or read, modify, or create items in public and private folders on their behalf.

(f) **Conferencing**. Participation in public, online discussions with others.

(g) **Assigning tasks**. A task request can be sent to a colleague who can accept, decline, or reassign the task. After the task is accepted, the groupware will keeps the task status up-to-date on a task list.

(h) **Voting** type facilities that can, say, request and tally responses to a multiple-choice question sent in a mail message (eg 'Here is a list of options for this year's Christmas party').

(i) **Hyperlinks** in mail messages. The recipient can click the hyperlink to go directly to a Web page or file server.

(j) **Workflow management** (see below) with various degrees of sophistication.

Workflow is a term used to describe the defined series of tasks within an organisation to produce a final outcome. Sophisticated workgroup computing applications allow the user to define different **workflows** for different types of jobs. For example, in a publishing setting, a document might be automatically routed from writer to editor to proofreader to production.

At **each stage** in the workflow, **one individual** or group is **responsible** for a specific task. Once the task is complete, the workflow software ensures that the individuals responsible for the **next** task are notified and receive the data they need to do their stage of the process.

Workflow systems can be described according to the type of process they are designed to deal with. There are three common types.

(a) **Image-based workflow systems** are designed to automate the flow of paper through an organisation, by transferring the paper to digital "images". These were the first workflow systems that gained wide acceptance. These systems are closely associated with 'imaging' (or 'document image processing' (DIP)) technology, and help with the routing and processing of digitised images.

(b) **Form-based workflow systems** (formflow) are designed to route forms intelligently throughout an organisation. These forms, unlike images, are text-based and consist of editable fields. Forms are automatically routed according to the information entered on them. In addition, these form-based systems can notify or remind people when action is due.

(c) **Co-ordination-based workflow systems** are designed to help the completion of work by providing a framework for **co-ordination** of action. Such systems are intended to improve organisational productivity by addressing the issues

NOTES

necessary to **satisfy customers,** rather than automating procedures that are not closely related to customer satisfaction.

Intranets

Definition

An **intranet** is an internal network used to share information. Intranets utilise Internet technology and protocols. The firewall surrounding an internet fends off unauthorised access.

The idea behind an 'intranet' is that companies set up their own **mini version of the Internet.** (We look at the Internet in detail in Chapter 5.) Intranets use a combination of the organisation's own networked computers and Internet technology. Each employee has a browser, used to access a server computer that holds corporate information on a wide variety of topics, and in some cases also offers access to the Internet.

Potential applications include company newspapers, induction material, online procedure and policy manuals, employee web pages where individuals post up details of their activities and progress, and **internal databases** of the corporate information store.

Most of the **cost** of an intranet is the **staff time** required to set up the system.

The **benefits** of intranets are diverse.

(a) Savings accrue from the **elimination of storage, printing** and **distribution** of documents that can be made available to employees on-line.

(b) Documents on-line are often **more widely used** than those that are kept filed away, especially if the document is bulky (eg manuals) and needs to be searched. This means that there are **improvements in productivity** and **efficiency**.

(c) It is much **easier to update** information in electronic form.

(d) Wider access to corporate information should open the way to **more flexible working patterns**, eg material available on-line may be accessed from remote locations..

Extranets

Definition

An **extranet** is an intranet that is accessible to authorised outsiders.

Whereas an intranet resides behind a firewall and is accessible only to people who are members of the same company or organisation, an extranet provides various levels of accessibility to outsiders.

Only those outsiders with a valid username and password can access an extranet, with varying levels of access rights enabling control over what people can view. Extranets are becoming a very popular means for **business partners to exchange information**.

Extranets therefore allow better use of the knowledge held by an organisation - by facilitating access to that knowledge.

4.4 Creating knowledge

Knowledge work systems (KWS)

Knowledge Work Systems (KWS) are information systems that facilitate the creation and integration of new knowledge into an organisation. They provide knowledge workers with tools such as:

- Analytical tools
- Powerful graphics facilities
- Communication tools
- Access to external databases
- A user-friendly interface

The workstations of knowledge workers are often designed for the specific tasks they perform. For example, a design engineer would require sufficient graphics power to manipulate 3-D Computer Aided Design (**CAD**) images; a financial analyst would require a powerful desktop computer to access and manipulate a large amount of financial data (an **investment workstation**).

The components of a KWS are shown in the following diagram.

Knowledge work system

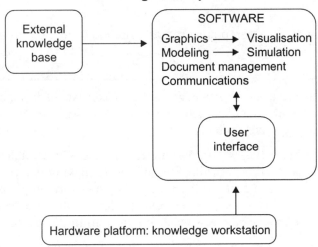

Virtual reality systems are another example of KWS. These systems create computer generated simulations that emulate real-world activities. Interactive software and hardware (eg special headgear) provide simulations so realistic that users experience sensations that would normally only occur in the real world.

EXAMPLE

Virtual reality

Burger King have used virtual reality stores to test new store designs.

Volvo have used virtual reality test drives in vehicle development.

4.5 Capturing and codifying knowledge

Artificial intelligence (AI)

Definition

Artificial intelligence (AI) is the development of computer-based systems designed to behave as humans. Artificial intelligence systems are based on human expertise, knowledge and reasoning patterns.

The field of AI includes:

- Robotics
- 'Natural language' programming tools
- Perceptive systems
- Expert systems

The main commercial applications of AI have involved **expert systems**.

Definition

An **expert system** is a computer program that captures human expertise in a limited domain of knowledge.

Expert system software uses a knowledge base that consists of facts, concepts and the relationships between them on a particular domain of knowledge and uses pattern-matching techniques to 'solve' problems.

Rules of thumb or ('heuristics') are important. A simple example might be 'milk in first' when making a cup of tea: this is a rule of thumb for tea making that saves people having to rethink how to make a cup of tea every time they do so. A simple business example programmed into a credit check may be: 'Don't allow credit to a person who has no credit history and has changed address twice or more within the last three years'.

For example, many financial institutions now use expert systems to process straightforward **loan applications**. The user enters certain key facts into the system such as the loan applicant's name and most recent addresses, their income and monthly outgoings, and details of other loans. The system will then:

(a) **Check the facts** given against its database to see whether the applicant has a good previous credit record.

(b) **Perform calculations** to see whether the applicant can afford to repay the loan.

(c) **Make a judgement** as to what extent the loan applicant fits the lender's profile of a good risk (based on the lender's previous experience).

(d) Suggest a decision.

A decision is then suggested, based on the results of this processing. This is why it is now often possible to get a loan or arrange insurance **over the telephone,** whereas in the past it would have been necessary to go and speak to a bank manager or send details to an actuary and then wait for him or her to come to a decision.

Other applications of expert systems include:

(a) **Legal** advice.

(b) **Tax** advice.

(c) **Forecasting** of economic or financial developments, or of market and customer behaviour.

(d) **Surveillance,** for example of the number of customers entering a supermarket, to decide what shelves need restocking and when more checkouts need to be opened, or of machines in a factory, to determine when they need maintenance.

(e) **Diagnostic systems,** to identify causes of problems, for example in production control in a factory, or in healthcare.

(f) **Education and training** (diagnosing a student's or worker's weaknesses and providing or recommending extra instruction as appropriate).

An organisation can use an expert system when a number of conditions are met.

(a) The problem is **well defined**.
(b) The expert can define **rules** by which the problem can be solved.
(c) The **investment** in an expert system is cost-justified.

The knowledge base of an expert system must be kept up-to-date.

Expert systems are not suited to high-level unstructured problems as these require information from a wide range of sources rather than simply deciding between a few known alternatives.

A diagram of an expert system follows.

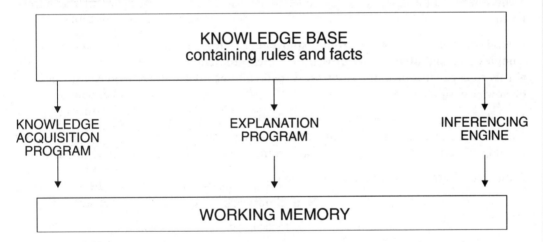

(a) The **knowledge base** contains facts and rules from past experience.

(b) The **knowledge acquisition program** is a program which enables the expert system to incorporate new knowledge and rules.

(c) The **working memory s**tores the facts and rules being used by the current enquiry, and the current information given to it by the user.

(d) The **inferencing engine** is the software that executes the reasoning. It decides which rules apply, and allocates priorities.

Activity 4 **(20 minutes)**

Why do you think organisations wish to automate reasoning or decision-making tasks which humans are naturally better able to perform than computers?

BPP
PUBLISHING

Advantages of expert systems include the following.

(a) AI and expertise is **permanent**, whereas human experts may leave the business.

(b) AI is **easily copied**.

(c) AI is **consistent**, whereas human experts and decision makers may not be.

(d) AI can be **documented**. The reasoning behind an expert recommendation produced by a computer will be recorded.

(e) Depending on the task the computer may be much **faster** than the human being.

Disadvantages of expert systems include the following:

(a) Systems are **expensive**.

(b) The technology is still relatively new. Systems will probably need extensive testing and debugging.

(d) People are naturally **more creative**.

(e) Systems have a very **narrow focus**.

Neural networks

Neural networks are another application of AI, seen by some as the 'next step' in computing. Neural computing is modelled on the biological processes of the human brain.

Neural networks can **learn from experience**. They can analyse vast quantities of complex data and **identify patterns** from which predictions can be made. They have the ability to cope with incomplete or 'fuzzy' data, and can deal with previously unspecified or **new situations**.

Neural techniques have been applied to similar areas as expert systems eg credit risks. Neural techniques are more advanced in that they don't rely on a set of hard rules, but develop a 'hidden' layer of experience and come to a decision based on this hidden layer.

A diagram showing a neural network follows.

Neural network

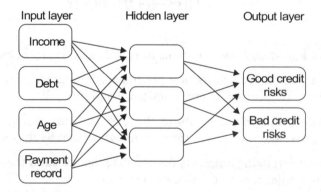

Fuzzy logic

Artificial intelligence applications are increasingly making use of 'fuzzy logic'. Traditionally computer programs have required precision such as 'yes' or 'no'.

Fuzzy logic involves using more complex rules than the traditional IF-THEN statements. For example, a traditional statement may say '*IF room temperature is less than 60 degrees THEN raise the heat*'.

A system using fuzzy logic would have a range of membership functions which are less precise than rules. A membership function may say '*If the temperature is warm or hot and the humidity is high lower the temperature and humidity.*'

The parameters for *warm, hot, high, low* etc would be defined elsewhere in the system (and may overlap). The program would combine the function readings and using weightings decide on the required course of action.

We look at the features of widely used information technology in Chapter 5.

5 DATA WAREHOUSING AND DATAMINING

Two techniques designed to utilise the ever increasing amounts of data held by organisations are **data warehousing** and **data mining**.

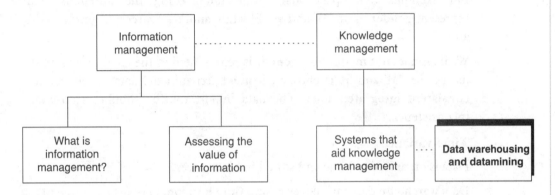

5.1 Data warehousing

Definition

> A **data warehouse** consists of a database, containing data from various operational systems, and reporting and query tools.

A data warehouse contains data from a range of internal (eg sales order processing system, nominal ledger) and external sources. One reason for including individual transaction data in a data warehouse is that if necessary the user can drill-down to access transaction level detail. Data is increasingly obtained from newer channels such as customer care systems, outside agencies or websites.

Data is copied to the data warehouse as often as required – usually either daily, weekly or monthly. The process of making any required changes to the format of data and copying it to the warehouse is usually automated.

The result should be a coherent set of information available to be used across the organisation for management analysis and decision making. The reporting and query tools available within the warehouse should facilitate management reporting and analysis.

The reporting and query tools should be flexible enough to allow multidimensional data analysis, also known as on-line analytical processing (**OLAP**). Each aspect of information (eg product, region, price, budgeted sales, actual sales, time period etc) represents a different dimension. OLAP enables data to be viewed from each dimension, allowing each aspect to be viewed and in relation to the other aspects.

Features of data warehouses

A data warehouse is subject-oriented, integrated, time-variant, and non-volatile.

(a) **Subject-oriented**

A data warehouse is focussed on data groups not application boundaries. Whereas the operational world is designed around applications and functions such as sales and purchases, a data warehouse world is organised around major **subjects** such as customers, supplier, product and activity.

(b) **Integrated**

Data within the data warehouse must be consistent in format and codes used – this is referred to as **integrated** in the context of data warehouses.

For example, one operational application feeding the warehouse may represent **gender** as an 'M' and an 'F' while another represents **gender** as '1' and '0'.

While it does not matter how **gender** is represented in the data warehouse (let us say that 'M' and 'F' is chosen), it **must** arrive in the data warehouse in a **consistent integrated** state. The data import routine should 'cleanse' any inconsistencies.

(c) **Time-variant**

Data is organised by time and stored in 'time-slices'.

Data warehouse data may cover **a long time horizon,** perhaps from five to ten years. Data warehouse data tends to deal with **trends** rather than single points in time. As a result, each data element in the data warehouse environment must carry with it the time for which it applies.

(d) **Non-volatile**

Data **cannot be changed** within the warehouse. Only load and retrieval operations are made.

Organisations may build a single central data warehouse to serve the entire organisation or may create a series of smaller **data marts**. A data mart holds a selection of the organisation's data for a specific purpose.

A data mart can be constructed more quickly and cheaply than a data warehouse. However, if too many individual data marts are built, organisations may find it is more efficient to have a single data warehouse serving all areas.

Advantages of data warehouses

Advantages of setting up a datawarehouse system include the following.

(a) Decision makers can access data without affecting the use of operational systems.

(b) Having a wide range of data available to be queried easily encourages the taking of a wide perspective on organisational activities.

(c) Datawarehouses have proved successful in some businesses for:

    (i) Quantifying the effect of marketing initiatives.

    (ii) Improving knowledge of customers.

    (iii) Identifying and understanding an enterprise's most profitable revenues streams.

Some organisations have found they have invested considerable resources implementing a datawarehouse for little return. To benefit from the information a datawarehouse can provide, organisations need to be flexible and prepared to act on what they find. If a warehouse system is implemented simply to follow current practice it will be of little value.

The components of a data warehouse are shown in the following diagram.

Components of a data warehouse

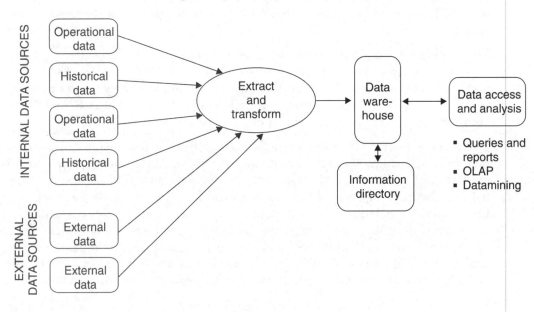

EXAMPLE: SEVEN STEPS TO BRING YOUR SYSTEMS INTO THE 21ST CENTURY

Step One. Implement a data warehouse

A data warehouse is a computer loaded with a database product such as Oracle or Microsoft SQL server. **This database is configured to hold the key information** you want to look at and is interfaced with the 'transaction processing' systems.

For larger volumes of data a toolset has been developed called **OLAP (on-line analytical processing)** which allows **summary information** to be created and stored across the different business performance metrics. As a consequence of this, on-line and instant enquiries can potentially be made on the balances of any combination of customer/product/regional performance by date/period range.

The performance of the transaction-processing systems will not be affected by heavy use of the data warehouse for a complex set of enquiries, as you will not be working with the live information.

Once this warehouse has been set up, information can be combined from the different operations systems into a consistent format and can be accessed by a wide variety of

reporting/analysis/web tools.

Step Two. Reporting tools

Time and time again finance directors say that their key IT issue is lack of reporting capabilities in the systems they are using. Reporting problems tend to fall into three categories.

First, the **inability to access the source data**. This is either because it is in a format that cannot be accessed by PC technology or it is held in so many places that its structure is incomprehensible to a member of the finance team.

Second, the **tools to make the enquiries** or produce the reports are often **difficult to use** and do not produce the reports in a 'user friendly' format with 'drill down' capabilities.

Third, there is the issue of **consistency of information** across systems. In order to get an overall picture of your organisation's performance you will usually need to access data from different operation applications. All too often the data is not the same across these systems.

The argument for replacing what you have is well rehearsed. New systems promise the latest technology for reporting and enquiries. **Enterprise Resource Planning (ERP)** packages promise to integrate your different applications smoothly and give you a single point of access to all data. **Customer Relationship Management (CRM)** software has been added to this recipe to give this approach a better chance of happening.

There are a myriad of reporting tools costing from a few pounds to hundreds of thousands of pounds. One that is regularly overlooked is the **spreadsheet**. Excel is the product most commonly used by accountants. With the advent of Microsoft Office 2000 there is a bewildering array of features to present information on your desktop or paper. **Pivot tables** are starting to be used more widely for multi-dimensional analysis and can be combined with the increasingly powerful **graphical capabilities** of Excel. Spreadsheets are much underrated and it is surprising how many organisations go out and buy expensive new knowledge-management tools when they already have a product on their computer that will deliver all the reporting/enquiry performance they require.

So, see how far your spreadsheet will take you and see if you can avoid the cost of another new IT tool.

Step Three. Intranet enable reporting/enquiries

Larger companies have by now started to implement a **corporate intranet**. This typically holds information on employee phone and contact details, standard forms for holiday requests, terms and conditions of employment and so on.

It is possible now to integrate financial reporting into an intranet. The leading web page development tools allow the display of information from a data warehouse. Excel has facilities to post spreadsheets and pivot table information straight to a web page and for users to drill down to the detail from a summary level. There are a number of **benefits** to this.

First, the information is presented in a **user-friendly** format and can be made 'idiot proof' for non-IT literate staff.

Second, the benefit of using a web browser is that it allows for **remote access** to the information quickly and easily. This means that people working at different parts of the organisation or away from the office can access this data rapidly.

Third, the web browser technology is becoming an **industry standard** and as such is well supported and increasingly reliable. So, start to use a web browser to access your reports and **publish these to your intranet** server rather than printing them out.

Step Four. Client/supplier access to information

So you have implemented the above and have your core business data from your different systems in **a single data warehouse**. You will be using PC tools like Excel to access this and will have developed part of your intranet so that staff can access key information quickly and easily wherever they are.

Why not consider making **some of this information available to your business partners**? For example, if you have customer sales order information in your data warehouse, why not make it available to your customers and even suppliers? If you have internal information on the products and services that you sell, why not do likewise?

This is where the Internet can really start to bite and give your organisation real commercial benefit.

Step Five. Streamlined transaction processing

The next step is to look at the possibility of **streamlining your business processes**. How many times are you capturing your transactions in your organisation?

Why not allow customers to generate their own orders via the web? If the data warehouse holds information on the clients, the products and services you sell, it could be relatively straightforward to create an order front-end with a web browser to this information.

You could populate the data warehouse with these incoming orders and use this to upload your core transaction processing systems. Most packages now have data import modules and this process may be more straightforward than you think and a lot cheaper and easier than replacing your core business systems. Why not extend this to allowing your employees and even customers to 'self service' the information in your systems and keep it up-to-date themselves.

Clearly there are lots of caveats to this option. **Security** is always a concern, as is the resilience of the IT infrastructure necessary to support on-line order processing by clients. However, a number of forward-thinking businesses have achieved this without replacing all their systems.

Step Six. Train staff in what you already have

Do your staff really understand the features of your accounting and business systems? Are they familiar with what the web can offer your organisation? Put together a **comprehensive training programme**.

Step Seven. Get board buy-in

A note of caution to conclude on: **you MUST get board and senior management buy-in to what you are planning.**

Source: Adapted from an article by John Tate, Management Accounting, April 2000

5.2 Datamining

Definition

> **Datamining** software looks for hidden patterns and relationships in large pools of data.

True datamining software discovers **previously unknown relationships**. Datamining provides insights that can not be obtained through OLAP. The hidden patterns and relationships the software identifies can be used to guide decision making and to **predict future behaviour**.

Datamining uses statistical analysis tools as well as neural networks, fuzzy logic and other **intelligent techniques**. The types of relationships or patterns that datamining may uncover may be classified as follows.

Relationship\Discovery	Comment
Classification or cluster	These terms refer to the identification of patterns within the database between a range of data items. For example, datamining may find that unmarried males aged between 20 and 30, who have an income above £50,000 are more likely to purchase a high performance sports car than people from other demographic groups. This group could then be targeted when marketing material is produced/distributed.
Association	One event can be linked or correlated to another event – such as in Wal-Mart example (1) below.
Forecasting	Trends are identified within the data that can be extrapolated into the future.

EXAMPLES: DATAMINING

(1) The American retailer Wal-Mart discovered an unexpected relationship between the sale of **nappies** and **beer!** Wal-Mart found that both tended to sell at the same time, just after working hours, and concluded that men with small children stopped off to buy nappies on their way home, and bought beer at the same time. Logically therefore, if the two items were put in the same shopping aisle, sales of both should increase. Wal-Mart tried this and it worked.

The Wal-Mart system, tracking sales by store, item and date, required a **4 terabyte** (4000 gigabyte) database. Even this enormous quantity of data will not support the market analysis techniques that Wal-Mart anticipates using in the future, which will require data on each sales transaction.

(2) Some credit card companies have used datamining to predict which customers are likely to switch to a competitor in the next few months. Based on the datamining results, the bank can take action to retain these customers.

EXAMPLE: DATAMINING SOFTWARE

The following is extracted from marketing material for a Datamining product called the NeoVista Decision Series.

Understand The Patterns In Your Business and Discover The Value In Your Data

Within your corporate database resides extremely valuable information - information that reflects how your business processes operate and how your customers behave. Every transaction your organisation makes is captured for accounting purposes, and with it, a wealth of potential knowledge.

When properly analysed, organised and presented, this information can be of enormous value. Conventional 'drill down' database query techniques may reveal some of these details, but much of the valuable **knowledge content will remain hidden**.

The NeoVista Decision Series is a suite of knowledge discovery software specifically designed to address this challenge. Analysing data without any preconceived notion of the patterns it contains, the Decision Series **seeks out relationships and trends**, and presents them in easy-to-understand form, enabling better business decisions. The Decision Series is being used today by leading corporations to discover the hidden value in their data, providing them with major competitive advantages and organisational benefits.

A Large Multi-National Retailer uses the Decision Series **to refine inventory stocking levels,** by store and by item, to dramatically reduce out-of-stock or overstocking situations and thereby improve revenues and reduce forced markdowns.

A Health Maintenance Group uses the Decision Series to **predict which of its members are most at risk** from specific major illnesses. This presents opportunities for timely medical intervention and preventative treatment to promote the patient's well-being and reduce the healthcare provider's costs.

An International Retail Sales Organisation uses the Decision Series to **optimise store and department layouts,** resulting in more accurate targeting of products to maximise sales within the scope of available resources.

NeoVista's unique software can be applied to a wide range of business problems, allowing you to:

Determine the relationships that lie at the heart of your business.

Make reliable **estimates of future behaviour** based on sophisticated analyses of past events.

Make **business decisions with a higher degree of understanding** and confidence.

Datamining is renowned for exposing important facts and anomalies within data warehouses. The NeoVista Decision Series' knowledge discovery methodology has the proven ability to expose the patterns that are not merely interesting, but which are critical to your business. These patterns provide you with an advantage through insight and knowledge that your competition may never discover.

NOTES

Chapter roundup

Information is a **valuable resource** that requires efficient management.

- Technology has changed how information is collected, stored and processed, as well as changing the information needs of organisations

- The cost and value of information are often not easy to quantify - but attempts should be made to do so.

- Knowledge management describes the process of collecting, storing and utilising the knowledge held by people and systems within an organisation.

- There are a wide range of systems available that encourage knowledge management including:

  ° Computer supported co-operative working

  ° Groupware

  ° Workflow and workgroup applications

  ° Intranets and extranets

- **Neural computing** utilises concepts such as artificial intelligence in an attempt to enable computers to 'learn' from experience.

- A **data warehouse** consists of a database, containing data from various operational systems, and reporting and query tools.

- Organisations may build a single central data warehouse to serve the entire organisation or may create a series of smaller **data marts**.

- **Datamining** software looks for **hidden** patterns and relationships in large pools of data. Datamining uses **statistical analysis tools** as well as **neural networks, fuzzy logic** and other **intelligent techniques**.

Quick quiz

1   List five tasks of information management. (See Section 1.1)

2   What factors should be considered when assessing the cost and value of information? (See Section 2.2)

3   Define knowledge and knowledge management. (See Section 3.1)

4   What is a 'learning-organisation' centred on? (See Section 3.2)

5   What is groupware? (See Section 4.3)

6   List four benefits of an intranet. (See Section 4.3)

7   What is an extranet? (See Section 4.3)

8   List four business applications of datamining. (See Section 5.2)

Answers to Activities

1   There are many possible suggestions, including those given below.

    (a)   The organisation's **bankers** take decisions affecting the amount of money they are prepared to lend.

(b)   The **public** might have an interest in information relating to an organisation's products or services.

(c)   The **media** (press, television etc) use information generated by organisations in news stories, and such information can adversely or favourably affect an organisation's relationship with its environment.

(d)   The **government** (for example the Department of Trade and Industry) regularly requires organisational information.

(e)   The **Inland Revenue** and **HM Customs and Excise** authorities require information for taxation and VAT assessments.

(f)   An organisation's **suppliers** and **customers** take decisions whether or not to trade with the organisation.

2   (a)   What information is provided?

    (b)   What is it used for?

    (c)   Who uses it?

    (d)   How often is it used?

    (e)   Does the frequency with which it is used coincide with the frequency of provision?

    (f)   What is achieved by using it?

    (g)   What other relevant information is available which could be used instead?

3

Method	Advantages	Disadvantages
Payback	(1) Easy to calculate (2) Favours project that offer quick returns	(1) Ignores cash flows after payback period (2) Only a crude measure of timing of a project's cash flows.
ARR	(1) Easy to calculate (2) Easy to understand	(1) Doesn't allow for timing of inflows/outflows of cash (2) Subject to accounting conventions.
NPV	(1) Uses relevant cost approach by concentrating on cash flows (2) Represents increase to company's wealth, expressed in present day terms	(1) Not easily understood by laymen. (2) Cost of capital may be difficult to calculate.
IRR	(1) Uses opportunity cost approach (2) Represents breakeven borrowing rate.	(1) Could get several IRRs or no IRRs (2) Ignores scale of project whereas NPV takes this into account.

4   The primary reason has to do with the relative cost of information. An expert can spend a great deal of time acquiring a specialised body of knowledge, but the commercial value of this expertise ceases with the expert's retirement or departure from the labour force.

Secondly, enshrining an expert's accumulated wisdom in a computer system means that this wisdom can be accessed by more people. Thus, the delivery of complicated services to customers, decisions whether or not to extend credit and so forth, can be made by less experienced members of staff if the expert's knowledge is available to them. If a manufacturing company has a complicated mixture of plant and machinery, then the repair engineer may accumulate a lot of knowledge over a period of time about the way it behaves: if a problem occurs, the engineer will be able to make a reasoned guess as to where the likely cause is to be found. If this accumulated expert information is made available to less experienced staff, it means that some of their learning curve is avoided.

An expert system is advantageous because it saves time, like all computer systems (in theory at least) but it is particularly useful as it possesses both knowledge and a reasoning ability.

Assignment 2 (30 minutes)

CC plc is a company employing 500 staff in 10 different offices within one country. The company offers a wide range of specialist consultancy advice to the building and construction industry. This includes advice on materials to be used, relevant legislation (including planning applications) and appropriate sources of finance.

The information to meet client requirements is held within each office of the company. Although most clients are serviced by a single office, a lot of the information used is duplicated between the different offices.

In the past there has been no attempt to share data because of the cost of transferring information and the lack of trust on the part of staff in other offices. Some senior managers tend to keep part of client data confidential to themselves.

The Marketing Director has suggested that an Intranet should be established in the company so that common information can be shared rather than each office maintaining its own data. This suggestion is meeting with come resistance from all grades of staff.

Task

Explain the objectives of an intranet and show how the provision of an intranet within CC plc should result in better provision of information.

Chapter 3 :
SYSTEM DESIGN

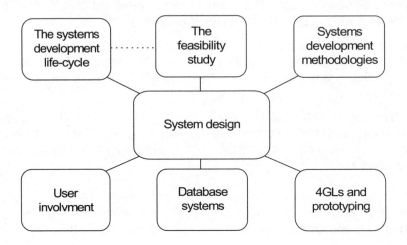

Introduction

Even very small organisations now tend to have computerised systems. In this chapter we discuss a variety of issues relating to the design and development of computerised Management Information Systems.

Your objectives

After completing this chapter you should understand:

(a)   The processes of system design and development.

(b)   The nature and purpose of systems maintenance and performance evaluation.

1 THE SYSTEMS DEVELOPMENT LIFE-CYCLE

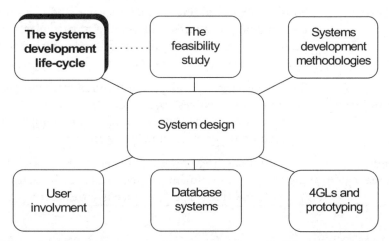

At least some elements of almost all Management Information Systems are now computerised.

In the early days of computing, systems were developed in a fairly haphazard fashion. Systems development usually involved the automation of existing procedures. The development of systems **was not properly planned**. The consequences were often poorly designed systems, which were not suited to users' needs. A more disciplined approach to systems development is known was developed, and became known as the **systems development life-cycle**. A six-stage **model** of the development life-cycle is explained below.

1.1 Stages of the systems development life-cycle

Stage	Comment
Identification of a problem	In the case of the development of a new information system, this stage will involve an analysis of the organisation's information requirements. Such an analysis should be carried out in conjunction with users, so that their **actual** requirements can be identified, rather than their **likely** requirements.
Feasibility study	This involves a brief review of the existing system and the identification of a range of possible alternative solutions. One will usually be recommended on the basis of its costs and benefits, although it is possible for a decision not to proceed to result.
Systems investigation	This is a fact finding exercise which investigates the existing system to assess its problems and requirements and to obtain details of data volumes, response times and other key indicators.
Systems analysis	Once the workings of the existing system have been documented, they can be analysed. This process examines why current methods are used, what alternatives might achieve the same, or better, results, what restricts the effectiveness of the system and what performance criteria are required from a system.

Stage	Comment
Systems design	This is a technical phase which considers both computerised and manual procedures, addressing, in particular, inputs, outputs, program design, file design and security. A detailed specification of the new system is produced.
Systems implementation	This stage carries development through from design to operations. It involves acquisition (or writing) of software, program testing, file conversion or set-up, acquisition and installation of hardware and 'going live'.
Review and maintenance	This is an ongoing process which ensures that the system meets the objectives set during the feasibility study, that it is accepted by users and that its performance is satisfactory.

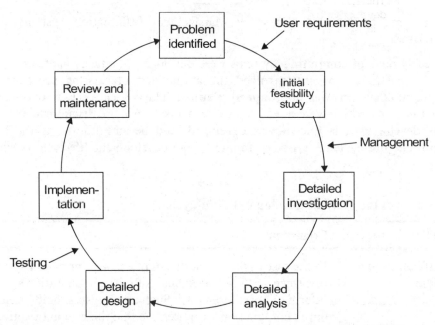

The systems development lifecycle approach to systems development was adopted by many organisations. It provided a model of how systems should be developed. It imposed a **disciplined** approach to the development process, it encouraged **communication** between systems professionals and 'ordinary' users and it recognised the importance of **analysis and design**, previously much neglected.

1.2 Drawbacks of the SDLC

While the basic SDLC approach has some advantages, it has a number of drawbacks **if not properly implemented**.

(a) While it was efficient at automating operational areas, the **information needs of middle and senior management were ignored**. Computerisation was a means of speeding up high-volume routine transaction processing, not providing information for decision-making.

(b) User input was obtained only early in the development process. This often resulted in the need for substantial (and costly) system modifications later.

(c) **New systems rarely lived up to users' expectations**. Even with packaged software, users may be disappointed. It becomes increasingly difficult to change system requirements the further a system is developed, and users were required to 'sign off' at an early stage.

(d) Much system documentation was **written for programmers and specialists**. It was highly technical, more of a technical manual than a guide for the user. Problems could also occur, if inadequately documented modifications led to 'bugs' elsewhere in the system.

(e) Many routine transaction processing systems **could not cope with unusual situations**, and so some complicated processing was still performed manually.

2   THE FEASIBILITY STUDY

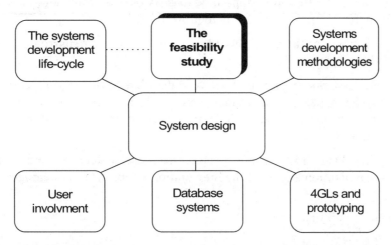

Before any system is implemented a feasibility study should be conducted. For very small systems the 'study' may involve only one individual and take less than a day. Complex systems may require a study involving a team of people and lasting months.

Definition

> A **feasibility study** is a formal study to decide what type of system can be developed which meets the needs of the organisation.

2.1 Terms of reference

The **terms of reference** for a feasibility study for a large information systems project might consist of the following items.

- To **investigate and report on an existing system**, its procedures and costs

- To define the **systems requirements**

- To establish **whether these requirements are being met** by the existing system

- To establish whether they could be met by an **alternative system**

- To specify **performance criteria** for the system

- To recommend the **most suitable system** to meet the system's objectives

- To prepare a **detailed cost budget**, within a specified budget limit

- To prepare a draft **plan for implementation** within a specified timescale

- To establish whether the hoped-for benefits could be realised

- To establish a detailed design, implementation and operating budget

- To compare the detailed budget with the **costs of the current system**

- To set the **date** by which the study group must report back

- To decide **which operational managers** should be approached by the study group

2.2 The feasibility study team

A feasibility study team should be appointed to carry out the study (although individuals might be given the task in the case of smaller projects).

(a) Members of the team should be drawn from the **departments affected by the project**.

(b) At least one person must have a **detailed knowledge of computers and systems design** (in a small concern it may be necessary to bring in a systems analyst from outside, or to rely on an accountant as the 'computer expert').

(c) The team must include people that have a **detailed knowledge of the organisation** and what the **information needs** of the system are

2.3 Areas of feasibility

The **study** itself will concentrate on **three key areas** in which a project must be feasible if it is to proceed.

- **Technical** feasibility
- **Operational** feasibility
- **Economic** feasibility

2.4 Technical feasibility

The requirements, as defined in the feasibility study, must be **technically achievable**. This means that any proposed solution must be capable of being implemented using available hardware, software and other equipment. The type of requirement which might depend for success on technical feasibility might be one of the following.

- **Volume** of transactions which can be processed within a given time

- **Capacity** to hold files or records of a certain size

- Response **times**

- **Number** of users which can be supported without deterioration in the other criteria

2.5 Operational feasibility

Operational feasibility is a key concern. If a solution makes technical sense but **conflicts with the way the organisation does business**, the solution is not feasible. Thus an organisation might reject a solution because it forces a change in management responsibilities and chains of command, or does not suit regional reporting structures, or because the costs of redundancies, retraining and reorganisation are considered too high.

2.6 Economic feasibility

A system which satisfies the above criteria must still be economically feasible. This means that it must be a 'good investment'. This has two strands.

(a) The project selected must be the **'best' option from those computerisation projects** under consideration.

(b) The project selected must **compete with other projects in other areas of the business** for funds. Even if it is projected to produce a positive return and satisfies all relevant criteria, it may not be chosen because a new warehouse is needed or the head office is to be relocated, and available funds are allocated to these projects instead.

2.7 Costs and benefits

Cost-benefit analysis before or during the development of information systems is complicated by the fact that many of the system cost elements are **poorly defined** (particularly for development projects) and that benefits can often be highly qualitative and subjective in nature.

The costs of a proposed system

In general the best cost estimates will be obtained for **complete systems** bought from an **outside vendor** who provides a cost quotation against a specification. Less concrete cost estimates are generally found with development projects where the work is performed by the organisation's own employees. The costs of a new system will include costs in a number of different categories.

Equipment costs (capital costs/leasing costs) include the following.

- Computer and peripherals
- Ancillary equipment
- The initial system supplies (disks, tapes, paper etc)

Installation costs relate to the infrastructure.

- New building (if necessary)
- The computer room (wiring, air-conditioning etc)

Development costs include costs of measuring and analysing the existing system and costs of looking at the new system. They include software/consultancy work and systems analysis and programming as well as changeover costs.

Personnel costs include all those one-off and ongoing costs not related to systems professionals.

- Staff training
- Staff recruitment/relocation
- Staff salaries and pensions
- Redundancy payments
- Overheads

Operating costs, which may in the long-term comprise up to 70% of overall systems costs, are the ongoing running costs.

- Consumable materials (tapes, disks, stationery etc)

- Maintenance
- Accommodation costs
- Heating/power/insurance/telephone
- Standby arrangements

A distinction can be made between **capital costs** and **revenue costs,** which may be either 'one-off' costs in the first year or regular annual costs. The distinction between capital costs and revenue costs is important.

(a) To establish the **cash outflows** arising from the system, the costs/benefit analysis of a system ought to be based on cash flows and DCF.

(b) The annual **charge against profits** is usually of interest! Capital items will be capitalised and depreciated, and revenue items will be expensed as incurred as a regular annual cost. The items treated as **'one-off' revenue costs** are costs which would usually fall to be treated as revenue which, by virtue of being incurred during the period of development only and in connection with the development are one-off. In practice, accounting treatment of such items may vary widely between organisations depending on their accounting policies and on agreement with their auditors.

Activity 1   **(30 minutes)**

Draw up a table with three headings: capital cost items, one-off revenue cost items and regular annual costs. Identify at least three items to be included under each heading. You may wish to refer back to the preceding paragraph for examples of costs.

Benefits of a proposed system

Among the criteria for **justifying** the cost of a new systems development may be the following.

(a) **Reduction in the danger of loss** through error or fraud. For example, customers may be prevented from exceeding their credit limits.

(b) **Sharing of information** through international **networks**.

(c) **Improved reputation and company image**, in terms of responsiveness to customer needs and the company's standing within the industry.

(d) **Better administrative and management control systems**, possibly using fewer but more highly trained staff.

(e) **Greater confidence in decision making,** through techniques of forecasting, planning, investment and modelling.

(f) **Increased responsiveness,** with the company being better placed to respond rapidly and flexibly to changing circumstances.

(g) **Enhanced job satisfaction** for staff. Self esteem, motivation and group cohesion may rise in line with highly regarded skills.

(h) **Better presentation** of all types of printed and on-screen inputs, both those generated for internal purposes and those which are communicated externally.

(i) Ultimately the benefits should add up to **increased profit** for the organisation.

Many of the benefits here are **intangible**. Convincing executives to invest in new systems development may require a powerful argument based on a combination of tangible and intangible benefits, using wherever possible, capital investment appraisal techniques.

2.8 The feasibility study report

Once each area of feasibility has been investigated a number of possible projects may be put forward. The results are included in a **feasibility report**. This should contain the following items.

- **Terms of reference**
- Description of **existing system**
- **System requirements**
- Details of the **proposed system(s)**
- **Cost/benefit analysis**
- **Development** and **implementation** plans
- **Recommendations** as to the preferred option

3 SYSTEMS DEVELOPMENT METHODOLOGIES

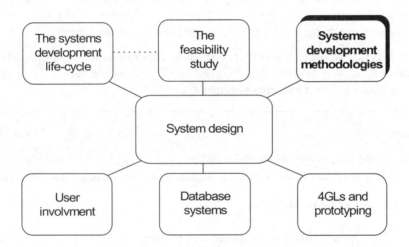

One popular approach to systems development and design is to use some kind of **methodology** such as **Structured Systems Analysis and Design**.

3.1 What is a systems development methodology?

Definition

> A systems development '**methodology**' of procedures, techniques, tools and documentation aids which will help systems developers in their efforts to implement a new information system.

When a methodology is used, hardware and software are developed or acquired that meet the demands of the information system specifications rather than developing a system acquired to fit hardware and software.

The needs of **users** are expressed in the outputs or potential outputs required of the system. The user's information requirements and potential requirements should determine the type of data collected or captured by the system.

3.2 Comparing and evaluating methodologies

Jayaratna (*Understanding and Evaluating Methodologies*, 1994) estimates that there are **over 1,000 brand named methodologies** in use in the world.

All methodologies seek to facilitate the '**best**' solution. But 'best' may be interpreted in a number of ways, such as **most rapid** or **least cost** systems. Some methodologies are highly **prescriptive** and require rigid adherence to stages whilst others are highly **adaptive** allowing for creative use of their components. The former may be viewed as following a recipe and the latter as selecting suitable tools from a toolkit.

In choosing the **most appropriate methodology**, an organisation must consider the following questions.

- How **open** is the system?
- To what extent does the methodology facilitate **participation**?
- Does it generate alternative solutions?
- Is it well documented, tried, tested and proven to work?
- Can **component 'tools'** be selected and used as required?
- Will it benefit from computer aided tools and prototyping?

It is **not necessary to be restricted** to the tools offered by just one methodology. For instance soft systems methodology may be useful at the outset, to get a system well-defined, and subsequently to review its performance. Elements of harder techniques and possibly prototyping might usefully be employed during development.

Ultimately it is important to remember that whilst methodologies may be valuable in the development their use is a matter of great skill and experience. They **do not, by themselves, produce good systems solutions**.

Activity 2	(10 minutes)
Why does it matter how 'open' a system is?	

3.3 Advantages of methodologies

(a) The **documentation** requirements are rigorous.

(b) **Standard methods** allow **less qualified staff** to carry out some of the analysis work, thus **cutting the cost** of the exercise.

(c) Using a standard development process leads to **improved system specifications**.

(d) Systems developed in this way are **easier to maintain and improve**.

(e) **Users are involved** with development work from an early stage and are required to sign off each stage.

(f) The emphasis on **diagramming** makes it easier for relevant parties, including users, to **understand** the system than if purely narrative descriptions were used.

(g) The structured framework of a methodology **helps with planning**. It defines the tasks to be performed and sets out when they should be done. Each step has an identifiable end product. This allows control by reference to actual achievements rather than to estimates of progress.

(h)   A logical design is produced that is **independent of hardware and software**. This logical design can then be given a physical design using whatever computer equipment and implementation language is required.

(i)   Techniques such as data flow diagrams, logical data structures and entity life histories **allow information to be cross-checked** between diagrams and ensure that the system delivers is what is required.

3.4   Disadvantages of methodologies

(a)   Methodologies were originally tailored to **large, complex organisations**. Only recently have they been adapted for PC-based systems.

(b)   It has been argued that methodologies are ideal for analysing and documenting processes and data items are operational level, but are perhaps **inappropriate for information of a strategic nature** that is collected on an ad hoc basis.

(c)   Some are a little **too limited in scope,** being too concerned with systems design, and not with their impact on actual work processes or social context of the system.

(d)   The conceptual basis of some is **not properly thought out**. Many methodologies grew out of diagramming conventions.

(e)   Arguably, methodologies are just as happy documenting a bad design as a good one.

4   FOURTH GENERATION LANGUAGES AND PROTOTYPING

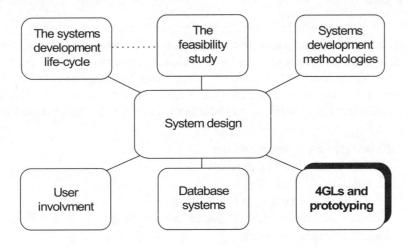

4.1   Fourth generation languages (4GLs)

As computer languages have developed over time, certain types of computer languages have become identified with a generation of languages. The four generations are explained in the following table.

BPP PUBLISHING

Generation	Comment
First	Machine code. Program instructions were written for individual machines in binary form (a series of 1s and 0s).
Second	Assembly languages. Still machine specific, programs were written using symbolic code which made them easier to understand and maintain.
Third	High-level languages such as COBOL, BASIC and FORTRAN. These languages have a wider vocabulary of words, enabling commands to be closer to everyday language. Programs produced are able to be moved between similar computers.
Fourth	There is no formal definition of a Fourth Generation Language (4GL). Fourth-generation languages are programming languages closer to human languages than typical high-level or third generation languages. Most 4GLs use simple query language such as 'FIND ALL RECORDS WHERE NAME IS 'JONES'

A fourth generation language is a programming language that is easier to use than languages like COBOL, PASCAL and C++. Well known examples include **Informix** and **Powerhouse**.

Definition

> A **Fourth Generation Language (4GL)** is a high-level computer language that uses commands that are closer to everyday speech than previous languages. 4GLs usually also include a range of features intended to automate software production.

Most fourth generation languages use a graphical user interface. Icons, objects, help facilities, pull down menus and templates present programmers with the options for building the software. Sections of code are often treated as components, which may be used (maybe with slight modifications) in a variety of applications. A 4GL will often include the following features (many of these features could also be provided by a CASE tool).

- Relatively easy to learn and use
- Often centred around a database
- Includes a data dictionary
- Uses a relatively simple query language
- Includes facilities for screen design and dialogue box design
- Includes a report generator
- Code generation is often automated

    Documenting and diagramming tools

4GLs are often used to facilitate **object-oriented programming**. With object-oriented programming, programmers define the types of operations (functions) that can be applied to data structures (in programming, a data structure refers to a scheme for organising related pieces of information). In this way, the data structure becomes an object that includes both data and functions. In addition, programmers can create relationships between one object and another. For example, objects can inherit characteristics from other objects.

One of the principal advantages of object-oriented programming techniques over procedural programming techniques is that they enable programmers to create modules that do not need to be changed when a new type of object is added. A programmer can simply create a new object that inherits many of its features from existing objects. This makes object-oriented programs easier to modify (a group of objects with some common properties may be referred to as a **class**).

4GLs enable a more flexible approach to be taken to software production than under the traditional Systems Development Lifecycle. Using a 4GL, changes to the program design and to the code itself can be made relatively easily and quickly. This allows development to follow a pattern like the Spiral model, with users able to make amendments based on prototypes.

Examples taken from 4GLs

The following screenshots are taken from the Metamill 4GL.

Example 1: Automated diagram production

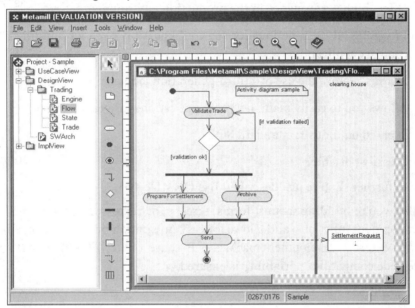

Example 2: Class properties window

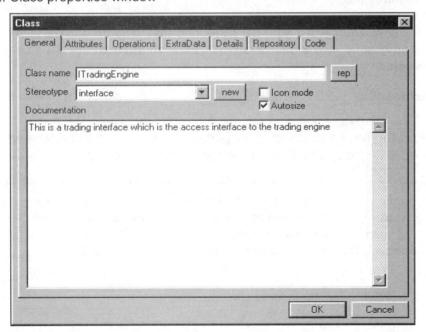

CASE EXAMPLE: INFORMIX

The following is an extract from marketing material on the Informix website.

The INFORMIX-4GL Product Family, comprised of INFORMIX-4GL Rapid Development System, INFORMIX-4GL Interactive Debugger, and INFORMIX-4GL Compiler, is a comprehensive fourth-generation application development and production environment that provides power and flexibility without the need for third-generation languages like C or COBOL. INFORMIX-4GL version 4.1 provides more enhancements to the product line than any other release since 4GL was introduced in 1986 giving you more functionality than ever before!

Wouldn't you like to find a self-contained application development environment that:

- Provides rapid development and interactive debugging capabilities

- Offers high performance in the production environment

- Integrates all the functionality you could possibly need for building even the most complex applications

- Doesn't require the use of a third-generation language

- Allows you to easily maintain your applications for years to come

- Is based on industry-standard SQL

- Is easily portable?

Look no further. You've just described INFORMIX-4GL.

Whether you're building menus, forms, screens, or reports, INFORMIX-4GL performs all development functions, and allows for easy integration between them, eliminating the need for external development packages. Because our INFORMIX-4GL products are source-code compatible, portability is ensured.

4.2 Prototyping

The use of 4GLs, together with the realisation that users need to see how a system will look and feel to assess its suitability, have contributed to the increased use of **prototyping**.

Definition

> A **prototype** is a model of all or part of a system, built to show users early in the design process how it is envisaged the completed system will appear.

As a simple example, a prototype of a formatted screen output from a system could be prepared using a graphics package, or even a spreadsheet model. This would describe how the screen output would appear to the user. The user could make suggested amendments, which would be incorporated into the next model.

Using prototyping software, the programmer can develop a **working model** of the system fairly quickly. The prototype can then be shown to users to establish whether it meets their needs. Changes may be requested at this stage and incorporated into the system more easily than if they were requested later in the development process.

The prototyping process

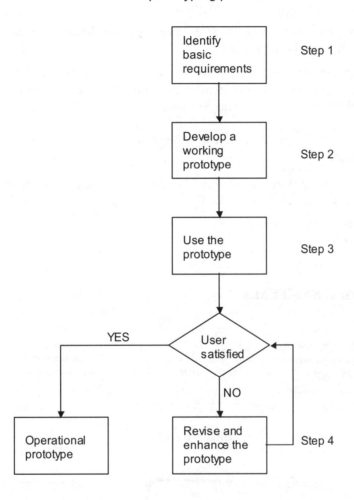

4.3 The advantages of prototyping.

(a) It makes it possible for programmers to present a 'mock-up' version of an envisaged system to users **before a substantial amount of time and money** have been committed. The user can judge the prototype before things have gone too far to be changed.

(b) The process facilitates the production of **'custom built' application software** rather than off-the-shelf packages which may or may not suit user needs.

(c) It makes efficient use of programmer time by helping programmers to develop programs more quickly. Prototyping may speed up the 'design' stage of the systems development lifecycle.

(d) A prototype does not necessarily have to be written in the language of what it is prototyping, so prototyping is not only a tool, but a **design technique**.

4.4 Disadvantages of prototyping

(a) Some prototyping tools are **tied** to a particular make of **hardware**, or a particular **database system**.

(b) It is sometimes argued that prototyping tools are **inefficient** in the program codes they produce, so that programs are bigger and require more memory than a more efficiently coded program.

(c) Prototyping may help users to steer the development of a new system towards an **existing system**.

(d) As prototyping encourages the attitude that changes and amendments are likely, some believe prototyping tools encourage programmers to produce programs quickly, but to neglect program quality.

FOR DISCUSSION

Has anyone in your group been involved in , or affected by, the implementation of a new system? How were user concerns addressed?

Was user involvement encouraged?

5 DATABASE SYSTEMS

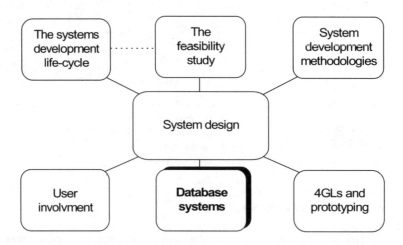

5.1 What is a database system?

The term 'database system' is used to describe a wide range of systems that utilise a central pool of data. In this context the term 'database system' involves much more than a single database package such as Microsoft Access.

Definitions

A **database** is a collection of structured data which may be manipulated to select or sort some or all of the data held. The database provides convenient access to data for a wide variety of users and user needs.

A **database management system (DBMS)** is the software that builds, manages and provides access to a database. It allows a systematic approach to the storage and retrieval of data.

The independence of logical data from physical storage, and the independence of data items from the programs which access them, is referred to as **data independence**

Duplication of data items is referred to as **data redundancy**

A database should have four major **objectives**.

(a) It should be **shared**.

(b) It should provide for the **needs of different users** who each have their own processing requirements and data access methods.

(c) The database should be **capable of evolving.** It must be able to meet the **future** data processing needs of users.

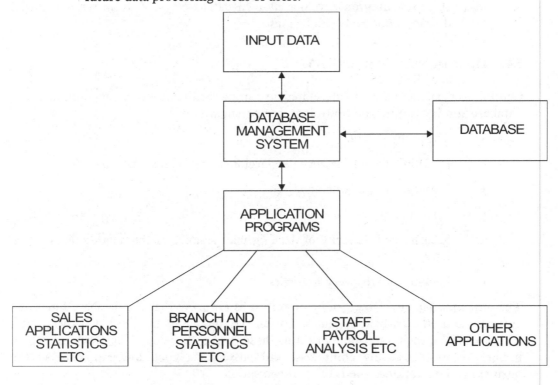

5.2 Advantages of a database system

(a) Avoidance of **unnecessary duplication** of data.

(b) Data is looked upon as serving the **organisation as a whole,** not just for individual departments. The database concept encourages management to regard data as a resource that must be **properly managed.**

NOTES

(c) The installation of a database system encourages management to **analyse data,** relationships between data items, and how data is used in different applications.

(d) **Consistency** - because data is only held once, the possibility of departments holding conflicting data on the same subject is reduced.

(e) Data on file is independent of the user programs that access the data. This allows **greater flexibility** in the ways that data can be used. New programs can be easily introduced to make use of existing data in a different way.

(f) Developing **new application programs** with a database system is easier because the programmer is not responsible for the file organisation.

5.3 Disadvantages of a database system

(a) There are problems of **data security** and **data privacy**. There is potential for unauthorised access to data. Administrative procedures for data security must supplement software controls.

(b) Since there is only one set of data, it is essential that the data should be **accurate** and free from corruption.

(c) Since data is held once, but its use is widespread, the impact of **system failure** would be greater.

(d) If an organisation develops its own database system from scratch, **initial development costs** will be high.

5.4 Database administrator (DBA)

Control over data and systems development can be facilitated by the appointment of a **database administrator,** who controls and sets standard for:

- The input of data
- Its definition, for instance the development of logical data models
- Physical storage structures
- System performance
- Security and integrity of data, eg maintenance of the data dictionary (see later)
- Back-up and recovery strategies

The principal role of a DBA can be described as ensuring that the database **functions correctly and efficiently** at all times. To achieve these aims the DBA will carry out a variety of tasks, including some or all of those discussed below. The DBA must be a person that is **technically competent** and possesses a **good understanding** of the **business and operational needs** of the organisation.

5.5 Data dictionary

Definition

A **data dictionary** is an index of data held in a database, used to assist in maintenance and any other access to the data.

A data dictionary is a feature of many database systems and CASE tools. As the term might suggest, it provides a method for **looking up the items of data** held in the database, to establish the following.

(a) **Field names, types, lengths and default values.** For instance a 'year' field would be numeric with four digits and may have a default value of the current year.

(b) A list of the entity, attribute and relationship types.

(c) A list of the **aliases** (see below).

(d) A list of all the **processes** which use data about each entity type.

(e) **How to access** the data in whatever manner is required (a data dictionary is sometimes called a data directory).

(f) What the data codes and symbols mean.

(g) The **origin** of the data.

(h) Possible range of values.

(i) **Ownership** of the data.

(j) Other comments.

A data dictionary is a record of each **data store** in the system and each **data flow** in the system.

The data dictionary is a form of technical documentation. It is also a **control tool** and ensures that all in the organisation define data **consistently**. This is extremely important for large projects which involve several programmers.

A data dictionary helps with systems analysis, systems design and systems maintenance.

(a) During systems analysis a data dictionary helps the analyst **organise information** about the data elements in the system, where they come from, where they go to what fields are used (name, type, length).

(b) During systems design a data dictionary helps the analyst and programmers to ensure that no data elements are missed out.

(c) Defining data items (ie building the dictionary) is a major part of the process of producing the physical system, and some data dictionaries can even generate program code automatically.

(d) Once the system is operational, and an **amendment** is required to a program, a data dictionary will help the programmer to understand what each data element is used for, so the impact of any amendments can be established. This is sometimes called **impact analysis.**

(e) Future **maintenance** work on the system is unlikely to be carried out by the people who originally wrote it. A data dictionary records the original work and helps to ensure continuity.

5.6 Using a database

There are four main operations in using a database.

(a) Creating the database **structure,** ie the structure of files and records.
(b) **Entering data** on to the database files, and **amending/updating** it.
(c) Retrieving and manipulating the data.
(d) Producing **reports**.

5.7 Creating the database structure

The creation of the database structure involves carrying out an **analysis** of the data to be included. It is necessary to specify what **files** will be held in the database, what **records** (entities) and the **fields** (attributes) they will contain, and how many **characters** will be in each field. The files and fields must be named, and the characteristics of particular fields (for example **all-numeric** or **all-alphabetic** fields) should be specified.

When the database structure has been established, the data user can **input data** and create a file (or files) or **derive data** from existing records.

Possible problems in **amalgamating data** are outlined below.

(a) The **compatibility** between systems is not just a matter of whether one system's files are computer-sensible to another system. It may extend to matters such as **different systems of coding**, different formats for personal data (with/without a contact name? with/without phone or fax number, and so on), different field sizes.

(b) There is potential for **loss or corruption of data** during the conversion process. This could mean a small amount of re-keying or it could be a disastrous, permanent loss of valuable information.

Full **back-ups** should be taken at the start of the process, and back-ups of information on the old system should continue during any period of parallel running.

(c) Existing application-specific systems are unlikely to have sufficient **storage** space to accommodate the combined data. This can easily be resolved, but it must be resolved with an eye to the **future growth** of the business and future use of the database.

(d) **Access to data must not suffer**. Operational users will be attempting to extract information from a much larger pool, and the system must be designed in such a way that they do not have to wade through large amounts of data that is irrelevant.

Those developing the system must consult those users who do the processing to ensure their information needs are met by the new data architecture.

(e) As well as offering the potential for new kinds of report the system must continue to **support existing reporting**.

Once more, **extensive consultation** with users is essential.

(f) Once the data has been amalgamated the business faces the task of ensuring that it is **secure**. A systems failure will now mean that no part of the business can operate, rather than at most just one part.

5.8 Retrieval and manipulation of data

Data can be retrieved and manipulated in a variety of ways.

(a) By **specifying the required parameters** - for example from a database of employee records, records of all employees in the sales department who have been employed for over 10 years and are paid less than £22,000 pa could be extracted. Search and retrieve parameters that are used regularly, can be stored on a search parameters file for future use.

(b) Retrieved data can be **sorted** on any specified field (for example for employees, sorting might be according to grade, department, age, experience, salary level etc).

(c) Some **calculations** on retrieved data can be carried out - such as calculating **totals** and **average** values.

5.9 Query languages

A database can be interrogated by a **query language**. A query language is a formalised method of constructing queries in a database system. A query language provides the ways in which you ask a database for data. Some query languages can be used to change the contents of a database.

The illustration below shows the screen from within the query building area of Microsoft Access.

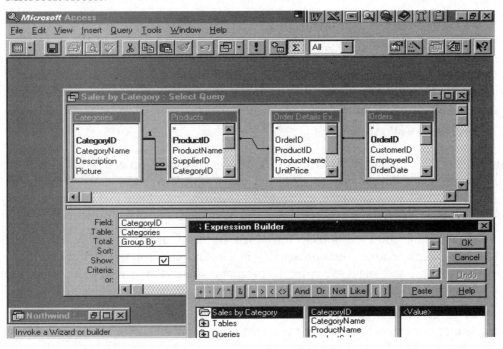

5.10 Report production

Most database packages include a **report generator facility** which allows the user to design report structures in a format which suits the user's requirements and preferences. Report formats can be stored on disk, if similar reports are produced periodically, and called up when required.

We explain some of the functions of the Microsoft Access database package in Chapter 7.

6 USER INVOLVEMENT

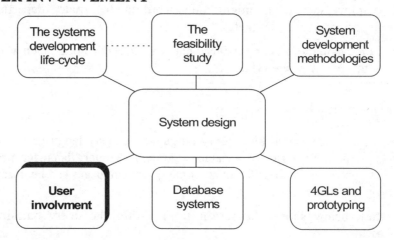

6.1 The importance of user involvement

The importance of user involvement in the development of a computerised Management Information System can not be over estimated. This section looks at a number of approaches intended to ensure that the required level of involvement is achieved.

6.2 Structured walkthroughs

Structured walkthroughs are a technique used by analysts and programmers to present their design to interested **user groups** – in other words to 'walk' them through the design. Structured walkthroughs are **formal meetings**, in which the **documentation produced during development is reviewed and checked** for errors or omissions.

These presentations are used both to **introduce and explain** the new systems to users and also to offer the users the opportunity of **making constructive criticism** of the proposed systems, and suggestions for further amendments/improvements, before the final systems specification is agreed.

Users are involved in structured walkthroughs because their knowledge of the desired system is more extensive than that of the systems development personnel. Walkthroughs are sometimes referred to as **user validation**.

6.3 The importance of signing off work

At the end of each stage of development, the resulting output is presented to users for their approval. There must be a **formal sign-off** of each completed stage before work on the next stage begins.

This **minimises reworking,** as if work does not meet user requirements, only the immediately preceding stage must be revisited. More importantly, it clarifies responsibilities and leaves little room for later disputes.

(a) If the systems developers fail to deliver something that both parties formally agreed to, it is the **developers' responsibility** to put it right, at their own expense, and compensate the user for the delay.

(b) If users ask for something extra or different, that was not formally agreed to, the developers cannot be blamed and **the user must pay** for further amendments and be prepared to accept some delay.

Activity 3   **(20 minutes)**

What, besides identification of mistakes (errors, omission, inconsistencies etc), would you expect the benefits of a walkthrough to be?

6.4 Joint applications development

Joint applications development is based on a **partnership between users and IT specialists**. When this was originally pioneered in the 1970s, it involved developers and users **specifying an entire application in just a few days**, right down to detailing screen layouts, by participating in day-long design sessions. Specific steps were followed to ensure that the design process was completed in those few days, and accomplished its goal, largely by bringing the decision makers together into one place at one time.

Joint Applications Development (JAD) was originally developed by **IBM** to promote a more participative approach to systems. The potential value to an organisation may be as follows.

(a)   It creates a **pool of expertise** comprised of interested parties from all relevant functions.

(b)   **Reduced risk of systems 'imposed'** by computer systems personnel.

(c)   This **increases the corporate ownership** and responsibility for systems solutions.

(d)   Emphasises the **information needs of users** and their relationship to business needs and decision making.

There are a number of possible **risks** affecting the potential value of JAD.

(a)   The relative **inexperience of many users** may lead to misunderstandings and possibly unreasonable expectations/demands on the system performance.

(b)   The danger of **lack of co-ordination** leading to fragmented, individual, possibly esoteric information systems.

The shift of emphasis to applications development by end-users must be well managed and controlled. An organisation may wish to set up an **information centre** to provide the necessary support and co-ordination.

6.5 Rapid applications development

JAD may also be used as a tool for users and IT specialists to build software using **rapid applications development (RAD)**. RAD can be described as a quick way of building software. It combines a management approach to systems development with the use of modern software tools such as **graphics-based user interfaces** and object oriented design methods. RAD also involves the **end-user** heavily in the development process.

At the start of the process, users and systems designers meet to **identify the overall business objectives** and to discuss the **technology required** to support these objectives. They produce a detailed definition of the required application, a description of the planned implementation and an indication of the flexibility required.

6.6 User groups

A user group is a forum for users of particular hardware or, more usually, software, so that they can **share ideas and experience** and, on occasions, acting as an arbiter in disputes with the supplier. The term is more commonly associated with users of **existing packaged software** who wish to contribute ideas for the continuing development and improvement of packages.

User groups are usually set up either by the **software manufacturers** themselves (who use them to maintain contact with customers and as a source of new product ideas) or by groups of users who were not satisfied with the level of support they were getting from suppliers of proprietary software.

Users of a particular package can meet, or more usually exchange views over the **Internet** to discuss **solutions, ideas or 'short cuts'** to improve productivity. An (electronic) **newsletter** service might be appropriate, based view exchanged by members, but also incorporating ideas culled from the wider environment by IT specialists.

Sometimes user groups are set up **within individual organisations**. Where an organisation has written its own application software, or is using tailor-made software, there will be a very small knowledge base initially, and there will obviously not be a national user group, because the application is unique.

6.7 Critical success factors

The use of **critical success factors** can help to determine the information requirements of managers which in turn assists in identifying the information systems required by an organisation. The critical success factors (CSF) method was developed by John Rockart in the late 1970s in order to define executive information needs.

Definition

> For each executive, **critical success factors** are the few key areas of the job where things must go right for the organisation to flourish.'
>
> (Sprague and McNurlin, **Information Systems Management in Practice**)

There are usually **fewer than ten** of these factors that any one executive should monitor. Furthermore, they are very time dependent, so they should be re-examined as often as necessary to keep abreast of the current business climate.

Two separate types of critical success factor can be identified. A **monitoring** CSF is used to keep abreast of existing activities and operations. A **building** CSF helps to measure the progress of new initiatives and is more likely to be relevant at senior executive level.

- **Monitoring** CSFs are important for **maintaining** business

- **Building** CSFs are important for **expanding** business

    'Let me stress that the CSF approach does not attempt to deal with information needs for strategic planning. Data needs for this management role are almost impossible to pre-plan. The CSF method centres, rather, on information needs for **management control** where data needed to **monitor and improve** existing areas of business can be more readily defined.'

    (Rockart, **Critical Success Factors** (Harvard Business Review))

6.8 Determining CSFs and performance indicators

One approach to determining the factors which are critical to success in performing a function or making a decision is as follows.

- List the organisation's corporate objectives and goals
- Determine which factors are critical for accomplishing the objectives
- Determine a small number of **performance indicators** for each factor

EXAMPLE

One of the **objectives** of an organisation might be to maintain a high level of service direct from stock without holding uneconomic stock levels. This is first quantified in the form of a **goal**, which might be to ensure that 95% of orders for goods can be satisfied directly from stock, while minimising total stockholding costs and stock levels.

CSFs might then be identified as the following.

- **Supplier performance** in terms of quality and lead times
- Reliability of **stock records**
- **Forecasting** of demand variations

6.9 Performance indicators

The determination of **performance indicators** for each of these CSFs is not necessarily straightforward. Some measures might use **factual**, objectively verifiable, data, while others might make use of **'softer' concepts**, such as opinions, perceptions and hunches.

For example, the reliability of stock records can be measured by means of physical stock counts, either at discrete intervals or on a rolling basis. Forecasting of demand variations will be much harder to measure.

Where measures use quantitative data, performance can be measured in a number of ways.

- In **physical quantities**, for example units produced or units sold
- In **money terms**, for example profit, revenues, costs or variances
- In **ratios** and **percentages**

FOR DISCUSSION

HJK Ltd is a light engineering company which produces a range of components, machine tools and electronic devices for the motor and aircraft industry. It employs about 1,000 people in 12 main divisions.

Discuss possible CSFs for HJK Ltd.

6.10 Data sources for CSFs

In general terms there are four **sources** of CSFs.

(a)   The **industry** that the business is in.

(b)   The **company** itself and its situation within the industry.

(c)   The **environment,** for example consumer trends, the economy, and political factors of the country in which the company operates.

(d)   Temporal organisational factors, which are **areas of corporate activity** which are currently **unacceptable** and represent a cause of concern, for example, high stock levels.

More specifically, possible internal and external data sources for CSFs include the following.

(a)   **The existing system**. The existing system can be used to generate reports showing **failures to meet CSFs.**

(b)   **Customer service department**. This department will maintain details of **complaints** received, **refunds** handled, **customer enquiries** etc. These should be reviewed to ensure all failure types have been identified.

(c)   **Customers**. A survey of customers, provided that it is properly designed and introduced, would reveal (or confirm) those areas where **satisfaction** is high or low.

(d)   **Competitors**. Competitors' operations, pricing structures and publicity should be closely monitored.

(e)   **Accounting system**. The **profitability** of various aspects of the operation is probably a key factor in any review of CSFs.

(f)   **Consultants**. A specialist consultancy might be able to perform a detailed review of the system in order to identify ways of satisfying CSFs.

We look at some of the activities carried out in the implementation, maintenance and review stages of the SDLC in Chapter 4.

Chapter roundup

- The **systems development life-cycle** aims to add discipline to many organisations' approach to system development. It is a model of how systems should be developed. However, in its original form it had a number of drawbacks, most notably that it ignored users' needs.

- The **feasibility study** is a formal study to decide what type of system can be developed which meets the needs of the organisation.

- There are three key areas in which a project must be **feasible** if it is to be selected. It must be justifiable on technical, operational and economic grounds.

- One of the most important elements of the feasibility study is the cost-benefit analysis. **Costs** may be analysed in different ways, but include equipment costs, installation costs, development costs, personnel costs and running costs. **Benefits** are usually more intangible, but include cost savings, revenue benefits and qualitative benefits.

- A **methodology** is a collection of procedures, techniques, tools and documentation aids which are designed to help systems developers in their efforts to implement a new system.

- A **4GL** enables programs to be constructed more quickly, as English-like commands can be taken to produce high-level code.

- **Database systems** are now common. The term 'database system' describes any system that utilises a central pool of information for a range of purposes.

- **Structured walkthroughs** are a technique used by those responsible for systems design to present their design to users. A structured walkthrough is a meeting in which the output from a phase or stage of development is presented to users for discussion and for formal approval.

- **Joint applications development** is an approach to development based on a partnership between users and IT specialists.

- One way of ensuring full user involvement in and commitment to design is the technique of **prototyping**. Prototyping assists programmers by helping them to write application programs much more quickly.

Quick quiz

1 What are the stages of the systems development lifecycle? (See Section 1.1)

2 What three areas must a project be feasible in? (See Section 2.3)

3 List five types of costs that may be incurred when developing a new system and five benefits. (See Section 2.7)

4 What is a methodology? (See Section 3.1)

5 What are the disadvantages of using a methodology? (See Section 3.4)

6   What are the advantages and disadvantages of prototyping? (See Sections 4.3 and 4.4)

7   List four approaches that may be utilised in systems development to ensure user needs are met. (See Sections 6.2 – 6.7)

Answers to Activities

1

Capital cost items	'One-off' revenue cost items	Regular annual costs
Hardware purchase costs	Consultancy fees	Operating staff salaries/wages
Software purchase costs	Systems analysts' and programmers' salaries	Data transmission costs
Purchase of accommodation (if needed)	Costs of testing the system (staff costs, consumables)	Consumable materials
		Power
Installation costs (new desks, cables, physical storage etc)	Costs of converting the files for the new system	Maintenance costs
	Staff recruitment fees	Cost of standby arrangements
		Ongoing staff training

2   An open system is much affected by unpredictable and rapidly changing environmental factors (a hospital admissions system, for instance) and it needs an approach that takes account of 'soft' problems. A highly stable system, such as a payroll system, simply needs to follow predefined rules (payroll rules change, but even the changes are relatively predictable).

3   (a)   Users become involved in the systems analysis process. Since this process is a critical appraisal of their work, they should have the opportunity to provide feedback on the appraisal itself.

     (b)   The output from the development is shown to people who are not systems development personnel. This encourages its originators to prepare it to a higher quality and in user-friendly form.

     (c)   Because the onus is on users to approve design, they are more likely to become committed to the new system and less likely to 'rubbish' it.

     (d)   The process focuses on quality of and good practice in operations generally.

     (e)   It avoids disputes about who is responsible for what.

Assignment 3 (35 minutes)

An important step in the implementation of any computer system is the feasibility study. Senior staff in an organisation may be unconvinced of the value of the study.

Tasks

(a) Briefly explain what is meant by a computer feasibility study, and what such a study should achieve.

(b) Give a justification for each of the main sections which should be contained in the feasibility study report.

(c) Identify three members of a 'typical' feasibility study team, and provide a one sentence description of their role.

(d) Comment briefly on the suggestion that if a special purpose package is to be purchased, then there is no need for such a study.

(e) List four major factors which might justify the introduction of a computer system for production planning and scheduling in a manufacturing company.

Chapter 4 :

SYSTEM IMPLEMENTATION, MAINTENANCE AND REVIEW

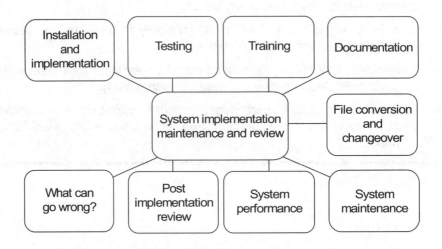

Introduction

Even if you have designed the best system in the world things can still go wrong when you actually try to put it in place. Implementation covers a **wide range of issues,** ranging from simple things like remembering that computers need desks to sit on and cables to link them up, the approach taken when changing to a new system.

Throughout its life, a system should operate effectively and efficiently. To do this, the system needs to be **maintained. We end this chapter with a** look at the **evaluation and review of systems.** This should be an ongoing process to ensure the system continues to meet requirements.

Your objectives

After completing this chapter you should understand:

(a) The nature and purpose of systems maintenance and performance evaluation.

(b) The main issues relating to the development of an Information Systems solution, and the risks involved in implementation.

(c) The role of training in ensuring users are able to fully utilise an MIS.

1 INSTALLATION AND IMPLEMENTATION

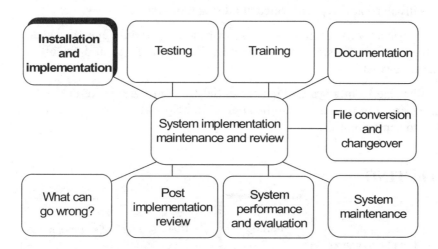

1.1 The stages of implementation

The implementation of a new computer system is a complex task, particularly with large systems. As with any complex task involving a number of related issues, planning is the key to success.

The main steps involved in a major computer system installation are outlined below. Note that this is only an example, the actual tasks and order will depend on the system being implemented and the organisation involved.

Step 1.	Select location/site
Step 2.	Choose and order hardware
Step 3.	Design and write software (or purchase off-the shelf)
Step 4.	Program testing
Step 5.	Staff training
Step 6.	Produce user documentation
Step 7.	Produce systems documentation
Step 8.	File conversion
Step 9.	Testing (including user acceptance testing)
Step 10.	System changeover (and further testing and training if required)

Software design and software/system testing have been covered in detail in previous chapters – the other main implementation issues are explained in the remainder of this chapter.

How the system implementation is conducted will have a significant impact on how users perceive the new system. A poorly planned implementation, that causes widespread disruption, is likely to result in users viewing the system negatively – which will hinder system operation.

It is important, therefore, that implementation procedures are designed so that likely problems are avoided and that unavoidable problems are managed to cause minimal disruption.

The introduction of a new system will change the way some people work, and will impact on established working relationships. To ensure staff support for change, users should be involved and kept informed at all stages of system development.

If the new system will result in some roles becoming redundant, management should handle these issues sensitively and openly. Re-training should be offered if other positions are available.

To get full value from a system, it is essential that staff are aware of what the systems capabilities are, and how these can be applied to help staff perform their roles. Training is the key to achieving this.

2   TESTING

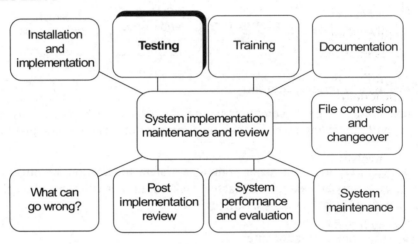

A system must be thoroughly tested before implementation, otherwise there is a danger that the new system will **go live with faults** that might prove costly. The scope of tests and trials will again **vary with the size** of the system.

Four basic stages of testing can be identified: system logic, program testing, system testing and user acceptance testing.

2.1   Testing system logic

Before any programs are written, the logic devised by the systems analyst should be checked. This process would involve the use of flow charts or structure diagrams such as data flow diagrams.

The path of different types of data and transactions are manually plotted through the system, to ensure all possibilities have been catered for and that the processing logic is correct. When all results are as expected, programs can be written.

2.2   Program testing

Program testing involves processing test data through all programs. Test data should be of the type that the program will be required to process and should include invalid/exceptional items to test whether the program reacts as it should. Program testing should cover the following areas:

- Input validity checks
- Program logic and functioning
- Interfaces with related modules \ systems
- Output format and validity

The testing process should be fully documented - recording data used, expected results, actual results and action taken. This documentation may be referred to at a later date, for example if program modifications are required.

Two types of program testing are unit testing and unit integration testing.

Unit testing and unit integration testing

Definitions

> **Unit testing** means testing one function or part of a program to ensure it operates as intended.
>
> Unit **integration testing** involves testing two or more software units to ensure they work together as intended. The output from unit integration testing is a debugged module.

Unit testing involves detailed testing of part of a program - refer back to the V model and you will see unit testing referred to at the lowest point of the V. If it is established during unit testing that a program is not operating as intended, the cause of the error must be established and corrected. Automated diagnostic routines, that step through the program line by line may be used to help this process.

Test cases should be developed that include test data (inputs), test procedures, expected results and evaluation criteria. Sets of data should be developed for both unit testing and integration testing. Cases should be developed for all aspects of the software.

2.3 System testing

When it has been established that individual programs and interfaces are operating as intended, overall system testing should begin. System testing has a wider focus than program testing. System testing should extend beyond areas already tested, to cover:

- Input documentation and the practicalities of input eg time taken

- Flexibility of system to allow amendments to the 'normal' processing cycle

- Ability to produce information on time

- Ability to cope with peak system resource requirements eg transaction volumes, staffing levels

- Viability of operating procedures

- Ability to produce information on time

System testing will involve testing both before installation (known as off-line testing) and after implementation (on-line testing). As many problems as possible should be identified before implementation, but it is likely that some problems will only become apparent when the system goes live.

2.4　User acceptance testing

Definition

> **User acceptance testing** is carried out by those who will use the system to determine whether the system meets their needs. These needs should have previously been stated as acceptance criteria. The aim is for the customer to determine whether or not to accept the system.

It is vital that users are involved in system testing to ensure the system operates as intended when used in its operating environment. Any problems identified should be corrected - this will improve system efficiency and should also encourage users to accept the new system as an important tool to help them in their work.

Users process test data, system performance is closely monitored and users report how they felt the system meets their needs. Test data may include some historical data, because it is then possible to check results against the 'actual' output from the old system.

2.5　Static testing and dynamic testing

Previous paragraphs have looked at the different stages of testing. Testing may also be described by reference to how it is performed. Software testing may be carried out in a static environment or a dynamic environment.

Definitions

> **Static testing** describes the process of evaluating a system or component based on its form, structure and content. The program or process is not executed or performed during static testing.
>
> **Dynamic testing** is testing that is performed by executing a program. It involves running the program and checking the results are as expected.

Both static and dynamic testing play an important role in software development. Static testing allows the program or part of program to be looked at in isolation - which means that other programs or parts of the system do not influence the test, and are not affected by the test. Many logical and coding errors are able to be found by simply checking and reviewing code.

However, it is only when actually running a program that some errors will be discovered. Dynamic testing will reveal any potential conflicts between the program and other elements of the system (hardware and software).

2.6　Performance testing

Tests can also be classified according to **what** they are testing – specifically performance and usability.

Definition

> **Performance testing** is conducted to evaluate the compliance of a system or component with specified performance requirements.

The specific performance requirements which performance testing uses will vary depending on the nature of the system. The initial specification for the software should provide suitable performance testing criteria.

As it is possible that the demands placed on the system and software may increase over time, it is useful to know what volume of transactions the system can cope with. Performance testing is therefore taken a 'step-further', to establish the volume of transactions or data the system can process before the software ceases to operate. This process is known as 'stress testing'.

2.7 Usability testing

Definition

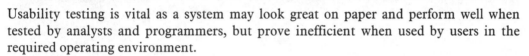

> **Usability testing** is conducted to establish the relative ease with which users are able to learn and use a system.

Usability testing is vital as a system may look great on paper and perform well when tested by analysts and programmers, but prove inefficient when used by users in the required operating environment.

Usability testing has a slightly different emphasis than user acceptance testing. Usability testing is concerned with lessons that could be learned regarding system design, in order to produce a system that is easier to learn and use. It is possible to improve usability without actually changing system capabilities - by making something more user-friendly. User acceptance testing is more specific – its purpose is to establish whether users are satisfied that the system meets the system specification when used in the actual operating environment.

2.8 Automated testing tools

Software testing can be very time consuming – often accounting for 30 percent of software development effort and budget. The need for thorough testing to achieve a quality product often conflicts with the requirement to produce the system on time and within budget.

The need for more efficient testing has led to the development of automated software testing. Automated testing involves using computer programs that automatically run the software to be tested, and record the results.

Automated testing tools are sometimes referred to as **Computer Aided Software Testing (CAST)** tools. There are products available that can automate a variety of tasks, including:

- Executing various command combinations and recording the results

- Testing software in a variety of operating environments and comparing results

- The debugging of some 'obvious' programming errors

- Facilities to track and document all testing and quality assurance information

Automated testing routines may be written by the same organisation that is writing the software, or, a specialised software testing product could be used. The following illustration shows how a software error is recorded in the testing package produced by a prominent testing software provider - Rational.

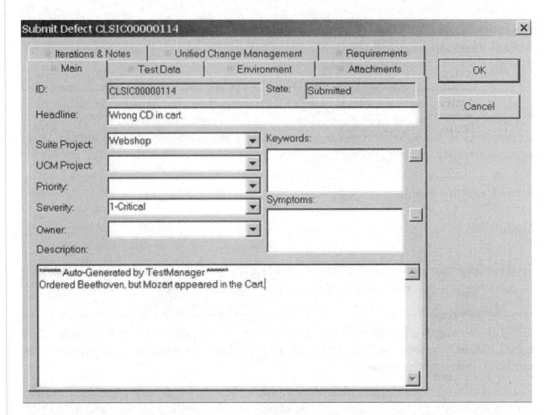

The facility provided by Rational to track software errors and testing is shown below.

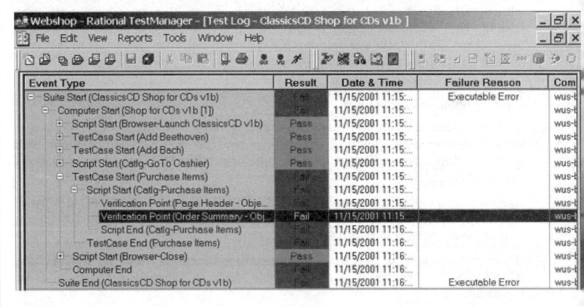

2.9 Beta versions

Commercial software producers often carry out user acceptance testing through the use of beta versions of software. A beta version is an almost finalised package, that has been tested in controlled conditions, but has not been used 'in the field'. Some users are prepared to use beta versions - and report any remaining bugs.

2.10 Developing a testing strategy

As we have seen in this chapter, there are numerous testing stages and techniques available to system developers. To ensure a coherent, effective approach to testing, a testing plan should be developed. This plan would normally form part of the overall software development quality plan.

A testing strategy should cover the following areas.

Testing strategy area	Comment
Strategy approach	A testing strategy should be formulated that details the approach that will be taken, including the tests to be conducted and the testing tools/techniques that will be used.
Test plan	A test plan should be developed that states: • What will be tested • When it will be tested (sequence) • The test environment
Test design	The logic and reasoning behind the design of the tests should be explained.
Performing tests	Detailed procedures should be provided for all tests. This explanation should ensure tests are carried out consistently, even if different people carry out the tests.
Documentation	It must be clear how the results of tests are to be documented. This provides a record of errors, and a starting point for error correction procedures.
Re-testing	The re-test procedure should be explained. In many cases, after correction, all aspects of the software should be re-tested to ensure the corrections have not affected other aspects of the software.

The presence of 'bugs' or errors in the vast majority of software/systems demonstrates that even the most rigorous testing plan is unlikely to identify all errors. The **limitations of software testing** are outlined below.

Limitation	Comment
Poor testing process	The test plan may not cover all areas of system functionality. Testers may not be adequately trained. The testing process may not be adequately documented.
Inadequate time	Software and systems are inevitably produced under significant time pressures. Testing time is often 'squeezed' to compensate for project over-runs in other areas.
Future requirements not anticipated	The test data used may have been fine at the time of testing, but future demands may be outside the range of values tested. Testing should allow for future expansion.
Inadequate test data	Test data should test 'positively' - checking that the software does what it should do, and test 'negatively' - that it doesn't do what it shouldn't. It is difficult to include the complete range of possible input errors in test data.
Software changes inadequately tested	System/software changes made as a result of testing findings or for other reasons may not be adequately tested as they were not in the original test plan.

3 TRAINING

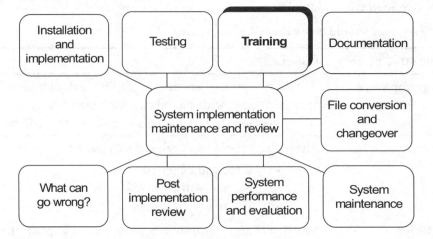

3.1 IT/IS training

Staff training in the use of information systems and information technology is essential if the return on investment in IS/IT is to be maximised.

Training is not simply an issue that affects operational staff. Training in information technology **affects all levels** in an organisation, from senior managers learning how to use an executive information system for example, to accounts clerks learning how to use an accounting package.

Training will be needed when:

- A new system is implemented
- An existing system is significantly changed
- Job specifications change
- New staff are recruited
- Skills have been forgotten

A **systematic approach** to training can be illustrated in a flowchart as follows.

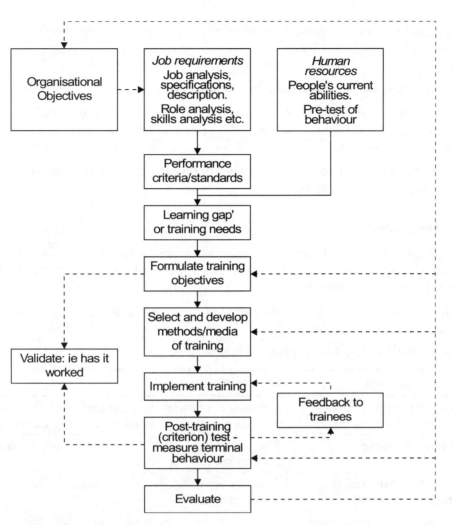

Note the following points in particular.

(a) Training is provided primarily to help the **organisation** achieve its **objectives**.

(b) An individual's **training need** is generally defined as follows.

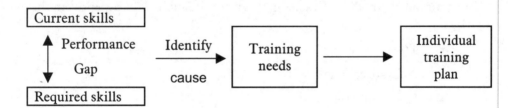

(c) Training should be **evaluated** to make sure that it has worked. If not the method may have been wrong. Whatever the cause, the training need still exists.

3.2 Senior management training

Senior manager are most likely to require training in the use of Executive Support Systems and Decision Support Systems (including spreadsheets).

Senior managers may also require an awareness of information technology in general, and project management skills to enable them to manage the acquisition and use of IS/IT within the organisation.

Training relevant to the management of information systems should therefore form part of a managers development plan.

3.3 Middle managers/supervisors training requirements

Staff operating at this level are likely to require a range of computing skills. They should be able to extract the information they require from various elements of the Management Information System.

Staff at this level should also be competent using 'office' type software (eg word-processing, spreadsheets, databases).

3.4 Operational staff

Operational staff are most likely to be involved in processing transactions. This could involve the use of bar-code readers (eg supermarket checkout operators), or keying into a transaction processing system.

Training should focus on the specific tasks the user is required to perform eg entering an invoice or answering a query.

There are a range of options available to deliver training.

Training method	Comment
Individual tuition 'at desk'	A trainer could work with an employee observing how they use a system and suggesting possible alternatives
Classroom course	The software could be used in a classroom environment, using 'dummy' data.
Computer-based training (CBT)	Training can be provided using CDs, or via an interactive website.
Case studies and exercises	Regardless of how training is delivered, it is likely that material will be based around a realistic case study relevant to the user.
Software reference material	Users may find on-line help, built-in tutorials and reference manuals useful.

The training method applicable in a given situation will depend on the following factors:

- Time available
- Software complexity
- User skill levels
- Facilities available
- Budget

BPP
PUBLISHING

4 DOCUMENTATION

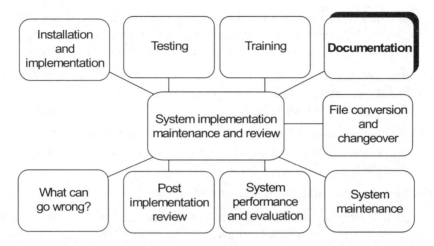

Definition

Documentation includes a wide range of technical and non-technical books, manuals, descriptions and diagrams relating to the use and operation of a computer system. Examples include user manuals, hardware and operating software manuals, system specifications and program documentation.

4.1 Technical manual

The technical manual is produced as a reference tool for those involved in producing and installing the system. The technical manual should include the following.:

- Contact details for the original developers
- System overview
- System specifications including performance details
- Hardware technical specification
- System objectives
- Flowcharts or Data Flow Diagrams
- Entity models and life histories
- Individual program specifications
- Data dictionary

The technical manual should be referred to when future modifications are made to the system. The technical manual should be updated whenever system changes are made.

4.2 User manual

The system should be documented from the point-of-view of **users**. User documentation is used to **explain** the system to users and in training. It provides a point of reference should the user have problems with the system. Much of this information may be available on-line using context-sensitive help eg 'Push F1 for help'.

The manual provides full documentation of the **operational procedures** necessary for the 'hands-on' running of the system. Amongst the matters to be covered by this documentation would be the following.

(a) **Systems set-up procedures**. Full details should be given for each application of the necessary file handling and stationery requirements etc.

(b) **Security procedures**. Particular stress should be placed on the need for checking that proper authorisation has been given for processing operations and the need to restrict use of machine(s) to authorised operators.

(c) **Reconstruction control procedures**. Precise instructions should be given in relation to matters such as back-up and recovery procedures to be adopted in the event of a systems failure.

(d) **System messages**. A listing of all messages likely to appear on the operator's screen should be given together with an indication of the responses which they should evoke.

(e) Samples, including input screens and reports.

When a system is developed in-house, the user documentation might be written by a systems analyst. However, it might be considered preferable for the user documentation to have some input from **users**. As user-documentation is intended to help users, it must be written in a way that users are able to understand. The aim is to **ensure the smooth operation of the system,** not to turn users into analysts.

As with the technical manual, the content of the user manual must be updated to reflect any system changes.

5   FILE CONVERSION AND CHANGEOVER

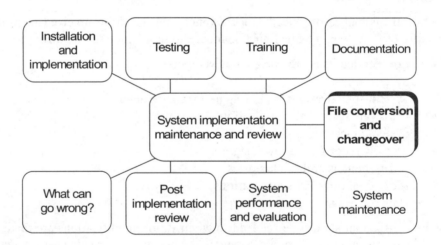

5.1   File conversion

Definition

> **File conversion**, means converting existing files into a format suitable for the new system.

Most computer systems are based around files containing data. When a new system is introduced, files must be created that conform to the requirements of that system.

The various scenarios that file conversion could involve are outlined in the following table.

Existing data	Comment
Held in manual (ie paper) files	Data must be entered manually into the new system – probably via the use of input forms, so that data entry operators have all the data they require in one document. This is likely to be a time-consuming process.
Held in existing computer files	How complex the process is in converting the files to a format compatible with the new system will depend on various technical issues such as whether coding systems are changing. It may be possible to automate much of the conversion process.
Held in both manual and computer files	Two separate conversion procedures are required
Existing data is incomplete	If the missing data is crucial, it must be researched and made available in a format suitable for the new-system – or suitable for the file conversion process.

The file conversion process is shown in the following diagram, which assumes the original data is held in manual files.

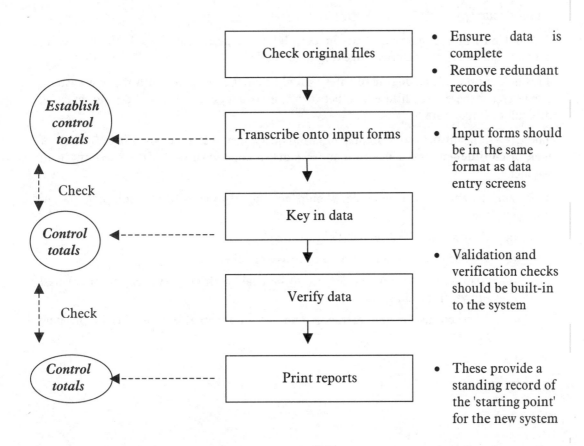

It is essential that the 'new' converted files are accurate. Various controls can be utilised during the conversion process.

    (a) **One-to-one checking** between records on the old and new systems.

    (b) **Sample checking**. Selecting and checking a sample of records, as there are too many to check individually.

    (c) **Built-in data validation** routines in automated conversion processes.

    (d) **Control totals** and **reconciliations**. These checks could include checking the total number of records, and the value of transactions.

5.2 Changeover

Once the new system has been fully and satisfactorily tested the changeover can be made. This may be according to one of four approaches.

- Direct changeover
- Parallel running
- Pilot operation
- Phased or 'staged' changeover

Direct changeover

The old system is **completely replaced** by the new system **in one move**.

This may be unavoidable where the two systems are substantially different, or where the costs of parallel running are too great.

While this method is comparatively **cheap** it is **risky** (system or program corrections are difficult while the system has to remain operational).

The new system should be introduced during **a quiet period**, for example over a bank holiday weekend or during an office closure.

Parallel running

The **old and new** systems are **run in parallel** for a period of time, both processing current data and enabling cross checking to be made.

This method provides a **degree of safety** should there be problems with the new system. However, if there are differences between the two systems cross-checking may be difficult or impossible.

There is a **delay** in the actual implementation of the new system, a possible indication of **lack of confidence,** and a need for **more staff** to cope with both systems running in parallel.

This cautious approach, if adopted, should be properly planned, and the plan should include:

    (a) A firm **time limit** on parallel running.

    (b) Details of **which data** should be **cross-checked**.

    (c) Instructions on how **errors** are to be dealt with eg previously undiscovered errors in the old system.

    (d) Instructions on how to report and act on any **major problems** in the new system.

Pilot operation

Pilot operation involves selecting part or parts of an organisation (eg a department or branch) to operate running the new system in parallel with the existing system. When the branch or department piloting the system is satisfied with the new system, they cease to use the old system. The new system is then piloted in another area of the organisation.

Pilot operation is **cheaper** and **easier to control** than running the whole system in parallel, and provides a **greater degree of safety** than does a direct changeover.

Phased changeover

Phased changeover involves selecting a complete section of the system for a direct changeover, eg in an accounting system the purchase ledger. When this part is running satisfactorily, another part is switched – until eventually the whole system has been changed.

A phased series of direct changeovers is less risky than a single direct changeover, as any problems and disruption experienced should be isolated in an area of operations.

The relative advantages and disadvantages of the various changeover methods are outlined in the following table.

Method	Advantages	Disadvantages
Direct changeover	Quick	Risky
	Minimal cost	Could disrupt operations
	Minimises workload	If fails, will be costly
Parallel running	Safe, built-in safety	Costly-two systems need to be operated
	Provides way of verifying results of new system	Time-consuming
		Additional workload
Pilot operation	Less risky than direct changeover	Can take a long time to achieve total changeover
	Less costly than complete parallel running	Not as safe as complete parallel running
Phased changeover	Less risky than a single direct changeover	Can take a long time to achieve total changeover
	Any problems should be in one area – other operations unaffected	Interfaces between parts of the system may make this impractical

FOR DISCUSSION

Has anyone in your group been involved in a system changeover? What method was used? Did the changeover proceed smoothly?

6 SYSTEM MAINTENANCE

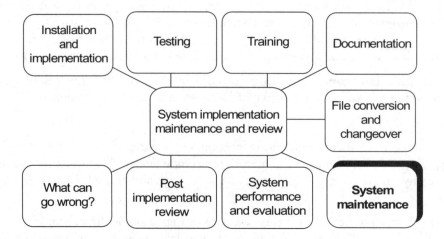

6.1 Types of maintenance

There are three types of maintenance activity.

- Corrective maintenance
- Perfective maintenance
- Adaptive maintenance

Definition

> **Corrective maintenance** is carried out in reaction to a system failure, for example in processing or in an implementation procedure. Its objective is to ensure that systems remain operational.
>
> **Perfective maintenance** is carried out in order to perfect the software, or to improve software so that the processing inefficiencies are eliminated and performance is enhanced.
>
> **Adaptive maintenance** is carried out to take account of anticipated changes in the processing environment. For example new taxation legislation might require change to be made to payroll software.

Corrective maintenance usually consists of action in response to a **problem**. Much **perfective** maintenance consists of making enhancements requested by **users** to improve or extend the facilities available. The user interface may be amended to make software more user friendly.

The key features of system maintenance ought to be **flexibility** and **adaptability**.

(a) The system, perhaps with minor modifications, should cope with changes in the computer user's procedures or volume of business.

(b) The computer user should benefit from advances in computer hardware technology without having to switch to another system altogether.

6.2   The causes of system maintenance

Besides environmental changes, three factors contribute to the need for maintenance.

Factor	Comment
Errors	However carefully and diligently the systems development staff carry out systems testing and program testing, it is likely that **bugs** will exist in a newly implemented system. Most should be identified during the first few runs of a system. The effect of errors can obviously vary enormously.
Changes in requirements	Although users should be consulted at all stages of systems development, problems may arise after a system is implemented because users may have found it difficult to express their requirements, or may have been concerned about the future of their jobs and not participated fully in development.
	Cost constraints may have meant that certain requested features were not incorporated. Time constraints may have meant that requirements suggested during development were ignored in the interest of prompt completion.
Poor documentation	If old systems are accompanied by poor documentation, or even a complete lack of documentation, it may be very difficult to understand their programs. It will be hard to update or maintain such programs. Programmers may opt instead to patch up the system with new applications using newer technology.

Corrective and adaptive maintenance should be carried out **as and when** problems occur, but perfective maintenance may be carried out on a more scheduled system-by-system basis (Sales system in January, Purchases in February, etc).

Assuming the system is intended to reflect business needs, it ought to be possible to predict with reasonable certainty when business **growth** will make maintenance necessary. It is possible to contend with increasing volumes and communication needs by enhancing the existing computer system on site, on a modular basis.

- Installing **disks** of **greater capacity** and **higher speed**
- Installing a **more powerful processor**
- Changing to **faster printers**
- Installing **additional terminals** or **network facilities**

As mentioned, systems analysts will always try to design **flexibility** into computer systems, so that the system can **adapt** to change.

However, there will come a point at which **redevelopment** is necessary, for example where hardware upgrades or the availability of new software make radical change necessary, or following a company restructuring.

7   SYSTEM PERFORMANCE AND EVALUATION

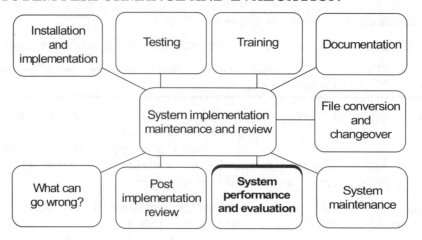

7.1   Performance measurement

It is not possible to identify and isolate every consequence of an implementation project and the impact of each on organisational effectiveness. To achieve some approximation to a complete evaluation, therefore, certain **indirect measures** must be used.

(a)   **Significant task relevance** attempts to observe the results of system use. For example, monthly management accounts should be available earlier if a manual accounting system is replaced by an accounting software package.

(b)   The **willingness to pay** of users might give an indication of value. Internal charge-out mechanisms could be implemented to introduce an element of 'user-pays'.

(c)   **Systems logs** may give an indication of the value of the system if it is a 'voluntary use' system, such as an external database.

(d)   **User information satisfaction** is a concept which attempts to find out, by asking users, how they rate their satisfaction with a system. They may be asked for their views on timeliness, quality of output, response times, processing and their overall confidence in the system.

(e)   The adequacy of system **documentation** may be measurable in terms of how often manuals are actually used and the number of errors found or amendments made. However, low usage of a user manual, for instance, could be due to the manual being poor, or may be because the system is very user-friendly.

Activity 1   (15 minutes)

Operational evaluation should consider, among other issues, whether input data is properly provided and output is useful. Output documents are often considered by users to be of marginal value, perhaps of use for background information only. In spite of this there is a tendency to continue producing existing reports.

How might you identify whether a report is being used?

Performance reviews will vary in content from organisation to organisation, but the matters which will probably be looked at are as follows.

(a) The **growth** rates in file sizes and the number of transactions processed by the system. Trends should be analysed and projected to assess whether there are likely to be problems with lengthy processing time or an inefficient file structure due to the volume of processing.

(b) The clerical **manpower** needs for the system, and deciding whether they are more or less than estimated.

(c) The identification of any **delays** in processing and an assessment of the consequences of any such delays.

(d) An assessment of the efficiency of **security** procedures, in terms of number of breaches, number of viruses encountered.

(e) A check of the **error rates** for input data. High error rates may indicate inefficient preparation of input documents, an inappropriate method of data capture or poor design of input media.

(f) An examination of whether **output** from the computer is being used to good purpose. (Is it used? Is it timely? Does it go to the right people?)

(g) Operational **running costs**, examined to discover any inefficient programs or processes. This examination may reveal excessive costs for certain items although in total, costs may be acceptable.

7.2 Improving performance

Computer systems efficiency audits are concerned with improving **outputs** from the system and their use, or reducing the costs of system **inputs**. With falling costs of computer hardware and software, and continual technological advances there should often be **scope for improvements** in computer systems, which an audit ought to be able to identify.

Outputs from a computer system

With regard to outputs, the efficiency of a computer system would be enhanced in any of the following ways.

(a) **More outputs** of some value could be produced by the **same input** resources.

For example:
(i) If the system could process **more transactions**.

(ii) If the system could produce **more management information** (eg sensitivity analysis).

(iii) If the system could make information **available to more people** who might need it.

(b) **Outputs of little value** could be **eliminated** from the system, thus making savings in the cost of inputs.

NOTES

For example:

(i) If reports are produced **too frequently**, should they be produced less often?

(ii) If reports are **distributed too widely**, should the distribution list be shortened?

(iii) If reports are **too bulky**, can they be reduced in size?

(c) The **timing** of outputs could be better.

Information should be available in good time for the information-user to be able to make good use of it. Reports that are issued late might lose their value. Computer systems could give managers **immediate** access to the information they require, by means of file enquiry or special software (such as databases or spreadsheet modelling packages).

(d) It might be found that outputs are not as satisfactory as they should be, perhaps because:

(i) **Access** to information from the system is limited, and could be improved by the use of a **database** and a **network** system.

(ii) Available outputs are **restricted** because of the **method of data processing** used (eg batch processing instead of real-time processing) or the **type of equipment** used (eg stand-alone PCs compared with client/server systems).

Depending on your current level of knowledge, you may need to refer to some parts of Chapter 5 before attempting the following activity.

Activity 2	(15 minutes)

What elements of hardware and software might restrict the capabilities of a system?

7.3 System evaluation

A system should be **reviewed** after implementation, and periodically, so that any unforeseen problems may be solved and to confirm that it is achieving the desired results.

The system should have been designed with clear, specified **objectives**, and justification in terms of **cost-benefit analysis** or other **performance criteria**.

Just as the feasibility of a project is assessed by reference to **technical, operational, social and economic factors,** so the same criteria can be used for evaluation. We need not repeat material that you have covered earlier, but here are a few pointers.

Cost-benefit review

A cost-benefit review is similar to a cost-benefit analysis, except that **actual** data can be used.

For instance when a large project is completed, techniques such as DCF appraisal can be performed **again**, with actual figures being available for much of the expenditure.

Activity 3	**(20 minutes)**

A cost-benefit review might categorise items under the five headings of direct benefits, indirect benefits, development costs, implementation costs and running costs.

Give two examples of items which could fall to be evaluated under each heading.

Efficiency and effectiveness

In any evaluation of a system, two terms recur. Two key reasons for the introduction of information systems into an organisation are to improve the **efficiency** or the **effectiveness** of the organisation.

Definition

Efficiency can be measured by considering the resource inputs into, and the outputs from, a process or an activity.

An activity uses **resources** such as staff, money and materials. If the same activity can be performed using **fewer resources**, for example fewer staff or less money, or if it can be completed **more quickly,** the efficiency of the activity is improved. An improvement in efficiency represents an improvement in **productivity**.

Automation of an organisation's activities is usually expected to lead to greater efficiency in a number of areas.

(a) The **cost** of a computer system is lower than that of the manual system it replaces, principally because jobs previously performed by human operators are now carried out by computer.

(b) The **accuracy** of data information and processing is improved, because a computer does not make mistakes.

(c) The **speed** of processing is improved. Response times, for example in satisfying customer orders, are improved.

Definition

Effectiveness is a measurement of how well the organisation is achieving its objectives.

Effectiveness is a **more subjective** concept than efficiency, as it is concerned with factors which are less easy to measure. It focuses primarily on the relationship of the organisation with its environment. For example, automation might be pursued because it is expected that the company will be more effective at **increasing market share** or at satisfying **customer needs**.

Computing was originally concerned with the automation of 'back office' functions, usually aspects of data processing. Development was concerned with improving **efficiency**.

Recent trends are more towards the development of **'front office'** systems, for example to improve an organisation's decision-making capability or to seek competitive advantage. This approach seeks to improve the **effectiveness** of the organisation.

Metrics

Definition

> **Metrics** are quantified measurements used to measure system performance.

The use of **metrics** enables **system quality** to be **measured** and the early identification of problems.

Examples of metrics include system response time, the number of transactions that can be processed per minute, the number of bugs per hundred lines of code and the number of system crashes per week.

Metrics should be devised that **suit the system in question** – those given above are simply typical examples.

Many facets of system quality are not easy to measure statistically (eg user-friendliness). Indirect measurements such as the number of calls to the help-desk per month can be use as an indication of overall quality/performance.

Metrics should be carefully thought out, objective and stated **clearly**. They must measure **significant aspects** of the system, be used consistently and **agreed with users.**

Hardware monitors

Computers themselves can be used in systems evaluation. Three methods used are hardware monitors, software monitors and systems logs.

Hardware monitors are devices which measure the presence or absence of electrical signals in selected circuits in the computer hardware.

They might measure **idle time** or **levels of activity** in the CPU, or peripheral activity. Data is sent from the sensors to counters, which periodically write it to disk or tape.

A program will then analyse the data and produce an analysis of findings as output. It might identify for example **inefficient co-ordination** of processors and peripherals, or **excessive delays** in writing data to backing storage.

Software monitors

Software monitors are computer programs which **interrupt the application in use** and record data about it. They might identify, for example, **excessive waiting** time during program execution. Unlike hardware monitors, they may slow down the operation of the program being monitored.

System logs

Many computer systems provide automatic log details, for example **job start and finish** times or which employee has used which program and for how long. The systems log can therefore provide useful data for analysis.

(a) Unexplained **variations in job running** times might be recorded.
(b) Excessive machine **down-time** is sometimes a problem.
(c) **Mixed workloads** of large and small jobs might be scheduled inefficiently.

Network systems are explained in Chapter 5.

BPP PUBLISHING

NOTES

8 POST-IMPLEMENTATION REVIEW

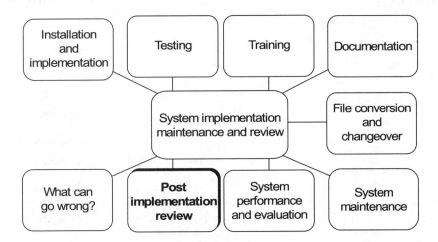

8.1 The post-implementation review

The post-implementation review should establish whether the objectives and targeted performance criteria have been met, and if not, why not, and what should be done about it.

In appraising the operation of the new system, comparison should be made between **actual and predicted performance**.

If the implementation has involved a **steering committee,** the committee may also be responsible for overseeing the post-implementation review. The **internal audit** department may be required to do much of the work involved in the review.

The post-implementation measurements should **not be made too soon** after the system goes live, or else results will be abnormally affected by 'teething' problems, lack of user familiarity and resistance to change.

The post-implementation review report

The findings of a post-implementation review team should be formalised in a **report**.

(a) A **summary** of their findings should be provided, emphasising any areas where the system has been found to be **unsatisfactory**.

(b) A review of **system performance** should be provided. This will address the matters outlined above, such as run times and error rates.

(c) A **cost-benefit review** should be included, comparing the forecast costs and benefits identified at the time of the feasibility study with actual costs and benefits.

(d) **Recommendations** should be made as to any **further action** or steps which should be taken to improve performance.

9 INFORMATION SYSTEMS PROJECTS – WHAT CAN GO WRONG?

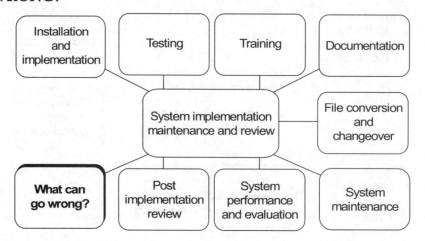

9.1 Conflicting demands

A systems development project is **affected by a number of factors, often in conflict with each other**. The requirement to keep to a specified **time** might for example increase **costs**, if there are delays and new staff have to be employed, or reduce **quality** if corners are cut. It is with these aims in mind that **management** of the project must be conducted.

(a) **Quality** of the system required, in terms of basic system requirements.

(b) The **resources**, both in terms of staff recruitment and work scheduling, and technology.

(c) **Time**, both to complete the project, and in terms of the opportunity cost of time spent on this project which could be spent on others.

(d) **Costs**, which are monitored and controlled, in accordance with the budget set for the project.

Perhaps the best way of understanding why active management of information systems projects is **necessary** is by seeing **what happens when they go wrong**. It is not uncommon for a systems development project to be late and over budget, and for the system produced still not to deliver what was expected. A number of factors can combine to produce these expensive disasters, as explained in the following paragraphs.

9.2 Project managers

The person appointed project manager in an Information Systems project is often an Information Technology specialist. Such an individual might be a highly proficient analyst or programmer, but **not a good manager**.

The project manager has a number of conflicting requirements.

(a) The **systems manager**, usually the project manager's boss, wants the project delivered on time, to specification and within budget.

(b) **Users,** and the **management** of the function to which they belong, want a system which does everything they require - but they are not always certain what they want. User input is vital to a project, but user management and staff may not be able to take time off from their normal duties to help out. If the project is late, over budget, and does not do all which is required of it, then users will be vocal critics.

(c) The project manager has to plan and supervise the work of **analysts** and **programmers**.

The project manager needs to develop an **appropriate management style**. As the project manager needs to encourage participation from users, an excessively authoritarian style is not suitable.

9.3 Other factors

Other factors can be identified.

(a) The project manager accepts an **unrealistic deadline** for having the system up and running. The timescale is fixed too early on in the planning process: the user's idea of when the system would be needed is taken as the deadline, before sufficient consideration is given to the realism of this timescale.

(b) **Poor or non-existent planning** is a recipe for disaster. Ludicrous deadlines would appear much earlier if a proper planning process was undertaken.

(c) **Control is non-existent** (ie no performance reviews).

(d) **Users change their requirements**, resulting in costly changes to the system as it is being developed.

(e) **Poor timetabling and resourcing** is a cause of problems. It is no use being presented on day 1 with a team of programmers, when there is systems analysis and design work to do. As the development and implementation of a computer project may take a considerable length of time (perhaps 18 months from initial decision to operational running for a medium-sized installation) a proper **plan** and time **schedule** for the various activities must be drawn up.

9.4 Steering committees

One tool used to reduce the likelihood of a poor system being developed is the steering committee. Some organisations set up a steering committee to oversee the development of information systems within the organisation. The steering committee's tasks are as follows.

(a) To **approve (or reject) projects** whose total budgeted cost is below a certain limit and so within their authorisation limit.

(b) To **recommend projects** to the board of directors for acceptance when their cost is high enough to call for approval at board level.

(c) To establish **company guidelines** within the framework of the IT strategy for the development of computer based processing and management information systems.

(d) The **co-ordination and control** of the work of the study group(s) and project development groups, in respect of the development time, the cost and the technical quality of the investigations.

(e) The **evaluation** of the feasibility study reports and system specifications. The steering committee must be satisfied that each new system has been properly justified.

(f) To monitor and **review each new system after implementation** to check whether the system has met its objectives. If it hasn't, to investigate the reasons for the system's failure, and take any suitable control or remedial measures.

(g) In an organisation which has a continuing programme of new DP projects, assessing the contribution of each project to the long term **corporate objectives** of the organisation, ranking projects in order of **priority** and assigning resources to the most important projects first, and taking decisions to defer projects when insufficient resources are available.

The steering committee might include the following.

- The **information director** or a senior IS staff member
- **Accountants** for technical financial advice relating to costs and benefits
- Senior **user management**

Activity 4 (40 minutes)

Tasks

(a) Describe the meaning and purpose of a post-implementation review.

The Human Resources Director of a large company wants to measure the success of the application software commissioned and implemented for a personnel system.

(b) Briefly describe three measures the Director could use to quantify the success of the application software and state what each of these three measures is attempting to assess.

It is expected that the user will define new requirements (and change old ones) throughout the life of the system.

(c) List the components of a procedure for recording, prioritising and implementing these changes.

NOTES

Chapter roundup

- The **implementation** of a new computer system is a complex task that requires careful planning.

- Staff should be **involved** and kept fully **informed** at all stages of system development and implementation.

- Staff **training** is essential to ensure that information systems are utilised to their full potential.

- Training is needed when

  ○ A **new** system is implemented
  ○ An existing system is significantly **changed**
  ○ Job specifications change
  ○ New staff are recruited
  ○ Skills have been forgotten

- Training should be targeted to ensure those involved receive training **relevant** to the tasks they perform.

- There are a range of options available to **deliver training**

  ○ Individual tuition 'at desk'
  ○ Classroom course
  ○ Computer based training (CBT)
  ○ Software reference material
  ○ Case studies and exercises

- The **technical manual** is produced as a reference tool for those involved in producing and installing the system.

- The user manual is used to explain the system to users.

- There are four approaches to **changeover**: direct changeover, parallel running, pilot operations and phased changeover. These vary in terms of time required, cost and risk.

- There are three types of systems **maintenance**. **Corrective** maintenance is carried out to correct an error, **perfective** maintenance aims to make enhancements to systems and **adaptive** maintenance takes account of anticipated changes in the processing environment.

- **Performance reviews** can be carried out to look at a wide range of systems functions and characteristics. Technological change often gives scope to improve the quality of outputs or reduce the extent or cost of inputs.

- During the **post-implementation review**, an evaluation of the system is carried out to see whether the targeted performance criteria have been met and to carry out a review of costs and benefits. The review should culminate in the production of a report and recommendations.

- Some organisations use **steering committees** to oversee the development of information systems.

Quick quiz

1 List the main stages in the implementation of a computer system (See section 1.1)

2 Name three types of testing. (See sections 2.1-2.7)

3 What options are available to deliver training? (See section 3.4)

4 Distinguish between the technical manual and the user manual. (See sections 4.1 – 4.2)

5 What is parallel running? (See section 5.2)

6 When might phased implementation be appropriate? (See section 5.2)

7 List three types of maintenance. (See section 6.1)

8 What factors contribute to the need for maintenance? (See section 6.2)

9 What is a computer system efficiency audit concerned with? (See section 7.2)

10 What should the post-implementation review establish? (See section 8.1)

Answers to Activities

1 There are a wide range of possible answers to this question. Two possibilities are:

(a) A study could be carried out to see what each recipient of the report does with it and assess its importance.

(b) A user-pays charge-out system could be implemented - this would be a strong incentive to cancel requests for unnecessary output.

2 A system's capabilities might be limited by the following restrictions.

(a) The size of the computer's memory.
(b) The power of the processor.
(c) The capacity of the computer's backing storage.
(d) The number of terminals linked to a mainframe.
(e) The software's capabilities.

3 *Direct benefits* might include reduced operating costs, for example lower overtime payments.

Indirect benefits might include better decision-making and the freeing of human 'brainpower' from routine tasks so that it can be used for more creative work.

Development costs include systems analysts' costs and the cost of time spent by users in assisting with fact-finding.

Implementation costs would include costs of site preparation and costs of training.

Running costs include maintenance costs, software leasing costs and on-going user support.

4

(a) **A post-implementation review** takes place a few months after system implementation is complete. The review is to receive feedback from users on how well the system is working and to check that the objectives of the project have been met. The review normally takes the form of a meeting between the project sponsor, systems analyst, developers and users.

The review will investigate both the procedures used throughout the project and the systems that have been produced. The purpose of doing this is to identify what features of the project went well, and what went wrong or badly, so that future projects will avoid these problems.

In reviewing the objectives of the project, the review will also check whether or not the business benefits expected from the project have been achieved. Where benefits have not been achieved, or other objectives of the project have not been met, the review may also recommend remedial action to ensure that the required benefits are obtained.

(b) **Measures of success for application software**

(i) **Number of calls to the help desk**

Ascertaining the number of help desk calls per 100 employees (or some other useful number) will help to determine how useable and user-friendly the system is. The number of calls may also give an indication of the effectiveness of the training provided.

(ii) **Number of errors reported**

A log can be maintained, either by individual users or the help desk, of the number and type of errors found in the system. The actual error rate provides an indication of the quality of programming and the effectiveness of the different stages of testing (user acceptance, system and module).

(iii) **Number of transactions processed**

The original software specification will indicate how many transactions should be processed. Comparing the specification with the actual number processed will provide information on the usefulness of the system (if the system is not useful then presumably it will be used less than expected). A small number of transactions being processed could also be indicative of poor programming or inadequate hardware specifications, so further analysis may be needed to determine which of these is relevant.

(iv) Number of change requests

Users may request changes to the system, either where that system did not meet their original requirements, or where the system as implemented does not meet their expectations in some way. Changes requested due to initial specifications not being met provides some measure on the quality of the design and testing processes. Changes requested because the software is not meeting expectations may indicate weaknesses in this method of obtaining data for the initial specification.

(c) The components of a procedure for recording, prioritising and **implementing changes requested for a live system** is outlined below.

- A means for the user to record and request a change to the system

- A method of collating these change requests

- A means of providing a impact analysis and business case for each change

- A process for reviewing each request with agreed criteria for accepting or rejecting a request

- A method of prioritising requests that have been accepted

- Provision of appropriate documentation to record each change request with analysis and design implications for the existing system

- A method of allocating amendments to programmers

- A process for reviewing the work of programmers and ensuring that the change meets the initial specification

- A process for testing the change within the whole program suite

- Procedures for informing users date and nature of the change

- Procedures for updating system and user documentation prior to the release of the change

---

Assignment 4   **(30 minutes)**

Investigating and documenting the current business system is one of the stages of the systems development life cycle.

Tasks

(a) Briefly explain three reasons why it is important that the analyst should investigate and document the current business system.

(b) Briefly describe four methods or models used in investigating and documenting the current business system.

Chapter 5 :

SELECTING AND MANAGING INFORMATION TECHNOLOGY

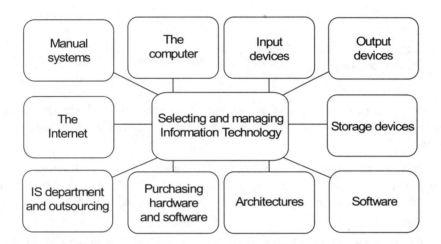

Introduction

Management Information Systems almost always utilise **Information Technology**. In this chapter we look at the features of Information Technology hardware and software in common use.

Many MIS are now offering access to the Internet, which is the subject of the final section in this chapter.

Your objectives

After completing this chapter you should have an understanding of:

(a) The various types of Information Technology hardware and software.

(b) Different system architectures.

(c) The main issues relating to the Internet.

NOTES

1 MANUAL SYSTEMS

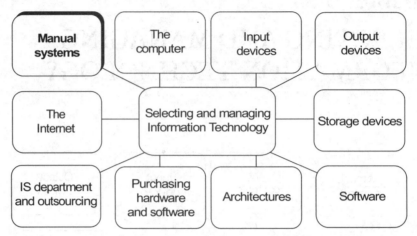

Many tasks (and people) are still better suited to manual methods of working, for example a single quick calculation may best be done mentally or by using a pocket calculator.

Many people also prefer **communicating face to face** with their colleagues, rather than using tools such as e-mail. People may prefer to interact both to fulfil social needs and because they find this form of communication more effective eg use of body language, tone of voice etc.

The use of poorly designed computer systems, or using 'good systems' with inadequately trained users, will result in inefficiencies that negate the benefits computerised processing should bring.

1.1 Manual systems v computerised systems

However, in many situations manual systems are inferior to computerised systems. Some **disadvantages of manual systems** are outlined in the following table.

Disadvantage	Comment
Productivity	**Productivity** is usually lower, particularly in routine or operational situations such as transaction processing.
Slower	Processing is **slower** where large volumes of data need to be dealt with.
	Slower processing means that some information that could be provided if computerised systems were used, will not be provided at all, because there is not time.
Risk of errors	The **risk of errors** is greater, especially in repetitive work like payroll calculations.
Less accessible	Information is generally **less accessible**. Access to information is often restricted to one user at a time. Paper files can easily be mislaid or buried in in-trays, in which case the information they contain is not available at all.

Disadvantage	Comment
Alterations	It is difficult to make **corrections**. If a manual document contains errors or needs updating it is often necessary to recreate the **whole** document from scratch, rather than just a new version with the relevant details changed.
Quality of output	**Quality of output** is less consistent and often not well-designed. At worst, hand-written records may be illegible and so completely useless. Poorly presented information may fail to communicate key points.
Bulk	Paper based systems are generally very **bulky** both to handle and to store, and office space is expensive.

2 THE COMPUTER

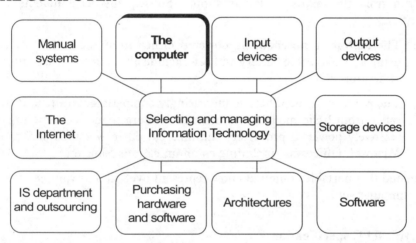

A computer is a device which accepts input data, processes it according to programmed rules, calculates results and then stores and/or outputs these results.

2.1 Types of computer

Computers can be classified as follows.

- Supercomputers
- Mainframe computers
- Minicomputers
- Microcomputers, now commonly called PCs

A supercomputer is used to process very large amounts of data very quickly. They are particularly useful for occasions where high volumes of calculations need to be performed, for example in meteorological or astronomical applications.

A mainframe computer system uses a powerful central computer, linked by cable or telecommunications to terminals. A mainframe has many times more processing power than a PC and offers extensive data storage facilities.

Mainframes are used by organisations such as banks that have very large volumes of processing to perform and have special security needs. Many organisations have now replaced their old mainframes with networked 'client-server' systems of mid-range computers and PCs because this approach is thought to be cheaper and offer more flexibility.

A minicomputer is a computer whose size, speed and capabilities lie somewhere between those of a mainframe and a PC. The term was originally used before PCs were developed, to describe computers which were cheaper but less well-equipped than mainframe computers.

With the advent of PCs and of mainframes that are much smaller than in the past, the definition of a minicomputer has become rather vague. There is really no definition which distinguishes adequately between a PC and a minicomputer.

PCs are now the norm for small to medium-sized business computing and for home computing, and most larger businesses now use them for day-to-day needs such as word-processing. Often they are linked together in a **network** to enable sharing of information between users.

2.2 Portables

The original portable computers were heavy, weighing around five kilograms, and could only be run from the mains electricity supply. Subsequent developments allow true portability.

(a) The **laptop** or **notebook** is powered either from the electricity supply or using a rechargeable battery and can include all the features and functionality of desktop PCs.

(b) The **palmtop** or handheld is increasingly compatible with true PCs. Devices range from basic models which are little more than electronic organisers to relatively powerful processors running 'cut-down' versions of Windows and Microsoft Office, and including communications features.

It is estimated that portable computers now represent over 50% in volume of all types of personal computer sold.

2.3 A typical PC specification

Here is the specification for a powerful PC, from an advertisement that appeared in mid 2002. This PC cost around £1000.

PC SPECIFICATION	
Intel 1.8 GHz Pentium 4 Processor	3.5" Floppy Disk Drive
25 GB hard disk drive	15" SVGA Monitor
56 kbps internal modem	Optical mouse
128MB RAM	2 serial ports, 1 parallel port
8 Speed CD-ROM/DVD Combo Drive	4 USB ports
Windows XP pre-loaded	

2.4 The processor

The processor is the 'brain' of the computer. The processor may be defined as follows. The processor (sometimes referred to as the central processing unit or CPU) is divided into three areas:

- Arithmetic and logic unit
- Control unit
- Main store or memory

The processing unit may have all its elements - arithmetic and logic unit, control unit, and the input/output interface on a single 'chip'. A chip is a small piece of silicon upon which is etched an integrated circuit, on an extremely small scale.

The chip is mounted on a carrier unit which in turn is 'plugged' on to a circuit board - called the motherboard - with other chips, each with their own functions.

The most common chips are those made by the Intel company. Each generation of Intel CPU chip has been able to perform operations in fewer clock cycles than the previous generation, and therefore works more quickly.

MHz and clock speed

The processor receives program instructions and sends signals to peripheral devices. The signals are co-ordinated by a **clock** which sends out a 'pulse' - a sort of tick-tock sequence called a cycle - at regular intervals.

The number of cycles produced per second is usually measured in **MegaHertz** (MHz) or **GigaHertz** (GHz).

- 1 MHz = one **million** cycles per second
- 1 GHz = one **billion** cycles per second

A typical modern business PC might run at 750 MHz, but models with higher clock speeds (eg 1 GHz) are now common.

2.5 Memory

Each individual storage element in the computer's memory consists of a simple circuit which can be switched **on** or **off**. These two states can be conveniently expressed by the numbers 1 and 0 respectively.

Each 1 or 0 is a bit. Bits are grouped together in groups of eight to form bytes. A byte may be used to represent a character, for example a letter, a number or another symbol.

Business PCs now make use of 32 bit processors. Put simply, this means that data travels around from one place to another in groups of 16 or 32 bits, and so modern PCs operate considerably faster than the original 8 bit models.

The processing capacity of a computer is in part dictated by the capacity of its memory. Capacity is calculated in kilobytes (1 kilobyte = 2^{10} (1,024) bytes) and megabytes (1 megabyte = 2^{20} bytes) and gigabytes (2^{30}). These are abbreviated to Kb, Mb and Gb.

RAM

RAM (Random Access Memory) is memory that is directly available to the processing unit. It holds the data and programs in current use. RAM in microcomputers is 'volatile' which means that the contents of the memory are erased when the computer's power is switched off.

The RAM on a typical business PC is likely to have a capacity of 32 to 128 megabytes. The amount of RAM available is extremely important. A computer with a 750 MHz clock speed and 64 Mb of RAM will not be as efficient as a 500 MHz PC with 128 Mb of RAM.

ROM

ROM (Read-Only Memory) is a memory chip into which fixed data is written permanently at the time of its manufacture. When you turn on a PC you may see a reference to BIOS (basic input/output system). This is part of the ROM chip containing all the programs needed to control the keyboard, screen, disk drives and so on.

Cache

The cache is a small but extremely fast part of memory which holds a second copy of data most recently read from or written to main memory – to enable quick retrieval. When the cache is full, older entries are 'flushed out' to make room for new ones.

RAM, ROM and cache are different to **hard disk storage**. Hard disks are storage devices that may hold vast amounts of data (eg 20 Gigabytes). Files are stored on storage media such as a hard disk. When files are opened to be referred to or amended, they are stored in RAM. We cover storage devices later in this chapter.

3   INPUT DEVICES

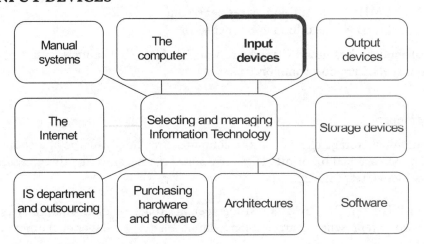

3.1   Data collection and input

A computerised information system receives data and instructions via input devices, stores data and programs on storage devices and outputs processed data (information) using output devices. The system may also interact with other systems via communications devices.

Data must be input into a computer system in a form the computer is able to interpret. There are a number of various methods of data input. When choosing a method of data input for a given situation, key considerations are:

- Speed
- Accuracy
- Cost
- Volume of data\transactions
- System reliability
- Flexibility required

Some common methods of input are explained in the following paragraphs.

The keyboard

Almost all computer terminals and personal computers include a keyboard based on the basic QWERTY typewriter keyboard. The user inputs data by hitting the relevant combination of keys.

Keyboard input is a labour-intensive process, but is the only suitable option in many circumstances eg producing a unique letter in which accuracy is vital.

The VDU or monitor

A VDU (visual display unit) or 'monitor' displays text and graphics. The screen's resolution is the number of pixels that are lit up. More and smaller pixels enable detailed high-resolution display. Super VGA, or SVGA, is the standard for newer monitors and offers resolutions up to $1,280 \times 1,024$.

Mouse

A wheeled mouse is a handheld device with a rubber ball protruding from a small hole in its base. The mouse is moved over a flat surface, and as it moves, internal sensors pick up the motion and convert it into electronic signals which instruct the cursor on screen to move in the same direction.

The wheeled mouse is slowly being replaced by the optical mouse. The optical mouse has a small light-emitting diode (LED) that bounces light off the surface the mouse is moved across. The mouse contains sensors that convert this movement into co-ordinates the computer can understand.

A typical mouse has two or three buttons which can be pressed (clicked) to send specific signals. For example, a 'click' on the left hand button can be used to send the cursor to a new cell in a spreadsheet and a 'double click' can select a particular application from a Windows menu. The latest variety also have a wheel to facilitate scrolling up and down a screen display.

Similar to the mouse is the trackball, which is often found on laptop computers. Trackballs comprise a casing fixed to the computer, and a ball which protrudes upwards. The user moves the ball by hand. Other mobile computers use a touch sensitive pad for mouse functions; others have a tiny joystick in the centre of the keyboard.

Magnetic ink character recognition (MICR)

Magnetic ink character recognition (MICR) involves the recognition by a machine of special formatted characters printed in magnetic ink. The characters are read using a specialised reading device. The main advantage of MICR is its speed and accuracy, but MICR documents are expensive to produce. The main commercial application of MICR is in the banking industry – on cheques and deposit slips.

Optical mark reading (OMR)

Optical mark reading involves the marking of a pre-printed form with a ballpoint pen or typed line or cross in an appropriate box. The card is then read by an OMR device which senses the mark in each box using an electric current and translates it into machine code.

Applications in which OMR is used include National Lottery entry forms (in the UK), and answer sheets for multiple choice questions.

Scanners and Optical Character Recognition (OCR)

A scanner is device that can read text or illustrations printed on paper and translate the information into a form the computer can use. A scanner works by digitising an image, the resulting matrix of bits is called a bit map.

To edit text read by an optical scanner, you need Optical Character Recognition (OCR) software to translate the picture into text format. Most scanners sold today come with OCR software.

Bar coding and EPOS

Bar codes are groups of marks which, by their spacing and thickness, indicate specific codes or values. Look at the back cover of this book for an example of a bar code.

Large retail stores have Electronic Point of Sale (EPOS) devices, which include bar code readers. This enables the provision of immediate sales and stock level information.

EFTPOS

Many retailers have now introduced EFTPOS systems (Electronic Funds Transfer at the Point of Sale). An EFTPOS terminal is used with a customers credit card or debit card to pay for goods or services. The customer's credit card account or bank account will be debited automatically. EFTPOS systems combine point of sale systems with electronic funds transfer.

Magnetic stripe cards

The standard magnetic stripe card contains machine-sensible data on a thin strip of magnetic recording tape stuck to the back of the card. The magnetic card reader converts this information into directly computer-sensible form. The widest application of magnetic stripe cards is as bank credit or service cards.

Smart cards

A smart card is a plastic card in which is embedded a microprocessor chip. A smart card would typically contain a memory and a processing capability. The information held on smart cards can therefore be updated (eg using a PC and a special device).

Touch screens

A touch screen is a display screen that enables users to make selections by touching areas of the screen. Sensors, built into the screen surround, detect which area has been touched. These devices are widely used in vending situations, such as the selling of train tickets.

Voice recognition

Computer software has been developed that can convert speech into computer-sensible form via a microphone. Users are required to speak clearly and reasonably slowly.

Activity 1

The next time you are at the supermarket check-out, think of the consequences of the operator simply scanning one bar code. What effect does this quick and simple action have?

---

4 OUTPUT DEVICES

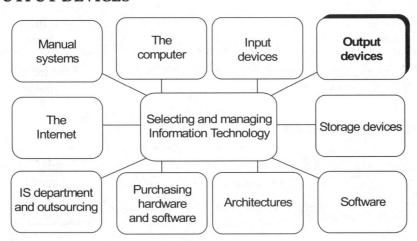

The two most common methods of computer output are output to a printer and output to the screen. Other methods include output to a computer file or onto microfilm (known as Computer Output on Microfilm or COM).

4.1 The choice of output medium

Choosing a suitable output medium depends on a number of factors.

Factor	Comment
Hard copy	Is a printed version of the output needed?
Quantity	For example, a VDU screen can hold a certain amount of data, but it becomes more difficult to read when information goes 'off-screen' and can only be read a 'page' at a time.
Speed	For example if a single enquiry is required it may be quicker to make notes from a VDU display.
Suitability for further use	Output to a file would be appropriate if the data will be processed further, maybe in a different system. Large volumes of reference data might be held on microfilm or microfiche.
Cost	The 'best' output device may not be justifiable on the grounds of cost - another output medium should be chosen.

Printers

Character printers, such as dot matrix printers, print a single character at a time. Dot matrix printers may still be found in some accounting departments. Their main drawback is their low-resolution. They are also relatively slow and noisy, but cheap to run.

Inkjet printers are small and reasonably cheap (under £100), making them popular where a 'private' output device is required. They work by sending a jet of ink on to the paper to produce the required characters – a line at a time. They produce print of a higher quality than dot matrix printers, and most models can print in colour. Running costs can be high.

Laser printers print a whole page at a time, rather than line by line. The quality of output with laser printers is very high. Compared with inkjet printers, running costs are relatively low.

The VDU

Screens were described earlier, as they are used together with computer keyboards for input. They can be used as an output medium, primarily where the volume of output is low, for example a single enquiry.

5   STORAGE DEVICES

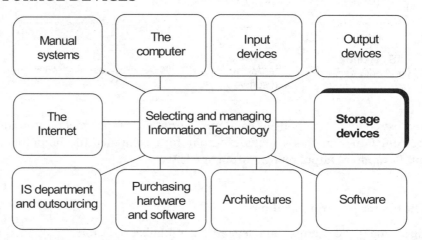

Hard disks

Disks offer **direct access** to data. A modern business PC invariably has an **internal hard disk**. At the time of writing the average new **PC** has a hard disk size of around 5 **Gigabytes,** but 15 Gb disks are not uncommon. In larger computer systems **removable disk packs** are commonly used.

Floppy disks

The floppy disk provides a **cost-effective** means of on-line storage for **small** amounts of information. A $3^{1}/_{2}$" disk can hold up to **1.44 Mb** of data.

A **Zip disk** is a different type of **removable** disk, with much larger capacity (100 Mb) that requires a special Zip drive. A Zip disk is suitable for back-up, storage or for moving files between computers.

Tape storage

Tape cartridges have a **much larger capacity** than floppy disks and they are still widely used as a backing storage medium. Fast tapes which can be used to create a back-up file very quickly are known as tape streamers.

Like an audio or video cassette, data has to be recorded along the length of a computer tape and so it is **more difficult to access** than data on disk (ie direct access is not possible with tape). Reading and writing are separate operations.

CD-ROM (Compact Disc – Read Only Memory)

A CD-ROM can store 650 megabytes of data.

The speed of a CD-ROM drive is relevant to how fast data can be retrieved: an eight speed drive is quicker than a four speed drive.

CD recorders are now available for general business use with blank CDs (CD-R) and **rewritable disks** (CD-RW) are now available.

DVD (Digital Versatile Disc)

The CD format has started to be superseded by DVD. DVD development was encouraged by the advent of multimedia files with video graphics and sound - requiring greater disk capacity.

Digital **Versatile Disk (DVD)** technology can store almost 5 gigabytes of data on one disk. Access speeds are improved as is sound and video quality. Many commentators believe DVD will not only replace CD-ROMs, but also VHS cassettes, audio CDs and laser discs.

Activity 2

Briefly outline two features and one common use of magnetic disks, magnetic tapes and optical disks (CD-ROMs).

---

6 SOFTWARE

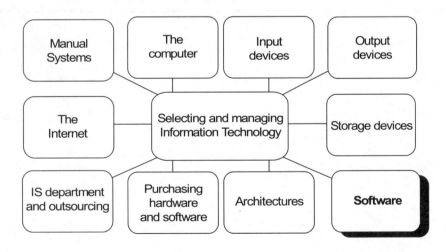

6.1 Types of software

The different types of computer software can be classified into five types, as shown in the following table.

Type	Comment
Operating systems	The operating system provides the interface between the computer hardware and both the user and the other software. An operating system will typically perform the following tasks. • Initial set-up of the computer, when it is switched on • Communication between hardware and software • Managing peripherals such as printers • File management The most widely-used operating system is Microsoft Windows. Other operating systems include UNIX, the Apple Macintosh O/S system and Linux.
Utilities	Software utilities are relatively small software packages, usually designed to perform a task related to the general operation of a computer system. An example of a utility is software designed to perform back-ups.
Programming tools	Some software is designed specifically to help programmers produce computer programs. Examples include program compilers and assemblers, and Computer Assisted Software Engineering (CASE) tools.
Off-the-shelf applications	This term is used to describe software produced by a software manufacturer and released in a form that is ready to use. 'Office' type software (spreadsheet, word-processing, database etc) and integrated accounting systems such as Sage Line 50 are examples.
Bespoke applications	Bespoke software is tailor-made to meet the needs of an organisation. Bespoke software is relatively expensive, but may be the only feasible solution in unusual situations.

7 ARCHITECTURES

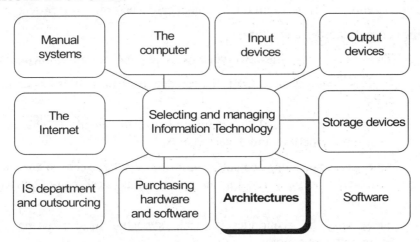

The term **system architecture** refers to the way in which the various components of an information system are linked together, and the way they relate to each other. In the following paragraphs we discuss the theory behind centralised and distributed systems. However, in reality many systems include elements of both.

7.1 Centralised architecture

Definition

> A **centralised architecture** involves all computer processing being carried out on a single central processor. The central computer is usually a mainframe or minicomputer designed to be accessed by more than one user.

A centralised system using a central mainframe linked to 'dumb terminals' (which do not include a CPU and therefore rely on the central computer for processing power) is shown below.

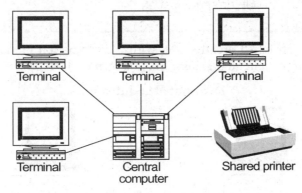

Many centralised systems also have shared peripherals, such as printers, linked to the central computer.

Centralised architectures could be based in a single location or spread over multiple locations. For example, both a local area network (LAN) and a wide area network (WAN) could utilise a centralised architecture.

A LAN is a network that spans a relatively small area. Most LANs are confined to a single building or group of buildings. A wide area network (WAN) is a computer network that spans a relatively large geographical area. A centralised WAN would have only one computer with processing power. (LANs may be linked to form a WAN – although such a configuration would not be considered a centralised architecture.)

Advantages of centralised architectures.

(a) There is one set of files. Everyone uses the same data and information.

(b) It gives better security/control over data and files. It is easier to enforce standards.

(c) Head office (where the computer is usually based) is able to control computing processes and developments.

(d) An organisation might be able to afford a very large central computer, with extensive processing capabilities that smaller 'local' computers could not carry out.

(e) There may be economies of scale available in purchasing computer equipment and supplies.

Disadvantages of centralised architectures.

(a) Local offices might experience processing delays or interruptions.

(b) Reliance on head office. Local offices rely on head office to provide information they need.

(c) If the central computer breaks down, or the software develops a fault, the entire system goes out of operation.

7.2 Decentralised or distributed architectures

Definition

> **Distributed architectures** spread the processing power throughout the organisation at several different locations. With modern distributed systems, the majority of processing power is held on numerous personal computers (PCs) spread throughout the organisation.

An example of a distributed architecture, with a combination of stand-alone PCs and networks spread throughout an organisation, is shown in the following diagram.

Distributed architecture

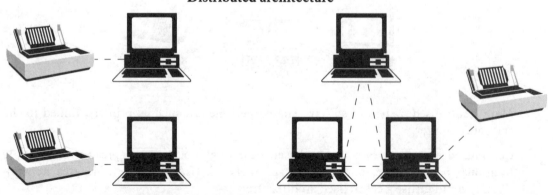

Key **features** of distributed architectures.

(a) Many computers have their own processing capability (CPU).

(b) Some sharing of information is possible via communication links.

(c) The systems are usually more user-friendly than mainframe based systems.

(d)   End-users are given responsibility for, and control over, programs and data.

7.3   Advantages of distributed architectures

(a)   There is greater flexibility in system design. The system can cater for both the specific needs of each local user of an individual computer and also for the needs of the organisation as a whole, by providing communications between different local computers in the system.

(b)   Since data files can be held locally, data transmission is restricted because each computer maintains its own data files which provide most of the data it will need. This reduces the costs and security risks in data transmission.

(c)   Speed of processing.

(d)   There is a possibility of a distributed database. Data is held in a number of locations, but any user can access all of it for a global view.

(e)   The effect of breakdowns is minimised, because a fault in one computer will not affect other computers in the system.

(f)   Allows for better localised control over the physical and procedural aspects of the system.

(g)   May facilitate greater user involvement and increase familiarity with the use of computer technology.

7.4   Disadvantages of distributed architectures

(a)   There may be some duplication of data on different computers, increasing the risk of data inaccuracies.

(b)   A distributed network can be more difficult to administer and to maintain, as several sites require access to staff with IT skills.

7.5   Client-server architecture

With a client-server architecture each computer or process on the network is either a 'client' or a 'server'. Servers are powerful computers or processes dedicated to managing disk drives (file servers), printers (print servers), or network traffic (network servers). Clients are PCs or workstations on which users run applications. Clients rely on servers for resources, such as files, devices, and sometimes processing power.

Definitions

A **client** is a machine which requests a service, for example a PC running a spreadsheet application which the user wishes to print out.

A **server** is a machine which is dedicated to providing a particular function or service requested by a client. Servers include file servers (see below), print servers, e-mail servers and fax servers.

A typical client-server system includes three **hardware** elements.

- A central server (sometimes called the corporate server)
- Local servers (sometimes called departmental servers)
- Client workstations

A server computer (such as a file server) may be a powerful PC or a minicomputer. As its name implies, it **serves** the rest of the network offering a generally-accessible hard disk and sometimes offering other resources, such as a **shared printer**.

A typical client-server architecture is shown in the following illustration.

Client-server architecture

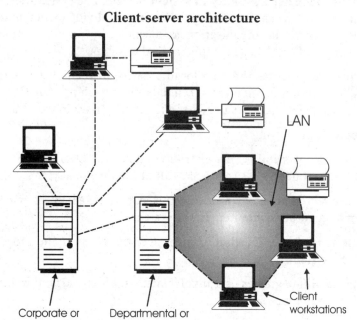

Client-server systems aim to locate software where it is most efficient - based on the number and location of users requiring access and the processing power required. There are three main types of software applications.

(a) **Corporate applications** are run on the central (or corporate) server. These applications are accessed by people spread throughout the organisation, and often require significant processor power (eg a centralised Management Information System).

(b) **Local applications** are used by users within a particular section or department, and therefore are run on the relevant local or departmental server (eg a credit-scoring expert system may be held on the server servicing the loans department of a bank).

(c) **Client applications** may be unique to an individual user, eg a specialised Executive Support System (ESS). Other software that may be run on client hardware could include 'office' type software, such as spreadsheet and word processing programs. Even though many people may use these applications, individual copies of programs are often held on client hardware - to utilise the processor power held on client machines.

7.6   The advantages of a client-server architecture

Advantage	Comment
Greater resilience	Processing is spread over several computers. If one server breaks down, other locations can carry on processing.
Scalability	They are highly scalable. Instead of having to buy computing power in large quantities you can buy just the amount of power you need to do the job.

Advantage	Comment
Shared programs and data	Program and data files held on a file server can be shared by all the PCs in the network. With stand-alone PCs, each computer would have its own data files, and there might be unnecessary duplication of data. A system where everyone uses the same data will help to improve data processing and decision making.
Shared work-loads	The processing capability of each computer in a network can be utilised. For example, if there were separate stand-alone PCs, A might do job 1, B might do job 2 and C might do job 3. In a network, any PC, (A, B or C) could do any job (1, 2 or 3). This is more efficient.
Shared peripherals	Peripheral equipment can be shared. For example, five PCs might share a single printer.
Communication	LANs can be linked up to the office communications network, thus adding to the processing capabilities in an office. Electronic mail, calendar and diary facilities can also be used.
Compatibility	Client/server systems are likely to include interfaces between different types of software used on the system, making it easier to move information between applications.
Flexibility	For example, if a detailed analysis of existing data is required, a copy of this data could be placed on a separate server, allowing data to be manipulated without disrupting the main system.

7.7 The disadvantages of a client-server architecture

The client/server approach has some drawbacks.

(a) A single **mainframe** may be more efficient performing some tasks, in certain circumstances. For example, where the process involves routine processing of a very large number (eg millions) of transactions.

(b) It is easier to **control** and **maintain** a centralised system. In particular it is easier to keep data **secure**.

(c) It may be **cheaper** to 'tweak' an existing mainframe system rather than throwing it away and starting from scratch: for example it may be possible to give it a graphical user interface and to make data exchangeable between Windows and non-Windows based applications.

(d) Each location may need its own **network administrator** to keep things running smoothly - there may be unnecessary duplication of **skills** and staff.

(e) Duplication of information may be a problem if individual users do not follow a disciplined approach.

7.8 Peer-to-peer architecture

'Peer-to-peer' refers to a type of network in which each workstation has equivalent capabilities and responsibilities. This differs from client-server architectures, in which some computers are dedicated to serving the others. Peer-to-peer networks are generally simpler, but they usually do not offer the same performance under heavy workloads.

8 PURCHASING HARDWARE AND SOFTWARE

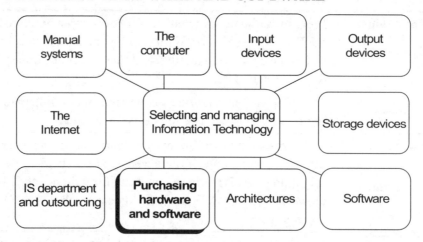

A computer user might buy hardware and software direct from a manufacturer, or through an intermediate supplier. Given that the expense is often considerable, the purchasing procedure must be carefully controlled.

8.1 Software sources

An organisation has a range of options when sourcing software for information systems. The four main options are described in the following table.

Source	Comment
Standard off-the-shelf package	This is the simplest option. The organisation purchases and installs a ready-made solution.
Amended standard package	A standard package is purchased, but some customisation is undertaken so that the software meets the organisations requirements. This may require access to the source code.
Standard package plus additions	The purchased standard package is not amended itself, but additional software that integrates with the standard package is developed. This also may require access to the source code.
Bespoke package	Programmers write an application to meet the specific needs of the organisation. This can be a time-consuming and expensive process.

In this section we discuss the process and relative advantages of the two main options - purchasing an application off-the-shelf and developing a bespoke solution. The other two options include elements of both of these two main options.

Definitions

Bespoke software is designed and written either 'in-house' by the IS department or externally by a software house.

An **off-the-shelf package** is one that is sold to a wide range of users. The package is written to handle requirements that are common to a wide range of organisations.

8.2 Choosing an application package off-the shelf

Off-the-shelf packages are generally available for functions that are likely to be performed similarly across a range of organisations eg accounting. The following table describes some of the factors to consider when choosing an off-the-shelf application package.

Factor	Comment
User requirements	Does the package fit the user's particular requirements? Matters to consider include data volumes, data validation routines, number of users and the reports available.
Processing times	Are the processing times fast enough? If response times to enquiries is slow, the user might consider the package unacceptable.
Documentation	Is there full and clear documentation for the user? A comprehensive user manual, a quick reference guide and on-line help should be considered.
Compatibility	Is the package compatible with existing hardware and software? Can data be exchanged with other related systems?
Controls	Access and security controls (eg passwords) should be included, as should processing controls that enable the accuracy of processing operations to be confirmed.
User-interface	Users are most affected by the user-interface design. The interface should be clear, logical, and consistent, and should follow standard interface conventions such as those used on most packages produced for use with the Microsoft Windows operating system.
Modification	Can the package be modified by the user - allowing the user to tailor it to meet their needs?
Support, maintenance and updates	The availability and cost of support, such as a telephone help-line, should be considered, as should the arrangements for updates and upgrades. This is particularly important if software is likely to be affected by changes in legislation eg a payroll package.
Cost	An organisation should aim to purchase a package that will meet their requirements. However, a package should not be purchased if the cost outweighs the value of the benefits it should bring.

8.3 Developing a bespoke application

Producing a bespoke software system involves all the tasks included in the software development and testing cycle.

The process is summarised in the diagram below, and explained in the table that follows.

The software development cycle

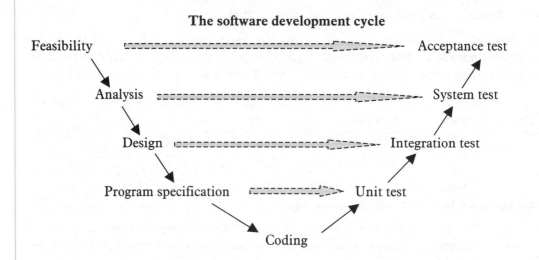

Stages of software development	Comment
Feasibility and analysis	The feasibility of software solutions would have usually been covered during the overall system feasibility study. An analysis of the software requirements should therefore be available.
Design and program specification	The software requirements are used to develop a systems design specification, which in turn is used to produce a detailed program specification. The specification would be used by in-house software developers, or would be distributed to software producers (as part of the invitation to tender - covered below).
Coding	Software producers will decide how to build the package, for example identifying parts of existing programs that may be used, and establishing what will need to be coded (ie written) from scratch. Prototyping may be used to help ensure user requirements are met.
Testing **Unit; Integration; System; Acceptance**	We covered testing, in Chapter 7. To briefly re-cap, unit testing tests individual programs (or units) operating alone. Integration testing tests how two or more units of the software interact with each other. System testing tests the complete package and how it interacts with other software programs. User acceptance testing aims to ensure all user requirements included in the software specification have been met.

8.4 Comparing supplier proposals

An organisation may receive a number of apparently viable tenders from software suppliers. Tenders are likely to have different strengths and weaknesses - a process to establish the 'best' tender needs to be established. Two common ways of comparing software or systems are benchmark tests and weighted ranking scores.

Benchmark tests

There are several factors involved in measuring the capability of a system. Benchmark tests are particularly useful to compare system speed and capacity.

Definition

> **Benchmark tests** test how long it takes a machine and program to run through a particular routine or set of routines.

Benchmark tests are carried out to compare the performance of a piece of hardware or software against pre-set criteria. Typical criteria which may be used as benchmarks include speed of performance of a particular operation, acceptable volumes before a degradation in response times is apparent and the general user-friendliness of equipment. Benchmarks can cover subjective tests such as user-friendliness, although it may be harder to reach definitive conclusions.

For example, an organisation comparing accounting software packages may test a number of different packages on its own existing hardware to see which performed the best according to various predefined criteria (eg speed of response, ability to process different volumes of transactions, reporting capabilities and so on).

Once the performance of the software package under consideration has been evaluated, the acquiring organisation should consider other features of the proposal, possibly using a weighted ranking system.

Weighted ranking

Definition

> A **weighted ranking** system involves establishing a number of factors important to a system, giving each factor a numerical weighting to reflect its importance, and using these weightings to calculate a score for each supplier (or software, or system).

The factors chosen to be used in the weighted ranking, and the relative importance of each factor will vary according to the purpose of the software/system under consideration. Judgements need to be made in the selection of criteria, the weightings applied to the criteria and the scores allocated. These judgements must be made by people who have a good understanding of the software/system requirements.

The following example shows how weighted ranking scores could be calculated.

EXAMPLE

An organisation must chose between three software suppliers.

The decision-makers within the organisation have decided on the relevant criteria and weightings that will be used to judge the suppliers. This information is shown in the following model, together with the scores that have been allocated to each supplier.

Weighted ranking							
Ranking scale: 3 = best supplier, 1 = worst		Supplier A software		Supplier B software		Supplier C software	
Criteria	**Weight**	Rank	Weighted rank score	Rank	Weighted rank score	Rank	Weighted rank score
User friendliness	9	2	18	3	27	1	9
Cost	4	1	4	2	8	3	12
Controls/Security	8	1	8	3	24	2	16
Processing speed	7	3	21	2	14	1	7
Support	10	2	20	1	10	3	30
		Total score	71	**Total score**	83	**Total score**	74

The weighted ranking calculation shows that the software supplied by Supplier B appears to best meet the organisation's needs.

8.5 The advantages and disadvantages of bespoke and off-the-shelf software

Bespoke software

Advantages of having software specially written include the following.

(a) If it is well-written, the software should meet the organisation's specific needs.

(b) Data and file structures may be chosen by the organisation rather than having to meet the structures required by standard software packages.

(c) The company may be able to do things with its software that competitors cannot do with theirs. In other words it is a source of competitive advantage.

(d) Similar organisations may wish to purchase the software.

(e) The software should be able to be modified to meet future needs.

Key **disadvantages** are.

(a) As the software is being developed from scratch, there is a risk that the package may not perform as intended.

(b) There is a greater chance of 'bugs'. Widely used off-the-shelf software is more likely to have had bugs identified and removed.

(c) Development will take longer than purchasing ready-made software.

(d) The cost is considerable when compared with a ready-made package.

(e) Support costs are also likely to be higher than with off-the-shelf software.

Overcoming the risks of bespoke development

Building a bespoke software application involves much time, effort and money. The risks associated with such an undertaking are that the resulting software:

- Does not meet user needs
- Does not interact as intended with other systems
- Is produced late
- Is produced over-budget

These risks can be minimised or overcome by:

(a) Good project management.

(b) Involving users at all stages of development.

(c) Ensuring in-house IT staff are able to maintain and support bespoke systems supplied from outside parties.

(d) Ensuring the ITT document includes details of all file structures required, and details of interfaces with other systems.

Off-the-shelf packages

Advantages of an off-the-shelf package

(a) The software is likely to be available immediately.

(b) A ready-made package will almost certainly cheaper because it is 'mass-produced".

(c) The software is likely to have been written by software specialists and so should be of a high quality.

(d) A successful package will be continually updated by the software manufacturer.

(e) Other users will have used the package already, and a well-established package should be relatively free of bugs.

(f) Good packages are well-documented, with easy-to-follow user manuals or on-line help.

(g) Some standard packages can be customised to the user's specific needs (see below).

The **disadvantages** of ready-made packages are as follows.

(a) The organisation is purchasing a standard solution. A standard solution may not be well suited to the organisation's particular needs.

(b) The organisation is dependent on the supplier for maintenance of the package - ie updating the package or providing assistance in the event of problems. It is unlikely that the supplier would give access to the code that would allow organisations with the relevant expertise to amend the software themselves.

(c) Competitors may well use the same package, removing any chance of using IS/IT for competitive advantage.

8.6 Customised versions of standard packages

Standard packages can be customised so that they fit an organisation's specific requirements. This can be done by purchasing the source code of the package and making modifications in-house, or by paying the producer of the package to customise it.

Advantages of customisation are similar to those of producing a bespoke system, with the additional advantages that:

(a) Development time should be much quicker, given that most of the system will be written already.

(b) If the work is done in-house the organisation gains considerable knowledge of how the software works and may be able to 'tune' it so that it works more efficiently with the company's hardware.

Disadvantages of customising a standard package include the following.

(a) It may prove more costly than expected, because new versions of the standard package will also have to be customised.

(b) Customisation may delay delivery of the software.

(c) Customisation may introduce bugs that do not exist in the standard version.

(d) If done in-house, the in-house team may have to learn new skills.

(e) If done by the original manufacturer disadvantages such as those for off-the-shelf packages may arise.

8.7 Choosing hardware

In general terms, the choice of computer hardware will depend on the following factors.

Factor	Comment
User requirements	The ease with which the computer configuration fits in with the user's requirements (eg direct access facilities, hard-copy output in given quantities).
Power	The power of the computer must be sufficient for current and foreseeable requirements. This is measured by: • Processor type • RAM in Mb • Clock speed in MHz • Hard disk size in Mb or Gb
Reliability	There should be a low expected 'break-down' rate. There should be back-up hardware available to limit any down-time in case of hardware failure.
Simplicity	Systems should be as simple as possible, whilst still capable of performing the tasks required.

Factor	Comment
Ease of communication	The system (hardware and software) should be able to communicate well with the user. Software is referred to as 'user-friendly' or 'user-unfriendly' but similar considerations apply to hardware (eg not all terminals are of standard screen size; the number and accessibility of terminals might also have a bearing on how well the user is able to put data into the computer or extract information).
Flexibility	The hardware should be able to meet new requirements as they emerge. More powerful CPUs tend to be more flexible.
Security	Keeping out 'hackers' and other unauthorised users is easier with more powerful systems, although security can be a major problem for any computer system.
Cost	The cost must be justified in terms of the benefits the hardware will provide.
Changeover	Whether the choice of hardware will help with a smooth changeover from the old to the new system.
Networking	Networking capacity, if a PC has been purchased.
Software	The hardware must be capable of running whatever software has been chosen.

9 IS DEPARTMENT AND OUTSOURCING

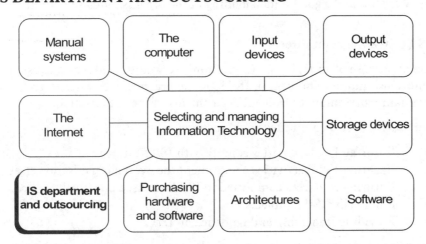

9.1 Information systems department

Most organisations choose have an information systems department, or team responsible for the tasks and responsibilities associated with information systems. Information systems increasingly utilise information technology.

At the head of the information systems/information technology function will be either the IS/IT manager, or the IS/IT director.

The IS/IT director would have responsibility for the following areas.

IS/IT director responsibility	Comment
IS/IT strategy development	The IS/IT strategy must compliment the overall strategy of the organisation. The strategy must also be achievable given budgetary constraints. Returns on investments in IS/IT should be monitored.
IS/IT risk management	This is a wide ranging area including legal risks, such as ensuring compliance with relevant data protection legislation, ensuring adequate IS/IT security measures and disaster recovery arrangements.
Steering committee	The IS/IT director should play a key role in a steering committee set up to oversee the role of IS/IT within the organisation. There is more on steering committees later in this chapter.
IS/IT infrastructure	Standards should be set for the purchase and use of hardware and software within the organisation.
Ensuring employees have the IS/IT support and tools the require	Efficient links are required between IS/IT staff and the rest of the organisation. Technical assistance should be easily obtainable.

An IS/IT director therefore requires a wide range of skills. The ideal person would possess technical know-how, excellent general management ability, a keen sense of business awareness and a good understanding of the organisations' operations.

9.2   IS/IT steering committee

The general purpose of an IS/IT steering committee would be to make decisions relating to the future use and development of IS/IT by the organisation. The steering committee should contain representatives from all departments of the organisation.

Common tasks of such a committee could include:

- Ensuring IS/IT activities comply with IS/IT strategy
- Ensuring IS/IT activities compliment the overall organisation strategy
- Ensuring resources committed to IS/IT are used effectively
- Monitoring IS/IT projects
- Providing leadership and guidance on IS/IT

Committee members should be chosen with the aim of ensuring the committee contains the wide range of technical and business knowledge required. The committee should liase closely with those affected by the decisions it will make.

9.3   Database administrator

A key information systems role is that of database administrator. A database administrator is responsible for all data and information held within an organisation. Key tasks include:

- Preparing and maintaining a record of all data held within the organisation (the data dictionary)

- Co-ordinating data and information use to avoid duplication and maximise efficiency

- Analysing the data requirements of new applications

- Implementing and controlling procedures to protect data integrity

- Recording data ownership

9.4 Systems development staff

In medium to large organisations in is likely that the IS department will include staff with programming and systems analysis skills. Key tasks for staff involved in systems development include:

- Systems analysis
- Systems design and specification
- Systems testing
- Systems evaluation and review

9.5 Data processing staff

Over the past two decades the traditional centralised data processing department has become less common. Most departments now process their own data using on-line systems, rather than batching up transactions and forwarding paper copies of them to a centralised department for processing.

Staff involved in data processing today are spread throughout the organisation, for example a call centre employee may input an order, an accounts clerk may process journal entries etc. Accurate data entry skills and an understanding of the task they are performing are key skills.

9.6 Information centre staff

Definition

An **Information Centre (IC)** is a small unit of staff with a good technical awareness of computer systems, whose task is to provide a support function to computer users within the organisation.

Information centres, sometimes referred to as **support centres**, are particularly useful in organisations which use distributed systems and so are likely to have hardware, data and software scattered throughout the organisation.

Help

An IC usually offers a Help Desk to solve IT problems. Help may be via the telephone, e-mail, through a searchable knowledge base or in person.

Remote diagnostic software may be used which enables staff in the IC to take control of a computer and sort out the problem without leaving their desk.

The help desk needs sufficient staff and technical expertise to respond quickly and effectively to requests for help. IC staff should also maintain good relationships with hardware and software suppliers to ensure their maintenance staff are quickly on site when needed.

Problem solving

The IC will maintain a record of problems and identify those that occur most often. If the problem is that users do not know how to use the system, training is provided.

Training applications often contain analysis software, drawing attention to trainee progress and common problems. This information enables the IC to identify and address specific training needs more closely.

If the problem is with the system itself, a solution is found, either by modifying the system or by investment in new hardware or software.

Improvements

The IC may also be required to consider the viability of suggestions for improving the system, and to bring these improvements into effect.

Standards

The IC is also likely to be responsible for setting, and encouraging users to conform to, common **standards**.

(a) Hardware standards ensure that all of the equipment used in the organisation is compatible and can be put into use in different departments as needed.

(b) Software standards ensure that information generated by one department can easily be shared with and worked upon by other departments.

(c) Programming standards ensure that applications developed by individual end-users (for example complex spreadsheet macros) follow best practice and are easy to modify.

(d) Data processing standards ensure that certain conventions such as the format of file names are followed throughout the organisation. This facilitates sharing, storage and retrieval of information.

Security

The IC may help to preserve the security of data in various ways.

(a) It may develop utility programs and procedures to ensure that back-ups are made at regular intervals.

(b) The IC may help to preserve the company's systems from attack by computer viruses, for instance by ensuring that the latest versions of anti-virus software are available to all users, by reminding users regularly about the dangers of viruses, and by setting up and maintaining 'firewalls', which deny access to sensitive parts of the company's systems.

End-user applications development

An IC can help applications development by providing technical guidance to end-user developers and to encourage comprehensible and well-documented programs. Understandable programs can be maintained or modified more easily. Documentation provides a means of teaching others how the programs work. These efforts can greatly extend the usefulness and life of the programs that are developed.

9.7   Outsourcing IT/IS services

Definition

> **Outsourcing** is the contracting out of specified operations or services to an external vendor.

There are four **broad classifications** of outsourcing.

Classification	Comment
Ad-hoc	The organisation has a short-term requirement for increased IS/IT skills. An example would be employing programmers on a short-term contract to help with the programming of bespoke software.
Project management	The development and installation of a particular IS/IT project is outsourced. For example, a new accounting system. (This approach is sometimes referred to as systems integration.)
Partial	Some IT/IS services are outsourced. Examples include hardware maintenance, network management or ongoing website management.
Total	An external supplier provides the vast majority of an organisation's IT/IS services. Eg a third party owns or is responsible for IT equipment, software and possibly staff.

Levels of service provision

The degree to which the provision and management of IS/IT services are transferred to the third party varies according to the situation and the skills of both organisations.

(a)   **Time-share**. The vendor charges for access to an external processing system on a time-used basis. Software ownership may be with either the vendor or the client organisation.

(b)   **Service bureaux** usually focus on a specific function. Traditionally bureaux would provide the same type of service to many organisations, eg payroll processing. As organisations have developed their own IT infrastructure, the use of bureaux has decreased.

(c)   **Facilities management (FM)**. The terms 'outsourcing' and 'facilities management' are sometimes confused. Facilities management traditionally involved contracts for premises-related services such as cleaning or site security.

In the context of IS/IT, facilities management involves an outside agency managing the organisation's IS/IT facilities. All equipment usually remains with the client, but the responsibility for providing and managing the specified services rests with the FM company. FM companies operating in the UK include Accenture, Cap Gemini, EDS and CFM.

The following table shows the main features of each of the outsourcing arrangements described above.

Feature	Outsourcing arrangement		
	Timeshare	Service	Facilities Management (FM)
Management responsibility	Mostly retained	Some retained	Very little retained
Focus	Operational	A function	Strategic
Timescale	Short-term	Medium-term	Long-term
Justification	Cost savings	More efficient	Access to expertise; higher quality service provision. Enables management to concentrate on the areas where they do possess expertise.

EXAMPLE

The retailer Sears outsourced the management of its vast information technology and accounting functions to Accenture. First year *savings* were estimated to be £5 million per annum, growing to £14 million in the following year, and thereafter. This is clearly considerable, although re-organisation costs relating to redundancies, relocation and asset write-offs are thought to be in the region of £35 million. About 900 staff were involved: under the transfer of undertakings regulations (which protect employees when part or all of a company changes hands), Accenture was obliged to take on the existing Sears staff. This provided new opportunities for the staff who moved, while those who remained at Sears are free to concentrate on strategy development and management direction.

9.8   Developments in outsourcing

Outsourcing arrangements are becoming increasingly flexible to cope with the ever-changing nature of the modern business environment. Three trends are:

(a)   **Multiple sourcing.** This involves outsourcing different functions or areas of the IS/IT function to a range of suppliers. Some suppliers may form alliances to present a stronger case for selection.

(b)   **Incremental approach.** Organisations progressively outsource selected areas of their IT/IS function. Possible problems with outsourced services are solved before progressing to the next stage.

(c)   **Joint venture sourcing.** This term is used to describe an organisation entering into a joint venture with a supplier. The costs (risks) and possible rewards are split on an agreed basis. Such an arrangement may be suitable when developing software that could be sold to other organisations.

(d)   **Application Service Providers (ASP).** ASPs are third parties that manage and distribute software services and solutions to customers across a Wide Area Network. ASP's could be considered the modern equivalent of the traditional computer bureaux.

NOTES

9.9 Advantages of outsourcing

The **advantages** of outsourcing are as follows.

(a) Outsourcing can remove uncertainty about **cost,** as there is often a long-term contract where services are specified in advance for a **fixed price.** If computing services are inefficient, the costs will be borne by the FM company. This is also an incentive to the third party to provide a high quality service.

(b) Long-term contracts (maybe up to ten years) encourage **planning** for the future.

(c) Outsourcing can bring the benefits of **economies of scale.** For example, a FM company may conduct research into new technologies that benefits a number of their clients.

(d) A specialist organisation is able to retain **skills and knowledge.** Many organisations would not have a sufficiently well-developed IT department to offer IT staff opportunities for career development. Talented staff would leave to pursue their careers elsewhere.

(e) New skills and knowledge become available. A specialist company can **share** staff with **specific expertise** (such as programming in HTML to produce Web pages) between several clients. This allows the outsourcing company to take advantage of new developments without the need to recruit new people or re-train existing staff, and without the cost.

(f) **Flexibility** (contract permitting). Resources may be able to be scaled up or down depending upon demand. For instance, during a major changeover from one system to another the number of IT staff needed may be twice as large as it will be once the new system is working satisfactorily.

An outsourcing organisation is more able to arrange its work on a **project** basis, whereby some staff will expect to be moved periodically from one project to the next.

9.10 Disadvantages of outsourcing arrangements

Some possible **drawbacks** are outlined below.

(a) It is arguable that information and its provision is **an inherent part of the business and of management.** Unlike office cleaning, or catering, an organisation's IS services may be too important to be contracted out. Information is at the heart of management.

(b) A company may have highly **confidential information** and to let outsiders handle it could be seen as **risky** in commercial and/or legal terms.

(c) Information strategy can be used to gain **competitive advantage.** Opportunities may be missed if a third party is handling IS services, because there is no onus upon internal management to keep up with new developments and have new ideas. Any new technology or application devised by the third party is likely to be available to competitors.

(d) An organisation may find itself **locked in** to an unsatisfactory contract. The decision may be very difficult to reverse. If the FM company supplies unsatisfactory levels of service, the effort and expense the organisation would incur to rebuild its own computing function or to move to another provider could be substantial.

(e)   The use of FM does not encourage awareness of the potential costs and benefits of IS/IT within the organisation. If managers cannot manage in-house IS/IT resources effectively, then it could be argued that they will not be able to manage an arrangement to outsource effectively either.

9.11   Insourcing

Outsourcing involves purchasing information technology services or expertise from outside the organisation. Several factors have led some to believe this is not the best solution in today's environment.

(a)   Many organisations have found there is a shortage of qualified **candidates** with the skills they require.

(b)   The **cost** of acquiring people with high-tech expertise and business skills, whether employing or outsourcing, fluctuates due to factors affecting supply and demand.

(c)   Third, there is increasing recognition that to do a good job, IT professionals must understand the **business principles** behind the systems that they develop and manage.

Insourcing involves recruiting IS/IT staff internally, from other areas of the business, and teaching these business-savvy employees about technology. The logic behind the idea is that it is easier (and cheaper) to teach technical skills to business people than to teach business skills to technical people.

Supporters of insourcing believe it has the potential to:

(a)   Create a better quality workforce that combines both technical and business skills.

(b)   Reduce costs.

(c)   Improve relationships and communication between IT staff and other departments.

(d)   Increase staff retention.

Possible disadvantages include:

(a)   The risk that non-technical employees will not pick up the IS/IT skills required.

(b)   Finding staff willing to make the change.

(c)   Replacing staff who do make the switch.

10 THE INTERNET

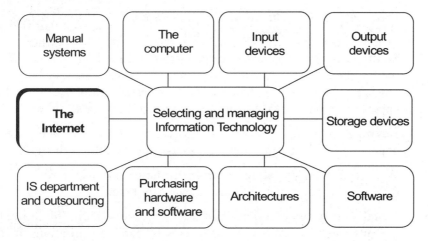

Definition

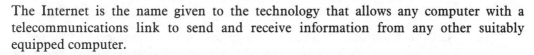

The **Internet** is a global network connecting millions of computers.

The Internet is the name given to the technology that allows any computer with a telecommunications link to send and receive information from any other suitably equipped computer.

The World Wide Web is the multimedia element which provides facilities such as full-colour, graphics, sound and video. Websites are points within the network created by those who wish to provide an information point for searchers to visit and benefit by the provision of information and/or by entering into a transaction.

Most companies now have a **website** on the Internet. A site is a collection of screens providing **information in text and graphic form**, any of which can be viewed simply by clicking the appropriate button, word or image on the screen.

10.1 Current uses of the Internet

The scope and potential of the Internet are still developing. Its uses already embrace the following:

(a) **Dissemination** of information.

(b) **Product/service development** - through almost instantaneous test marketing.

(c) **Transaction processing** (electronic commerce or e-commerce) - both business-to-business (B2B) and business-to-consumer (B2C).

(d) **Relationship enhancement** - between various groups of stakeholders.

(e) **Recruitment** and job search - involving organisations worldwide.

(f) **Entertainment** - including music, humour, art, games and some less wholesome pursuits!

It is estimated that over 40% of households in the UK will have Internet access by the end of 2002.

The Internet provides opportunities to organise for and to automate tasks which would previously have required more costly interaction with the organisation. These have often been called low-touch or zero-touch approaches.

Tasks which a **website may automate** include:

(a)   **Frequently-Asked Questions (FAQs)**: carefully-structured sets of answers can deal with many customer interactions.

(b)   **Status checking**: major service enquiries (Where is my order? When will the engineer arrive? What is my bank balance?) can also be automated, replacing high-cost human service processes, and also providing the opportunity to proactively offer better service and new services.

(c)   **Keyword search**: the ability to search provides web users with opportunities to find information in large and complex websites.

(d)   **Wizards (interview style interface)**: these can help ensure people are directed to the information most relevant to them.

(e)   **E-mail and systems to route and track inbound e-mail**: the ability to route and/or to provide automatic responses will enable organisations to deal with high volumes of e-mail from actual and potential customers.

(f)   **Bulletin boards**: these enable customers to interact with each other, thus facilitating self-activated customer service and also the opportunity for product/service referral. Cisco in particular has created communities of Cisco users who help each other - thus reducing the service costs for Cisco itself.

(g)   **Call-back buttons**: these enable customers to speak to someone in order to deal with and resolve a problem; the more sophisticated systems allow the call-centre operator to know which web pages the users were consulting at the time.

(h)   **Transaction processing**: usually referred to as e-commerce.

10.2   Problems with the Internet

To a large extent the Internet has grown organically **without any formal** organisation. There are specific communication standards, but it is not owned by any one body and there are no clear guidelines on how it should develop.

The quality of much of the information on the Internet leaves much to be desired.

Speed is a major issue. Data only downloads onto the user's PC at the speed of the slowest telecommunications link - downloading data can be a painfully slow procedure.

So much information and entertainment is available that employers worry that their staff will spend too much time browsing through non-work-related sites.

Connecting an information system to the Internet exposes the system to numerous **security issues**.

Definition

> A **virus** is a piece of software which infects programs and data and possibly damages them, and which replicates itself.

Viruses may cause damage to files or attempt to destroy files and damage hard disks. The programmers of viruses therefore place viruses where they have the opportunity to spread. In the early days of computing most viruses spread via floppy disk – now most spread via mass e-mails.

Another security issue associated with external networks such as the Internet is that unauthorised people (**hackers**) may be able to get into the company's network, either to steal data or to damage the system.

Systems usually have **firewalls** (which disable part of the telecoms technology) that aim to prevent unauthorised intrusions, but a determined hacker may be able to bypass these.

Information transmitted from one part of an organisation to another may be **intercepted**. Data can be 'encrypted' (scrambled) in an attempt to make it unintelligible to eavesdroppers.

10.3 Encryption and other safety measures

Encryption aims to prevent eavesdropping on data during transmission. Encryption involves scrambling the data at one end of the line, transmitting the scrambled data, and unscrambling it at the receiver's end of the line.

Authentication involves adding an extra field to a record, with the contents of this field derived from the remainder of the record by applying an algorithm that has previously been agreed between the senders and recipients of data.

Dial-back security operates by requiring the person wanting access to the network to dial-in and identify themselves first. The system then dials the person back on their authorised number before allowing access.

10.4 Jokes and hoaxes

More common than the genuine e-mail virus is the e-mail hoax – a message warning of a supposed virus with instructions to inform all other computer users you know. People pass along the warning because they are trying to be helpful, but they are in fact wasting the time of all concerned.

FOR DISCUSSION

How many of your group have purchased a product or service over the Internet? What was purchased? Did the purchase process run smoothly?

NOTES

Chapter roundup

- **Computers** can be classified as supercomputers, mainframes, minicomputers and PCs. The amount of **RAM** and the **processor speed** are key determinants of computer performance. Hard drive size is another important factor.

- The **operating system** provides the interface between hardware, software and user.

- There are a range of **input** and **output** devices available. The most efficient method will depend on the circumstances of each situation.

- Hard disks are used for internal **storage** - external storage may be on floppy disk, zip drive, CD-ROM or DVD.

- The term **system architecture** refers to the way in which the various components of an information system are linked together, and the way they relate to each other. A **centralised** architecture involves all computer processing being carried out on a single central processor. **Distributed** architectures spread the processing power throughout the organisation at several different locations.

- **Off-the-shelf software** is produced to meet requirements that are common to many organisations. The software is likely to be available **immediately** and **cost significantly less** than bespoke solutions. However, as it has not been written specifically for the organisation, it may not meet all of their requirements.

- **Bespoke software** should be written so as to **match** the organisation's requirements exactly. However, the software is likely to be considerably **more expensive** than an off-the-shelf package.

- Some organisations **outsource** their IT function to external organisations. Outsourcing has advantages (eg access to specialised expertise) and disadvantages (eg lack of control over a key resource).

- Many organisations are now utilising **the Internet** as a means of gathering and disseminating information, and conducting transactions. This has security implications such as exposure to **viruses** and **hackers**.

Quick quiz

1. List four types of computer. (See section 2.1)
2. List four input devices. (See section 3.1)
3. What factors influence the choice of output medium? (See section 4.1)
4. List five types of software. (See section 6.1)
5. What is a client-server system? (See section 7.5)
6. List four advantages of client-server computing? (See section 7.6)

Answers to Activities

1   (a)   The price of the item is added to your bill.

(b)   The supermarket stock 'number on shelf' is reduced by one, and if the predetermined minimum has been reached the 'shelf restock required' indicator will be activated.

(c)   The overall stock on hand figure will be reduced, and if the minimum stock holding has been reached the 'reorder from supplier' indicator will be activated.

(d)   The relevant accounting entries will be made, or be sent to a pending file awaiting the running of the month-end routine.

(e)   Marketing information will be obtained – what time the purchase was made, what else was purchased and if your loyalty card was swiped – who purchased it.

You may have thought of others. The key point to grasp from this exercise is that **efficient information collection** can be achieved using appropriate technology.

2   (a)   *Magnetic disks* offer fast access times, direct access to data and offer suitability for multi-user environments. Magnetic disk storage is therefore the predominant storage medium in most commercial applications currently. Direct access is essential for many commercial applications (eg databases) and in addition speed is necessary for real-time applications.

(b)   *Magnetic tapes* offer cheap data storage, portability and serial or sequential access only. Magnetic tape is most valuable as a backup medium.

(c)   Optical disks (eg CD-ROMs) offer capacity to store vast amounts of data but offer slower access speeds than magnetic disks. They are most suitable for backup and archiving, or keeping old copies of files which might need to be retrieved. However, the technology behind optical drives is still in development, and it may not be too long before they are a viable alternative to magnetic disk drives for most applications.

Assignment 5   **(35 minutes)**

AB plc is a national freight distribution company with a head office, five regional offices and a hundred local depots spread throughout the country. It is planning a major computerisation project. The options which are being considered are as follows.

(a)   A central mainframe system with terminals at each depot.

(b)   Distributed minicomputers at each regional office.

Task

Draft a report to the board of AB plc describing the ways in which each of the options would suit the company's structure and explaining the advantages and disadvantages of each.

BPP
PUBLISHING

Chapter 6 :
USING SOFTWARE: WORD PROCESSING AND SPREADSHEETS

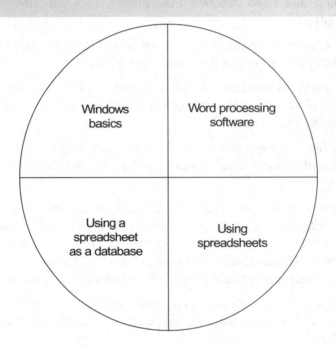

Introduction

The chapter aims to teach you the basics of using a PC and some commonly used software. We shall assume that you are a complete novice.

For many students this won't be true. You may have been using PCs since you were at school. Use the chapter in a way that best suits your needs. If you are a regular user of Windows you should skim read the parts of the chapter already familiar to you.

There are usually at least two (and often more) different ways of doing the same thing. If you can find a faster way to do something, or a way that you find easier to remember, or more comfortable for whatever reason, then use it.

Your objective

After completing this chapter you should understand the practical use of word processors and spreadsheets to provide information.

1   WINDOWS BASICS

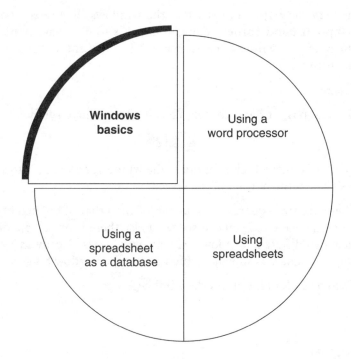

The initial screen used in the Microsoft Windows operating system is called the **Desktop**. The illustration below shows the desktop (in the background), with a Window that has been called up using the Start button.

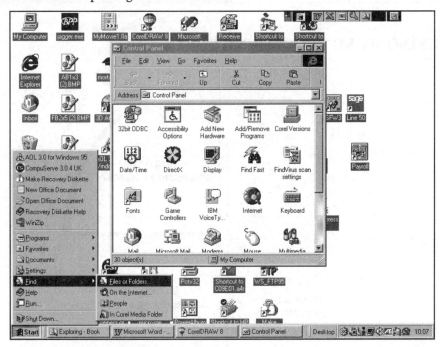

Nearly all windows have the following three features.

Title bar

A title, shown in a strip at the top the window. This is sometimes called the **title bar**.

Top left hand corner

Look up at the very top left-hand corner of the windows illustrated above. There is a symbol in the **top-left hand corner**. You can use this to do a variety of things, but its main use is to *close* the window. (The symbol is different depending upon which program you are using.)

Top right-hand corner

Now look up at the top **right hand** corner. You should see three symbols.

(a) There is a line, which minimises the window, reducing it to a button on the 'task bar' at the bottom of the screen.

(b) There are two squares, one on top of the other. This makes the window a little bit smaller so you can see what else there is on screen, or allows you to view two different windows. If your window is already in its 'smaller' state only one square is shown – which makes the window bigger.

(c) There is an **X.** This closes the window altogether.

FOR DISCUSSION

What are the advantages and disadvantages for the computer user of one operating system (Windows) dominating the market?

2 USING WORD PROCESSING SOFTWARE

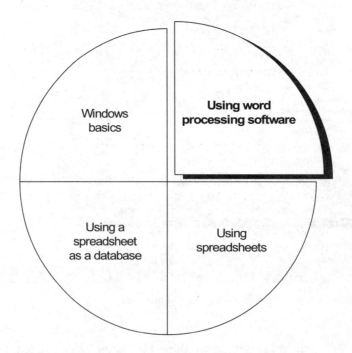

We could devote a whole book to the many facilities offered by a modern word processing package. All we are going to do here is give you an overview. Word processors are increasingly being seen as part of an integrated software package eg Microsoft Word is the word processing tool of Microsoft Office.

2.1 Integrated software

Definition

> Integrated software refers to programs, or packages of programs, that perform a variety of different processing operations, using **data which is compatible** with whatever operation is being carried out.

The term is generally used in two different situations.

(a) **Accounts packages** often consist of program **modules** that can be integrated into a larger accounting system. There will be a module for each of the sales ledger system, the purchase ledger system, the nominal ledger, and so on. Output from one 'module' in an integrated system can be used as input to another, without the need for re-entry of data.

(b) There are some PC software packages that allow the user to carry out a **variety of processing operations**, such as word processing, using spreadsheets and creating and using a database. Examples of integrated software packages that provide these varied facilities are Lotus Smartsuite and Microsoft Office.

Such packages allow **data to be freely transferred** between elements of the package, for example data from a spreadsheet can be imported into a report which is being word processed.

A potential **disadvantage** of such packages is that they may not offer the range of features which a specialist user of a stand-alone element.

2.2 Word processing

Definition

> A **word processing** program is used primarily to produce text based documents.

We are going to tell you a bit about Microsoft Word, one of the most commonly used word processors. There is little difference between the main competitors these days: manufacturers are quick to copy each others' good features, and it is in their interests that users find it easy to transfer from another system to the one that they make.

If you start up Word you will be presented with a window something like (but not exactly like) the following.

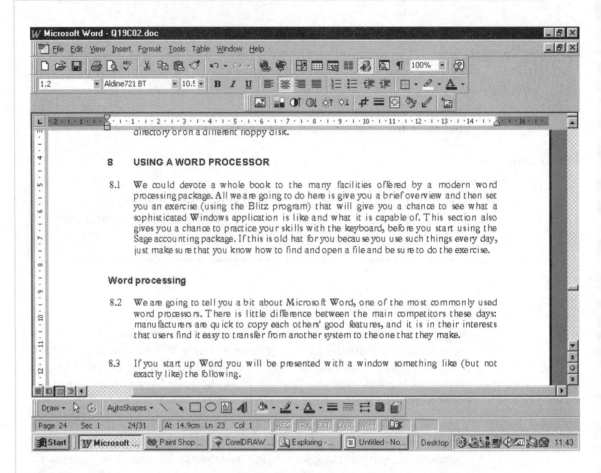

The main part of the screen is the area where you type, of course. At the top of the screen there is a bank of buttons and arrows that do useful things like **embolden** or *italicise* a word or words that you have selected, change the font style or size of selected text, or place text in the centre of the page, or set it to one side of the page. A host of other things can be done and you can create your own customised buttons to do them if you like.

In recent versions of Word, if you let the mouse pointer linger over a particular button (without clicking on it) a little label soon pops up telling you what it does. This is more fun than reading a book about it so we won't describe the buttons further.

The ruler below the buttons is used to set the left and right margins of the page and to indent paragraphs. You do this by dragging and dropping the triangular markers that you can see at either end of the ruler. The paragraphs on this page that you are reading now, for example, are indented by moving the lower of the two left-hand triangles in to the 1 mark.

The menu choices just below the title bar of the screen offer a huge range of further options. We are going to look at several of the most commonly used.

File: Open

Click on the word **File** and a menu will drop down which includes the item **Open.** If you click on this, a window like the following will appear.

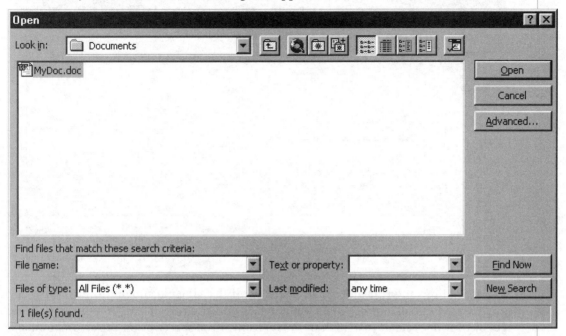

To open a particular file you would click on the **Look in** box arrow to specify the drive (if it is not the one shown already) then *double-click* in the directories box to pick the directory. A list of all the Word type files in the chosen directory will appear. Click on the file name that you want and that name will appear in the File Name box. Then you click on OK to open the file.

Double-clicking on a file name has the effect of both selecting it and clicking on OK to open it.

File: Save As

This option enables you to open a file that has one name, make some changes to it, and then save it with another name. The effect is that the file you originally opened remains in its original form, but the file with the new name retains all of your changes..

File: Close

Once you have finished with your file you should close it. Click on **File** and then on **Close** in the drop down menu. If you haven't already done so you will be asked if you want to save any changes you made.

File: Print

If you have a document open and you wish to print it, click on the **Print** option in the **File** menu. The following box will appear.

Core Unit 7: Management Information Systems

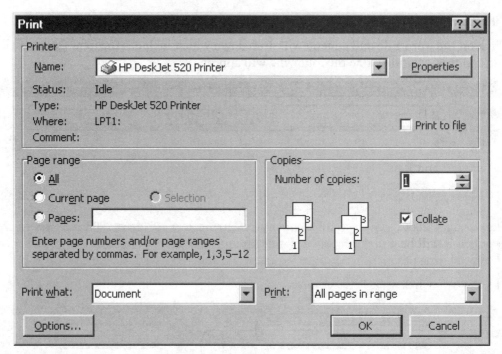

There are options to print more than one copy of the same document, to print only the page that your cursor was on when you clicked on the Print option or to print specific pages of your document. Just click in the relevant white spaces or on the arrows to make changes to any of the settings that come up when the window is first displayed.

An important point to check before you click on OK is the first line, which tells you which printer the document will be printed on.

Edit: Cut, Copy and Paste

The cut, copy and paste facilities are so useful that there are probably toolbar buttons for them as well as menu items. They are used as follows.

(a)　Select some text. Do this by positioning the mouse pointer at the beginning of the first word, holding down the left mouse button and, keeping the button held down, moving the mouse to the end of the last word (not forgetting any punctuation marks) and then releasing the button. This portion of text will now be highlighted.

(b)　Click on **Edit** at the top of the screen. A menu drops down.

(i)　To retain the highlighted text in its current place and also to make a copy of it which is retained temporarily in the computer's memory, click on **Copy.**

(ii)　To remove the highlighted text from its current place, but also keep it temporarily in the computer's memory, click on **Cut.** The highlighted text will disappear.

(c)　Move the cursor to the point in your document where you want to move the highlighted text or place a copy of it. Do this using the direction arrow keys or by pointing and clicking with the mouse.

(d)　Click on Edit again and choose **Paste.** The text you highlighted will reappear in this new place.

Note that what you paste will be the last thing you cut or copied. If you cut out some text meaning to put it in later, but before you get there you cut or copy something else, the first thing you cut will be lost.

Note also that there are keyboard shortcuts for cutting, copying and pasting. These are listed on the **Edit** menu. In Word you can even *drag* the selected text and *drop* it in the new place. Try this with a sentence of the text you typed in at the beginning of this section.

Edit: Find and Replace

The **Find** and **Replace** options on the **Edit** menu are very useful. Suppose you had a document that included lots of references to a certain product made by your company: the 'Widget 2000', say. If your company releases a new 'Widget 2003' version of the product, it will be a slow process to scroll through the entire document and retype every instance of the product name when you see it. Fortunately you don't have to.

(a)   Click on **Edit** and then on **Replace.**

(b)   A window appears that allows you to type what you wish to replace in one box (eg 'Widget 2000'), and what you wish to replace it with in another box (eg 'Widget 2003').

(c)   You then have a choice of buttons to click.

    (i)   The **Find next** button will take you directly to each successive instance of 'Widget 2000' in the document.

    (ii)   The **Replace** button will replace a particular instance of 'Widget 2000' with 'Widget 2003'.

    (iii)   The **Replace All** button will automatically replace *every* instance of 'Widget 2000' with 'Widget 2003'. This sounds better than option (ii), but there may be cases where you only want *some* of the examples of 'Widget 2000' replaced, such as 'This is the new improved version of the well-loved Widget 2000'.

Format: Paragraph

This item on the **Format** menu offers you (amongst other things) a better way of spacing out paragraphs than pressing return several times to leave blank lines.

Clicking on the **Paragraph** option in the **Format** menu brings up a window with a Spacing section which allows you to specify the number of 'points' (small units of vertical space) before paragraphs and after them. For example there are '18 pts' between this paragraph and the previous one.

Tools: Spelling

Finally we come to what is the best feature of word processors for bad spellers and clumsy typists. Click on **Tools** and then on **Spelling** in the drip down menu. Word will work right through your document seeing if the spelling matches the spelling of words in the computer's dictionary. If not it suggests alternatives from which you choose the correct one. For example, if you type 'drp', the choices you are offered include 'drip', 'drop', 'dry' and 'dip'. Do you think this paragraph has been spell-checked?

People sometimes forget that computer spell-checkers only recognise mistakes if they don't match a word in the computer's dictionary. For example, if you type 'form' instead of 'from' the computer will not realise you have made a mistake. It is also easy to make mistakes with a spell-checker if you are too eager to accept its first suggestion. The previous paragraph has a deliberate example.

3 USING SPREADSHEETS

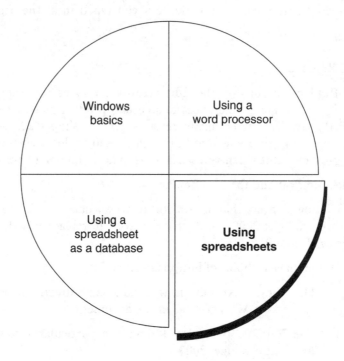

3.1 What is a spreadsheet?

Definition

> A **spreadsheet** is essentially an **electronic piece of paper** divided into **rows and columns**. It provides an automated way of performing calculations.

Below is a spreadsheet processing budgeted sales figures for three geographical areas for the first quarter of the year.

	A	B	C	D	E	F	G	H
1	BUDGETED SALES FIGURES							
2		Jan	Feb	Mar	Total			
3		£'000	£'000	£'000	£'000			
4	North	2,431	3,001	2,189	7,621			
5	South	6,532	5,826	6,124	18,482			
6	West	895	432	596	1,923			
7	Total	9,858	9,259	8,909	28,026			
8								
9								
10								
11								
12								
13								
14								
15								
16								
17								
18								
19								
20								

Spreadsheets save time. For example, the spreadsheet above has been set up to calculate the totals **automatically.** If you changed your estimate of sales in February for the North region to £3,296, when you input this information the totals would change accordingly.

The main examples of spreadsheet packages are Lotus 1-2-3 and Microsoft Excel. We will be referring to Microsoft Excel, as this is the most widely-used spreadsheet.

3.2 Uses of spreadsheets

Since spreadsheets can be used to build a wide variety of models, spreadsheet packages are '**general purpose**' software packages, as distinct from software packages which are designed for specific applications (for example a sales ledger package).

Some of the more **common applications** of spreadsheets are:

- Management accounts
- Cash flow analysis and forecasting
- Reconciliations
- Job cost estimates
- Market share analysis and planning
- Budgets
- Sales and profit projections

What all these have in common is that they all involve data processing with:

- **Numerical** data
- **Repetitive**, time-consuming calculations
- A **logical** processing structure

3.3 The appearance of a spreadsheet

A 'blank' spreadsheet is shown below. It consists of 'empty' rows and columns. **Rows** are **horizontal** and **columns vertical.** The **rows** are **numbered** 1, 2, 3 . . . etc and the **columns lettered** A, B C . . . etc.

	A	B	C	D	E	F	G	H
1								
2								
3								
4								
5								
6								
7								
8								
9								
10								
11								
12								
13								
14								
15								
16								
17								
18								
19								
20								

Each square is called a 'cell'. A cell address consists of its row and column reference. Some have the cells in the sheet below have been labelled with their references.

	A	B	C	D	E	F	G	H
1	A1	B1	C1	D1	E1	F1	G1	H1
2	A2	B2						
3	A3		C3					
4	A4			D4				
5	A5				E5			
6	A6					F6		
7	A7						G7	
8	A8							H8

The **cursor** shows the 'active' cell - in the previous illustration it is placed over cell C6.

At the top or bottom of the screen, the spreadsheet program will display such information as:

(a) The reference of the cell where the cursor lies.

(b) The width of the column where the cursor lies (you can alter column widths to suit yourself, without changing the total number of columns available on the spreadsheet).

(c) The contents of the cell where the cursor lies, if there is anything there.

The contents of any cell can be one of the following.

(a) **Text**. A cell so designated contains **words** or numerical data (eg a date) that will not be used in computations. On newer versions of all popular spreadsheets, text can be formatted in a similar way to what is possible using a word processing package. Different fonts can be selected, text can be emboldened or italicised, and the point size of the lettering can be changed.

(b) **Values**. A value is a **number** that can be used in a calculation.

(c) **Formulae**. A formula **refers to other cells** in the spreadsheet, and performs some sort of computation with them. For example, if cell C1 contains the formula =A1-B1 this means that the contents of cell B1 should be subtracted from the contents of cell A1 and the result displayed in cell C1. Note that a formula starts with a specific command or choice or symbols in most packages to distinguish it from text.

(i) In Excel, a formula always begins with an equals sign: =

(ii) Where a long row or column of cells (referred to as a range) is to be added together, a '**sum**' function can be used. In Excel this would be entered as =SUM(B7:B18)

Activity 1

This activity tests some basic ideas about spreadsheets.

(a)   What is a spreadsheet?

(b)   Give five uses of a spreadsheet.

(c)   In the spreadsheet below, what is the reference for the cell over which the cursor is positioned?

(d)   What is meant by the term 'the active cell'?

(e)   A cell in a spreadsheet can contain one of three things: text, values or formulae. Briefly explain the purpose of each of these.

	A	B	C	D	E	F	G
1							
2							
3							
4							
5							
6							
7							
8							
9							
10							
11							
12							
13							
14							
15							
16							
17							
18							
19							
20							

EXAMPLE: FORMULAE

The simple spreadsheet encountered earlier which totals sales figures follows.

	A	B	C	D	E	F	G	H
1	BUDGETED SALES FIGURES							
2		Jan	Feb	Mar	Total			
3		£'000	£'000	£'000	£'000			
4	North	2,431	3,001	2,189	7,621			
5	South	6,532	5,826	6,124	18,482			
6	West	895	432	596	1,923			
7	Total	9,858	9,259	8,909	28,026			
8								
9								
10								
11								
12								
13								
14								
15								
16								
17								
18								
19								
20								
21								

(a)   Which of the cells require a value to be typed in? Which cells would perform calculations, ie which cells contain a formula?

(b)   What formula would you put in each of the following cells?

    (i)   Cell B7

    (ii)   Cell E6

    (iii) Cell E7

(c)   If the February sales figure for the South changed from £5,826 to £5,731, what other figures would change as a result? Give cell references.

SOLUTION

You will notice in these solutions that we introduce the quick way, noted above, of adding up ('casting') a row or column of cells. This is not essential where only three cells are involved, but obviously useful for longer series of numbers.

(a)   Cells into which you would need to enter a value are: B4, B5, B6, C4, C5, C6, D4, D5 and D6. Cells which would perform calculations are B7, C7, D7, E4, E5, E6 and E7.

(b)   (i)   =B4+B5+B6 *or better* =SUM(B4:B6)

    (ii)   =B6+C6+D6 *or better* =SUM(B6:D6)

    (iii)   =E4+E5+E6 *or better* =SUM(E4:E6) Alternatively, the three monthly totals could be added across the spreadsheet: = SUM (B7: D7)

(c)   The figures which would change, besides the amount in cell C5, would be those in cells C7, E5 and E7. (The contents of E7 would change if *any* of the sales figures changed.)

Activity 2

The following spreadsheet shows sales of two products, the Ego and the Id, for the period July to September.

Devise a suitable formula for each of the following cells.

(a)   Cell B7
(b)   Cell E6
(c)   Cell E7

	A	B	C	D	E	F	G
1	**Sigmund Ltd**						
2	*Sales analysis - Q3 X7*						
3		M7	M8	M9	Total		
4		£	£	£	£		
5	Ego	3000	4000	2000	9000		
6	Id	2000	1500	4000	7500		
7	Total	5000	5500	6000	16500		
8							
9							
10							

Activity 3

The following spreadsheet shows sales, exclusive of VAT, in row 6.

Your manager has asked you to insert formulae to calculate VAT at 17½% in row 7 and also to produce totals.

(a)   Devise a suitable formula for each of the following cells.

   (i)   Cell B7
   (ii)   Cell E8

(b)   How could the spreadsheet be better designed?

	A	B	C	D	E	F	G	H
1	**Taxable Supplies plc**							
2	*Sales analysis - Branch C*							
3	*Six months ended 30 June XX*							
4		Jan	Feb	Mar	Apr	May	Jun	Total
5		£	£	£	£	£	£	£
6	Net sales	2,491.54	5,876.75	3,485.01	5,927.70	6,744.52	3,021.28	27,546.80
7	VAT							
8	Total							
9								
10								

Activity 4

The following balances have been taken from the books of Ed Sheet, a sole trader, at 31 December 200X.

	Dr £	Cr £
Plant and machinery (NBV)	20,000	
Motor vehicles (NBV)	10,000	
Stock	2,000	
Debtors	1,000	
Cash	1,500	
Creditors		2,500
Overdraft		1,500
Drawings	1,000	
Captial (1 Jan 200X)		28,000
Profit for year	3,500	

Your manager has tried to use a spreadsheet to produce a balance sheet. He has set up the basic structure and input the numbers, but he cannot remember how to do formulae. He has therefore highlighted with a border the cells which require a formula to be inserted and left the rest up to you. The spreadsheet is shown below.

	A	B	C	D	E	F
1	**Ed Sheet**					
2	*Balance sheet as at 31 Dec 200X*					
3		£	£			
4	*Fixed assets*					
5	Plant	20000				
6	Vehicles	10000				
7			⬚			
8	*Current assets*					
9	Stock	2000				
10	Debtors	1000				
11	Cash	1500				
12		⬚				
13	*Current liabilities*					
14	Creditors	2500				
15	Overdraft	1500				
16		⬚				
17	Net current assets		⬚			
18	Net assets		⬚			
19						
20	*Represented by:*					
21	Opening capital		28000			
22	Profit for year		3500			
23	Drawings		1000			
24	Closing capital		⬚			
25						
26						

(a) Devise and list the formulae required to go in the cells highlighted.

(b) Using the diagram above, show how the spreadsheet would appear when the correct formulae have been entered.

3.4   Getting started

Start your spreadsheet software by finding and double-clicking on the Excel **icon** or button (it will look like an X), or by choosing Excel from somewhere in the **Start** menus (maybe from within the **Microsoft Office** option).

3.5   Moving about (F5)

Press the function key labelled **F5** at the top of the keyboard. A **Go To** dialogue box will appear with the 'cursor' (a flashing line or lit up section) in a box. Delete anything that is in the box with the Delete key and then type C5 (or c5 – case does not matter) and press Enter. The 'cursor' will now be over cell C5. This is the **active cell** and it will have a thick black line all round it.

Press **Ctrl** + ↑ and then **Ctrl** + ←. (This means that you hold down one of the keys marked Ctrl and, keeping it held down, press the other key.)

The cursor will move back to cell A1. Try holding down Ctrl and pressing each of the direction arrow keys in turn to see where you end up. Try using the **Page Up** and **Page Down** keys and also try **Home** and **End** and Ctrl + these keys. Try **Tab** and **Shift + Tab**, too. These are all useful shortcuts for moving quickly from one place to another in a large spreadsheet.

> **TIP**
>
> The F5 key is not needed for small spreadsheets, but it is a handy way of getting around larger ones.

3.6   Entering data and the active cell

Get your cursor back to cell A1. Then type in 123. Then press the ↓ key. Note that the cell below (A2) now becomes the **active cell**.

Type 456 in cell A2 and then press the → key. The cell to the left (B2) is now the active cell.

Get back to cell A1. Above cell A1 you should be able to see a rectangle at the top left *telling* you that you are in cell A1 and, to the right of this a line containing the numbers 123. In other words this line at the top of the screen shows you the **cell reference** and the **contents** of the currently **active cell**.

3.7   Editing data (F2)

Assuming you have now made cell A1 the active cell, type 45. Note what happens both in the cell and in the line above. The previous entry (123) is replaced by the number 45. Press ↓. The active cell is now A2 (check in the line at the top of the screen).

Suppose you wanted to **change the entry** in cell A2 from 456 to 123456. You have four options. Option (d) is the best.

(a)   **Type** 123456 and press **Enter**.

To undo this and try the next option press **Ctrl + Z**: this will always undo what you have just done.

(b)   **Double-click** in cell A2. The cell will keep its thick outline but you will now be able to see a vertical line flashing in the cell. You can move this line by using the direction arrow keys or the Home and the End keys. Move it to before the 4 and type 123. Then press Enter.

When you have tried this press Ctrl + Z to undo it.

(c) **Click** *once* on the number 456 in the line that shows the active cell reference and cell contents at the top of the screen. Again you will get the vertical line and you can type in 123 before the 4. Then press Enter, then Ctrl + Z.

(d) Press the **function key F2**. The vertical line cursor will be flashing in cell A2 at the *end* of the figures entered there (after the 6). Press Home to get to a position before the 4 and then type in 123 and press Enter, as before.

> ## TIP
>
> **Option (d)** - F2 - may not seem much better than the other options at the moment, but after a bit of experience you will soon find that it is usually **quicker and more convenient** than the other methods.

Now make cell A3 the active cell. Type **1 2** (a 1, a space, and then a 2) in this cell and press Enter. Note that because the software finds a space it thinks you want **text** in this cell. It **aligns it to the left**, not the right. If you ever need to enter a number to be treated as text, you should enter an **apostrophe** before it. eg '1.

3.8 Deleting

Get to cell A3 if you have not already done so and press **Delete**. The contents of this cell will disappear.

Move the cursor up to cell A2. Now hold down the Shift key (the one above the Ctrl key) and keeping it held down press the ↑ arrow. Cell A2 will stay white but cell A1 will go black. What you have done here is selected the range A1 and A2. Anything you do next will be done to both cells A1 and A2.

Press Delete. The contents of cells A1 and A2 will disappear.

> **Activity 5**
>
> (a) What is the purpose of the F5 key?
>
> (b) What are four ways of editing the data in a cell?
>
> (c) What happens in a Windows program if you press Ctrl + Z?
>
> (d) How do you select a cell or a range of cells using:
>
>   (i) The mouse?
>   (ii) The keyboard?

3.9 Filling cells automatically

You should now have a blank spreadsheet on screen. Type the number 1 in cell A1 and the number 2 in cell A2. Now *select* cells A1: A2, this time by positioning the mouse pointer over cell A1, holding down the left mouse button and moving the pointer down to cell A2. When cell A2 goes black you can release the mouse button.

Now position the mouse pointer at the **bottom right hand corner** of cell A2. (You should be able to see a little black lump in this corner: this is called the 'fill handle'.) When you have the mouse pointer in the right place it will turn into a black cross.

Hold down the left mouse button again and move the pointer down to cell A10. You will see an outline surrounding the cells you are trying to 'fill'.

Release the mouse button when you have the pointer over cell A10. You will find that the software **automatically** fills in the numbers 3 to 10 below 1 and 2.

There are a number of variations on this technique that you can now experiment with.

(a)   Delete what you have just done and type in **Jan** in cell A1. See what happens if you select cell A1 and fill down to cell A12: you get the months **Feb, Mar, Apr** and so on.

(b)   Type the number 2 in cell A1. Select A1 and fill down to cell A10. What happens? The cells should fill up with 2's.

(c)   Type the number 2 in cell A1 and 4 in cell A2. Then select A1: A2 and fill down to cell A10. What happens? You should get 2, 4, 6, 8, and so on.

(d)   Can you **fill across** as well as down? You should be able to.

(e)   What happens if you click on the bottom right hand corner using the **right mouse button**, drag down to another cell and then release the button? You should get a menu giving you a variety of different options for how you want the cells to be filled in.

(f)   In Excel you can fill in any direction.

> **TIP**
>
> We suggest you spend some time playing with your package's fill facility: it is a useful skill to acquire.

3.10 The sum function

Load a clean spreadsheet if you wish to follow this explanation hands-on. Click on the button in the top left hand corner (above row number 1 and to the right of column letter A) and the **whole spreadsheet** will be selected: it will all go black. Press **Delete** to clear away any figures you may have entered in the last exercise. Then press ↑ or ← to clear away the highlighting.

Now enter the following figures in cells A1:B5. Make sure the **Num Lock light** on your keyboard is lit up (press the Num Lock key if not) to enable you to **use the numeric keypad**.

	A	B
1	400	582
2	250	478
3	359	264
4	476	16
5	97	125

To check that you have entered the figures correctly make cell A6 the active cell and *double-click* on the button labelled with a '**sum**' sign at the top of the screen. (The button has a Σ symbol, the mathematical sign for 'the sum of'.)

The number 1582 should shortly appear in cell A6.

Now select cell B6 and click *once* on the sum button. A formula will appear in the cell saying =SUM(B1:B5). Above cell B6 you will see a flashing dotted line encircling cells B1:B5. Click **anywhere within** the encircled area, hold down the left mouse button and move the mouse about a little from cell to cell. Watch the **formula** in cell B6 and the **boundary** of the dotted line change as you redefine the cells that are to be summed.

To finish up, click on cell B5, hold down the left mouse button and move the pointer up to cell B1. Then click on the Σ button. The formula =SUM(B1:B5) will be entered and the number 1465 will be appear in cell B6.

Next select cell C1. Type in an = sign then click on cell A1. Now type in an **asterisk** * (which serves as a **multiplication sign** in spreadsheets) and click on cell B1. Watch how the formula in cell C1 changes as you do this. (Alternatively you can enter the cell references by moving the direction arrow keys.) Finally press Enter. Cell C1 will show the result (232,800) of multiplying the figure in Cell A1 by the one in cell B1.

Your next task is to select cell C1 and **fill in** cells C2 to C5 automatically using the **dragging technique** described above. If you then click on each cell in column C, and look above at the line showing what the cell contains, you will find that the software has automatically filled in the correct cell references for you: A2*B2 in cell C2, A3*B3 in cell C3 and so on.

The sum function is a basic feature, but can be very useful function for carrying out simple but potentially time consuming calculations quickly, and without errors.

> **Activity 6**
>
> Use the sum *button* in your spreadsheet package to sum figures shown in the following spreadsheet. Cell D5 should show the total of cells A5 to C5, cell E5 the total of cells E1 to E3 and cell C11 the sum of cells B8 to B10.

	A	B	C	D	E	F
1					1	
2					2	
3					3	
4						
5	4	6	5			
6						
7						
8		10				
9		20				
10		70				
11						
12						
13						

3.11 Inserting columns and rows

When working with spreadsheets you may find that you need to insert cells or maybe a whole new column between existing cells.

(a) To insert cells, say between existing cells B1 to C5, highlight cells C1 to C5, position the mouse pointer anywhere **within** column C and click on the **right** mouse button. A menu will appear offering you an option **Insert...** . If you click on this you will be asked where you want to shift the cells that are being moved. In this case you want to move them to the *right* so choose this option and click on OK.

(c) To insert a whole new **column,** click on the letter at the top of the column (here C) to highlight the column, then proceed as in (b) or select Insert, Column from the main menu at the top of the screen.

You can also insert a **new row** in a similar way (or stretch rows).

(a) To insert *one* row – for headings say – click on the row number to highlight it, click with the right mouse button and choose insert. One row will be inserted **above** the one you highlighted. Try putting some headings above the figures in columns A to C.

(b) To insert **several** rows click on the row number **immediately below** the point where you want the new rows to appear and, holding down the left mouse button select the number of extra rows you want – rows 1, 2 and 3, say, to insert three rows above the current row 1. Click on the highlighted area with the right mouse button and choose insert.

3.12 Layout

Clear the contents of your spreadsheet, as described in paragraph 2.22. Then type the following text in cell A1: **This is far too wide to fit in the column.** Press Enter. The text **will** be too wide to fit in the column, but it will overlap into columns B, C, and possibly D so you will still be able to see what you typed.

Now click on where cell B1 should be (it will be covered up with words, but you can still work out where it should be: look at the box at the top left-hand corner if you are not sure you have clicked in the right place. Now type the number 1,234,567,890. Press Enter.

The result is likely to be something like the following.

	A	B	C	D	E
1	This is far	########			
2					
3					
4					
5					

You cannot see much of the text that you typed in cell A1, and you cannot see *any* of the figures that you typed in cell B1.

The reason for this is simply that the **columns are not wide enough**. To solve this there are two options.

(a) One is to **decide for yourself** how wide you want the columns to be. Position the mouse pointer at the head of column A directly over the little line dividing the letter A from the letter B. The mouse **pointer** will change to a sort of **cross**. Hold down the left mouse button and, by moving your mouse, stretch Column A to the right, to about the middle of column D, until the words you typed fit. You can do the same for column B. Then make your columns too narrow again so you can try option (b).

(b) The software can automatically resize the column. Position the mouse pointer over the little dividing line as before and get the cross symbol. Then double-click with the left mouse button. The column automatically adjusts to an appropriate width to fit the widest cell in that column.

TIP

You can either adjust the width of each column individually or you can do them all in one go. To do the latter click on the button in the top left hand corner to **select the whole sheet** and then **double-click** on just one of the dividing lines: all the columns will adjust to the 'best fit' width.

Activity 7

(a)   Enter the following data in a spreadsheet.

	A	B	C	D	E	F
1	1	2	3			
2	2					
3	3					
4						
5						
6						
7						

Without typing any data and without dragging and dropping data use the mouse to make the spreadsheet look like this.

	A	B	C	D	E	F
1	1		2		3	
2						
3	2					
4						
5	3					
6						
7						

(b)   Enter the text 'Profit and loss account' in cell A1 of a spreadsheet and the number 6,427,983.24 in cell B1.

Widen columns A and B so that the entries you have made can be clearly seen. Use the mouse to do this.

(c)   ˙ Drag the data you have just entered in cells A1 and B1 into cells E12 and F12. Widen columns E and F so that the data fits properly.

3.13   More keyboard shortcuts and buttons

Finally a few tips to improve the **appearance** of your spreadsheets and speed up your work. To do any of the following to a cell or range of cells, first **select** the cell or cells and then:

(a)   Press Ctrl + B to make the cell contents **bold.**

(b)   Press Ctrl + I to make the cell contents *italic.*

(c)   Press **Ctrl + C** to **copy** the contents of the cells.

(d)   Move the cursor and press **Ctrl + V** to **paste** the cell you just copied into the new active cell or cells.

(When you copy cells the highlighted area will have a **moving dotted border** until you paste them somewhere or else press the **Esc** key.)

There are also **buttons** at the top of the screen that carry out these and other functions. Enter some numbers and text into a spreadsheet and try out the above keyboard shortcuts and any buttons you fancy to see what effect they have. You cannot break the spreadsheet by using its facilities and you do not have to save what you do unless you want to.

EXAMPLE: CONSTRUCTING A CASH FLOW PROJECTION

Suppose you wanted to set up a simple six-month cash flow projection, in such a way that you could use it to estimate how the **projected cash balance** figures will **change** in total when any **individual item** in the projection is **altered**. You have the following information.

(a) Sales were £45,000 per month in 20X5, falling to £42,000 in January 20X6. Thereafter they are expected to increase by 3% per month (ie February will be 3% higher than January, and so on).

(b) Debts are collected as follows.

  (i) 60% in month following sale.
  (ii) 30% in second month after sale.
  (iii) 7% in third month after sale.
  (iv) 3% remains uncollected.

(c) Purchases are equal to cost of sales, set at 65% of sales.

(d) Overheads were £6,000 per month in 20X5, rising by 5% in 20X6.

(e) Opening cash is an overdraft of £7,500.

(f) Dividends: £10,000 final dividend on 20X5 profits payable in May.

(g) Capital purchases: plant costing £18,000 will be ordered in January. 20% is payable with order, 70% on delivery in February and the final 10% in May.

Headings and layout

The first job is to put in the various **headings** that you want on the cash flow projection. At this stage, your screen might look as follows.

	A	B	C	D	E	F	G
1	EXCELLENT PLC						
2	*Cash flow projection - six months ending 30 June X6*						
3		*Jan*	*Feb*	*Mar*	*Apr*	*May*	*Jun*
4		£	£	£	£	£	£
5	Sales						
6	*Cash receipts*						
7	1 month in arrears						
8	2 months in arrears						
9	3 months in arrears						
10	Total operating receipts						
11							
12	Cash payments						
13	Purchases						
14	Overheads						
15	Total operating payments						
16							
17	Dividends						
18	Capital purchases						
19	Total other payments						
20							
21	Net cash flow						
22	Cash balance b/f						
23	Cash balance c/f						
24							

A couple of points to note at this stage.

(a) We have **increased the width** of column A to allow longer pieces of text to be inserted. Had we not done so, only the first part of each caption would have been displayed (and printed).

(b) We have developed a **simple style for headings**. Headings are essential, so that users can identify what a spreadsheet does. We have **emboldened** the company name and *italicised* other headings.

(c) When **text** is entered into a cell it is usually **left-aligned** (as for example in column A). We have **centred** the headings above each column by highlighting the cells and using the relevant buttons at the top of the screen.

(d) **Numbers** should be **right-aligned** in cells.

(e) We have left **spaces** in certain rows (after blocks of related items) to make the spreadsheet **easier to use and read**.

Inserting formulae

The next stage is to put in the **calculations** you want the computer to carry out, expressed as **formulae**. For example, in cell B10 you want total operating receipts, so you move to cell B10 and put in the formula =SUM(B7:B9).

Look for a moment at cell C7. We are told that sales in January were £42,000 and that 60% of customers settle their accounts one month in arrears. We could insert the formula =B5*0.6 in the cell and fill in the other cells along the row so that it is replicated in each month. However, consider the effect of a change in payment patterns to a situation where, say, 55% of customer debts are settled after one month. This would necessitate a **change to each and every cell** in which the 0.6 ratio appears.

An alternative approach, which makes **future changes much simpler** to execute, is to put the relevant ratio (here, 60% or 0.6) in a cell **outside** the main table and cross-refer each cell in the main table to that cell.

This means that, if the percentage changes, the change need only be reflected in **one cell**, following which all cells which are dependent on that cell will **automatically use the new percentage**.

We will therefore input such values in separate parts of the spreadsheet, as follows over the page. Look at the other assumptions which we have inserted into this part of the spreadsheet.

	A	B	C	D	E	F	G
24							
25							
26	*This table contains the key variables for the*		*X6 cash flow projections*				
27							
28	Sales growth factor per month		1.03				
29	Purchases as % of sales		-0.65				
30							
31	Debts paid within 1 month		0.6				
32	Debts paid within 2 months		0.3				
33	Debts paid within 3 months		0.07				
34	Bad debts		0.03				
35							
36	Increase in overheads		1.05				
37							
38	Dividends (May)		-10000				
39							
40	Capital purchases		-18000				
41	January		0.2				
42	February		0.7				
43	May		0.1				
44							
45							
46	*This table contains relevant opening balance data as at Jan*		*X6*				
47							
48	Monthly sales X5		45000				
49	January X6 sales		42000				
50	Monthly overheads X5		-6000				
51	Opening cash		-7500				
52							

Now we can go back to cell C7 and input =B5*C31 and then fill this in across the '1 month in arrears' row. (Note that, as we have no December sales figure, we will have to deal with cell B7 separately.) If we assume for the moment that we are copying to cells D7 through to G7 and follow this procedure, the contents of cell D7 would be shown as =C5*D31, and so on, as shown below.

	A	B	C	D	E	F	G
3		Jan	Feb	Mar	Apr	May	Jun
4		£	£	£	£	£	£
5	Sales						
6	*Cash receipts*						
7	1 month in arrears		=B5*C31	=C5*D31	=D5*E31	=E5*F31	=F5*G31
8	2 months in arrears						
9	3 months in arrears						
10	Total operating receipts						

You may notice a problem if you look at this closely. While the formula in cell C7 is fine - it multiplies January sales by 0.6 (the 1 month ratio stored in cell C31) - the remaining formulae are useless, as they **refer to empty cells** in row 31. This is what the spreadsheet would look like (assuming, for now, constant sales of £42,000 per month).

	A	B	C	D	E	F	G
3		Jan	Feb	Mar	Apr	May	Jun
4		£	£	£	£	£	£
5	Sales	42000	42000	42000	42000	42000	42000
6	*Cash receipts*						
7	1 month in arrears		25200	0	0	0	0
8	2 months in arrears						
9	3 months in arrears						
10	Total operating receipts						

3.14 Relative and absolute references (F4)

There is a very important distinction between **relative** cell references and **absolute** cell references.

Usually, cell references are **relative**. A formula of =SUM(B7:B9) in cell B10 is relative. It does not really mean 'add up the numbers in cells B7 to B9'; it actually means '**add up the numbers in the three cells above this one**'. If the formula were copied to cell C10 (as we will do later), it would become =SUM(C7:C9).

This is what is causing the problem encountered above. The spreadsheet thinks we are asking it to 'multiply the number two up and one to the left by the number twenty-four cells down', and that is indeed the effect of the instruction we have given. But we are actually intending to ask it to 'multiply the number two up and one to the left by the number in cell C31'. This means that we need to create an **absolute** (unchanging) **reference** to cell C31. This is done by adding a pair of **dollar signs** ($) to the relevant formula, one before the column letter and one before the row number.

TIP

Don't type the dollar signs, add them as follows.

(a) Make cell C7 the active cell and press F2 to edit it.

(b) Note where the cursor is flashing: it should be after the 1. If it is not move it with the direction arrow keys so that it is positioned somewhere next to or within the cell reference C31.

(c) Press F4

The **function key F4** adds dollar signs to the cell reference: it becomes $C$31. Press F4 again: the reference becomes C$31. Press it again: the reference becomes $C31. Press it once more, and the simple relative reference is restored: C31.

(a) A dollar sign **before a letter** means that the **column** reference stays the same when you copy the formula to another cell.

(b) A dollar sign **before a number** means that the **row** reference stays the same when you copy the formula to another cell.

EXAMPLE: BACK TO THE CASH FLOW PROJECTION

In our example we have now altered the reference in cell C7 and filled in across to cell G7, overwriting what was there previously. This is the result.

(a) Formulae

	A	B	C	D	E	F	G
3		*Jan*	*Feb*	*Mar*	*Apr*	*May*	*Jun*
4		£	£	£	£	£	£
5	Sales	42000	42000	42000	42000	42000	42000
6	*Cash receipts*						
7	1 month in arrears		=B5*$C$31	=C5*$C$31	=D5*$C$31	=E5*$C$31	=F5*$C$31
8	2 months in arrears						
9	3 months in arrears						
10	Total operating receipts						

(b)   Numbers

	A	B	C	D	E	F	G
3		Jan	Feb	Mar	Apr	May	Jun
4		£	£	£	£	£	£
5	Sales	42000	42000	42000	42000	42000	42000
6	*Cash receipts*						
7	1 month in arrears		25200	25200	25200	25200	25200
8	2 months in arrears						
9	3 months in arrears						
10	Total operating receipts						

Other formulae required for this projection are as follows.

(a)   **Cell B5** refers directly to the information we are given - **sales of £42,000** in January. We have input this variable in cell C49. The other formulae in row 5 (sales) reflect the predicted sales growth of 3% per month, as entered in cell C28.

(b)   Similar formulae to the one already described for row 7 are required in rows 8 and 9.

(c)   **Row 10** (total operating receipts) will display simple **subtotals**, in the form =SUM(B7:B9).

(d)   **Row 13 (purchases)** requires a formula based on the data in row 5 **(sales)** and the value in cell C29 **(purchases** as a % of sales). This model assumes no changes in stock levels from month to month, and that stocks are sufficiently high to enable this. The formula is B5 * $C$29. Note that C29 is negative.

(e)   **Row 15** (total operating payments), like row 10, requires **formulae** to create **subtotals**.

(f)   **Rows 17 and 18** refer to the **dividends and capital purchase data** input in cells C38 and C40 to 43.

(g)   **Row 21** (net cash flow) requires a **total** in the form =B10 + B15 + B21.

(h)   **Row 22** (balance b/f) requires the contents of the **previous month's closing cash** figure.

(i)   **Row 23** (balance b/f) requires the **total** of the **opening cash** figure and the **net cash flow** for the month.

Once the formulae have been inserted, the following illustration shows the formulae the spreadsheet would contain. (Remember, it does not normally look like this on screen, as formulae are not usually displayed in cells.)

	A	B	C	D	E	F	G
1	EXCELLENT PLC						
2	Cash flow projection - six months						
3		Jan	Feb	Mar	Apr	May	Jun
4		£	£	£	£	£	£
5	Sales	=C49	=B5*$C$28	=C5*$C$28	=D5*$C$28	=E5*$C$28	=F5*$C$28
6	Cash receipts						
7	1 month in arrears	=$C$48*$C$31	=B5*$C$31	=C5*$C$31	=D5*$C$31	=E5*$C$31	=F5*$C$31
8	2 months in arrears	=$C$48*$C$32	=$C$48*$C$32	=B5*$C$32	=C5*$C$32	=D5*$C$32	=E5*$C$32
9	3 months in arrears	=$C$48*$C$33	=$C$48*$C$33	=$C$48*$C$33	=B5*$C$33	=C5*$C$33	=D5*$C$33
10	Total operating receipts	=SUM(B7:B9)	=SUM(C7:C9)	=SUM(D7:D3)	=SUM(E7:E9)	=SUM(F7:F9)	=SUM(G7:G9)
11							
12	Cash payments						
13	Purchases	=B5*$C$29	=C5*$C$29	=D5*$C$29	=E5*$C$29	=F5*$C$29	=G5*$C$29
14	Overheads	=$C$50*$C$36	=$C$50*$C$36	=$C$50*$C$36	=$C$50*$C$36	=$C$50*$C$36	=$C$50*$C$36
15	Total operating payments	=SUM(B13:B14)	=SUM(C13:C14)	=SUM(D13:D14)	=SUM(E13:E14)	=SUM(F13:F14)	=SUM(G13:G14)
16							
17	Dividends	0	0	0	0	=C38	0
18	Capital purchases	=C40*C41	=C40*C42	0	0	=C40*C43	0
19	Total other payments	=SUM(B17:B18)	=SUM(C17:C18)	=SUM(D17:D18)	=SUM(E17:E18)	=SUM(F17:F18)	=SUM(G17:G18)
20							
21	Net cash flow	=B10+B15+B19	=C10+C15+C19	=D10+D15+D19	=E10+E15+E19	=F10+F15+F19	=G10+G15+G19
22	Cash balance b/f	=C51	=B23	=C23	=D23	=E23	=F23
23	Cash balance c/f	=SUM(B21:B22)	=SUM(C21:C22)	=SUM(D21:D22)	=SUM(E21:E22)	=SUM(F21:F22)	=SUM(G21:G22)
24							

Negative numbers

In a spreadsheet, you must be very careful to sort out the approach which you wish to take when manipulating negative numbers. For example, if total operating payments in row 15 are shown as **positive**, you would need to **subtract** them from total operating receipts in the formulae in row 23. However if you have chosen to make them **negative**, to represent outflows, then you will need to **add** them to total operating receipts. This becomes even more important when you are dealing with accounts or balances which may be sometimes positive and sometimes negative, for example the cash balances rows.

Opening balances

It is important, in an exercise like this, to get the opening balances right. However good your budgeting of income and expenses is, if you have made a **poor estimate** of the opening cash balance, this will be **reflected right through the forecast**.

Integration

In practice, you might well **integrate** a cash flow projection like this with a forecast profit and loss account and balance sheet. This would give a high degree of **re-assurance** that the numbers 'stacked up' and would enable you to present a 'cleaner' projection: for example, sales would appear on the profit and loss account, and the cash receipts formulae could refer direct to that part of the spreadsheet (or even to a separate spreadsheet in some packages). Similarly, cash not collected could be taken straight back into the profit and loss account as **bad debt expense**.

Here is the spreadsheet in its normal 'numbers' form.

	A	B	C	D	E	F	G
1	EXCELLENT PLC						
2	Cash flow projection - six months ending 30 June X6						
3		Jan	Feb	Mar	Apr	May	Jun
4		£	£	£	£	£	£
5	Sales	42000	43260	44558	45895	47271	48690
6	Cash receipts						
7	1 month in arrears	27000	25200	25956	26735	27537	28363
8	2 months in arrears	13500	13500	12600	12978	13367	13768
9	3 months in arrears	3150	3150	3150	2940	3028	3119
10	Total operating receipts	43650	41850	41706	42653	43932	45250
11							
12	Cash payments						
13	Purchases	-27300	-28119	-28963	-29831	-30726	-31648
14	Overheads	-6300	-6300	-6300	-6300	-6300	-6300
15	Total operating payments	-33600	-34419	-35263	-36131	-37026	-37948
16							
17	Dividends					-10000	
18	Capital purchases	-3600	-12600			-1800	
19	Total other payments	-3600	-12600			-11800	
20							
21	Net cash flow	6450	-5169	6443	6521	-4894	7302
22	Cash balance b/f	-7500	-1050	-6219	224	6746	1852
23	Cash balance c/f	-1050	-6219	224	6746	1852	9154
24							

Core Unit 7: Management Information Systems

This needs a little **tidying up**. We will do the following.

(a)   Add in **commas** to denote thousands of pounds.

(b)   Put **zeros** in the cells with no entry in them.

(c)   Change **negative numbers** from being displayed with a **minus sign** to being displayed in **brackets**.

	A	B	C	D	E	F	G
1	EXCELLENT PLC						
2	*Cash flow projection - six months ending 30 June X6*						
3		*Jan*	*Feb*	*Mar*	*Apr*	*May*	*Jun*
4		£	£	£	£	£	£
5	Sales	42,000	43,260	44,558	45,895	47,271	48,690
6	*Cash receipts*						
7	1 month in arrears	27,000	25,200	25,956	26,735	27,537	28,363
8	2 months in arrears	13,500	13,500	12,600	12,978	13,367	13,768
9	3 months in arrears	3,150	3,150	3,150	2,940	3,028	3,119
10	Total operating receipts	43,650	41,850	41,706	42,653	43,932	45,250
11							
12	*Cash payments*						
13	Purchases	(27,300)	(28,119)	(28,963)	(29,831)	(30,726)	(31,648)
14	Overheads	(6,300)	(6,300)	(6,300)	(6,300)	(6,300)	(6,300)
15	Total operating payments	(33,600)	(34,419)	(35,263)	(36,131)	(37,026)	(37,948)
16							
17	Dividends	0	0	0	0	(10,000)	0
18	Capital purchases	(3,600)	(12,600)	0	0	(1,800)	0
19	Total other payments	(3,600)	(12,600)	0	0	(11,800)	0
20							
21	Net cash flow	6,450	(5,169)	6,443	6,521	(4,894)	7,302
22	Cash balance b/f	(7,500)	(1,050)	(6,219)	224	6,746	1,852
23	Cash balance c/f	(1,050)	(6,219)	224	6,746	1,852	9,154
24							

3.15   More features of spreadsheets

Spreadsheets are versatile tools. Some useful features include:

(a)   **Print commands**. Print options are achieved by selecting **File** and then **Page Setup**. You then specify the range to be printed, the paper orientation and choose from any other options, for example which printer to send the output to.

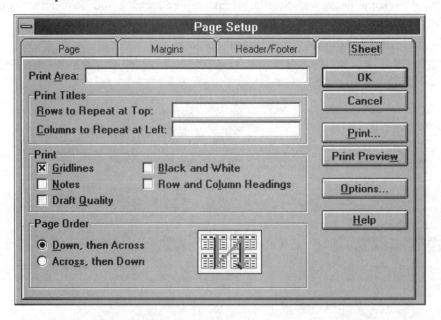

(b) **Database and sorting facilities.** Lists of tables of data can be sorted by criteria selected by the user. In Excel, after highlighting the cells containing data, select Data, Sort from the menu. The options selected will depend on how you wish to sort the data. Experiment with this function. Database type facilities are looked at in more depth in the following section.

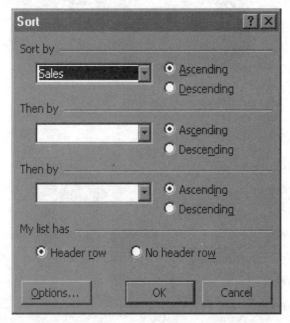

(c) **Graphics facility.** It is usually possible to convert tabulated data in a spreadsheet into a variety of bar chart or graphical formats. We will look again at the Discount Traders Ltd example, reproduced below.

	A	B	C	D	E
1	**Discount Traders Ltd**				
2	*Sales analysis - April 200X*				
3	Customer	Sales	5% discount	Sales (net)	
4		£	£	£	
5	Arthur	956.00	0.00	956.00	
6	Dent	1423.00	71.15	1351.85	
7	Ford	2894.00	144.70	2749.30	
8	Prefect	842.00	0.00	842.00	
9					
10					

This could be used to generate any of the following charts.

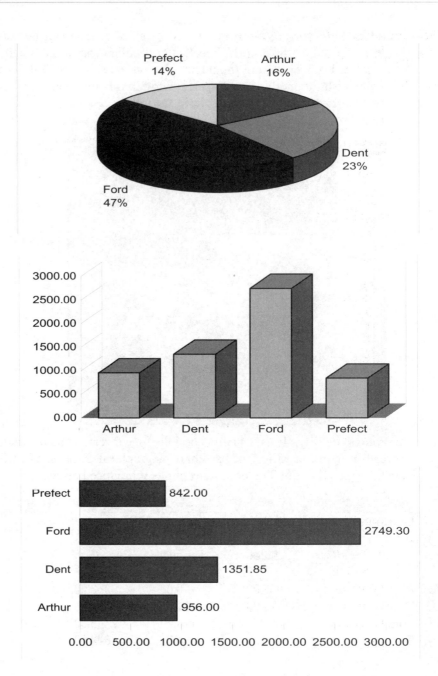

Impressive looking charts can be generated simply by **selecting the range** of figures to turn into a chart and then clicking on a **chart icon** and following the step-by-step instructions on screen.

In this case we are trying to draw charts showing **net sales** to different **customers** and the relevant data to select is in cells A5 to A8 and D5 to D8. Don't worry about the fact that the data is not in **adjacent** columns. Select cells A5:A8 in the normal way, then move your pointer to cell D5, hold down **Ctrl** and drag to select cells D5:D8.

Next, look at the **toolbars** at the top of the screen until you see an **icon** that looks like a little bar chart. Click on this. A 'Chart Wizard' appears. This is explained below.

3.16 Creating a chart - step by step

The following paragraphs explain how to use the Microsoft Excel Chart Wizard.

Step 1. Pick the type of chart you want. To create a chart similar to the second of the charts shown above we need to choose chart type **Column** and then select the sub-type we think will be most effective, as shown below.

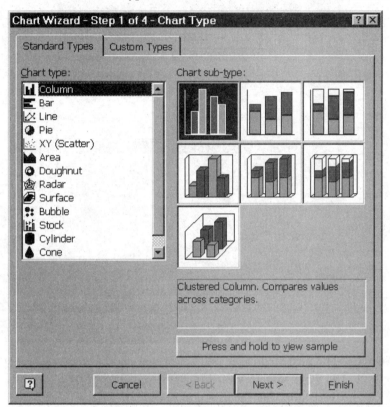

Step 2. This gives us the opportunity to confirm that the data we selected earlier was correct and to decide on how the **data series** should be shown: in other words whether the chart should be based on **columns** (eg Customer, Sales, Discount etc) or **rows** (Arthur, Dent etc). In this case, because there is only one series - net sales - it makes no difference, but you will see the effect of the different options when you try the next Activity.

A **data series** is a group of related data points plotted in a chart that originate from rows or columns on a single worksheet. Each data series in a chart has a unique colour or pattern. You can plot one or more data series in a chart. Pie charts have only one data series.

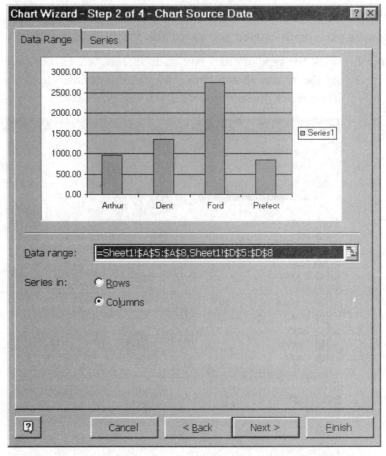

Step 3. The next step is the one where you do all the things you usually forget to do when you are drawing charts and graphs by hand: giving your chart a **title**, **labelling** the axes and so on.

The lack of **labels and titles** is the main fault of the charts shown earlier. (Incidentally, one way of remembering which is the **X axis** and which is the **Y axis** is to look at the letter Y: it is the only letter that has a vertical part pointing straight up, so it must be the vertical axis!)

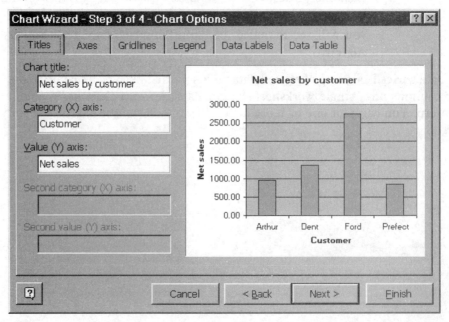

As you can see, there are many other index tabs available. You can see the effect of selecting or deselecting each one in **preview** - experiment with these options as you like.

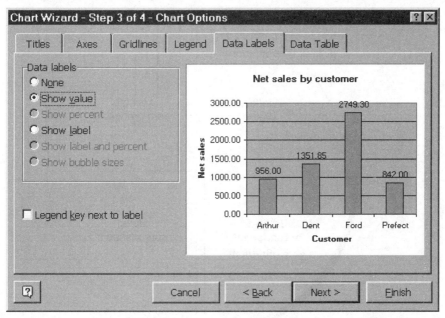

Step 4. The final step in Excel 97 is to choose whether you want the chart to appear on the same worksheet as the data or on a separate sheet of its own.

Even after your chart is 'finished', you can change it.

(a) You can **resize it** simply by selecting it and dragging out its borders.

(b) You can change **each element** by **double clicking** on them and choosing from a variety of further options.

(c) You could also select any item of **text** and alter the wording, size or font, or change the **colours** used.

(d) In the following illustration, the user has double-clicked on the Y axis because they have decided to **change the scale**.

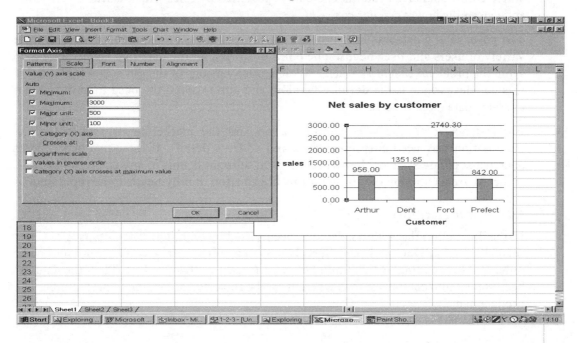

4   USING A SPREADSHEET AS A DATABASE

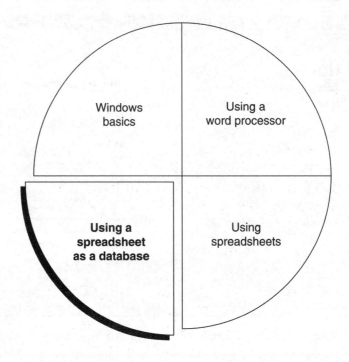

Windows basics

Using a word processor

Using a spreadsheet as a database

Using spreadsheets

Definition

> A database is a collection of **structured data.** Any item of data within the database can be used as a subject of enquiry.

4.1   Spreadsheets and databases

Spreadsheet packages are **not true databases,** but they often have database-like facilities for manipulating tables of data, if only to a limited extent compared with a true database.

A database is a **collection of data** which is integrated and organised so as to provide a **single comprehensive system.** The data is governed by rules which define its structure and determine how it can be accessed.

The **purpose** of a database is to provide **convenient access** to common data for a **wide variety** of **users** and **user needs.** The point of storing all the data in a single place is to avoid the problems that arise when several similar versions of the same data exist, so that it is not clear which is the **definite version,** and also to avoid the need to have to input the same data more than once.

For instance, both the sales administration and the marketing departments of an organisation may need **customer name and address details.** If these two departments operated **separate** systems they will **both** need to input details of any change of address. If they **share a common database** for this information, it **only needs to be input once.**

4.2   Sorting facilities

In the illustration that follows, data has been sorted by highlighting columns A to C and then clicking on **Data** and then **Sort.** It has been sorted into **ascending** product name order and **descending** order of number of parts used in that product. Then the data has been copied into columns E to G where it can be **re-sorted** according to part number and product name.

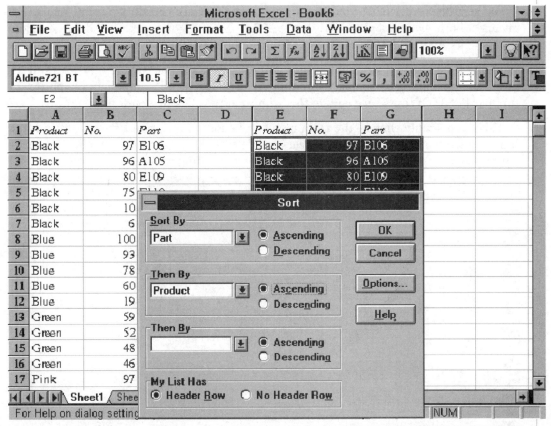

EXAMPLE: SPREADSHEETS AND DATABASES

Here is a spreadsheet used for **stock control**.

	A	B	C	D	E	F	G	H	I
1	Component	Product	Quantity	In stock	Re-order level	Free stock	Reorder quantity	On order	Supplier
2	A001	A	1	371	160	211	400	-	P750
3	A002	B	5	33	40	-	100	100	P036
4	A003	A	5	206	60	146	150	-	P888
5	A004	D	3	176	90	86	225	-	P036
6	A005	E	9	172	120	52	300	-	P750
7	A006	C	7	328	150	178	375	-	P684
8	A007	C	2	13	10	3	25	-	P227
9	A008	C	6	253	60	193	150	-	P036
10	A009	E	9	284	90	194	225	-	P888
11	A010	B	3	435	100	335	250	-	P720
12	A011	B	2	295	110	185	275	-	P036
13	A012	A	3	40	190	-	475	475	P036
14	A013	A	7	23	120	-	300	300	P227
15	A014	C	4	296	110	186	275	-	P750
16	A015	D	7	432	40	392	100	-	P684
17	A016	D	4	416	100	316	250	-	P141
18	A017	A	3	463	150	313	375	-	P888

If you scrutinise this table you may notice that there are certain common items. For instance both components A001 and A003 are used to make Product A. Both components A001 and A005 are bought from supplier P750.

Wouldn't it be handy if we could **manipulate** this data in some way, say, to get a full list of all components used to make product A, or a list of all components supplied by supplier P750? Of course, we **can** do this, almost at the click of a button.

In Excel you simply click in the **Data** menu and choose the option **Filter ... Auto filter.** A downward pointing arrow now appears beside each heading, and if you click on one of the arrows a list of each different item in the corresponding column drops down.

	A	B	C	D	E	F	G	H	I
1	Component	Product	Quantity	In stock	Re-order level	Free stock	Reorder quantity	On order	Supplier
2	A001	A	1	371	160	211	400	-	(All)
3	A002	B	5	33	40	-	100	100	(Top 10...)
4	A003	A	5	206	60	146	150	-	(Custom...)
5	A004	D	3	176	90	86	225	-	P036
6	A005	E	9	172	120	52	300	-	P141
7	A006	C	7	328	150	178	375	-	P227
8	A007	C	2	13	10	3	25	-	P684
9	A008	C	6	253	60	193	150	-	P720
10	A009	E	9	284	90	194	225	-	P750
11	A010	B	3	435	100	335	250	-	P888
12	A011	B	2	295	110	185	275	-	P036
13	A012	A	3	40	190	-	475	475	P036
14	A013	A	7	23	120	-	300	300	P227
15	A014	C	4	296	110	186	275	-	P750
16	A015	D	7	432	40	392	100	-	P684
17	A016	D	4	416	100	316	250	-	P141
18	A017	A	3	463	150	313	375	-	P888

Sheet1 / Sheet2 / Sheet3 /

In this illustration the user has clicked on the arrow in the Supplier column and is about to select Supplier 750. This is what happens.

	A	B	C	D	E	F	G	H	I
1	Component	Product	Quantity	In stock	Re-order level	Free stock	Reorder quantity	On order	Supplier
2	A001	A	1	371	160	211	400	-	P750
6	A005	E	9	172	120	52	300	-	P750
15	A014	C	4	296	110	186	275	-	P750

Sheet1 / Sheet2 / Sheet3 /

This shows that supplier P750 supplies components A001, A005 and A014, that there is nothing on order from this supplier at present, that this supplier is important for products A, E and C only, and so on.

If the original data were restored (by clicking on the Supplier arrow and choosing All) and then we clicked on the arrow in the **Product** column we would be able to see at a glance all the components used for product A and all the suppliers for those components, whether any components were on order at present (possibly meaning delays in the availability of the next batch of Product A) and so on.

Activity 8 (20 minutes)

Construct the spreadsheet shown on the previous page. You may have to use the on-line help facility (press the F1 key) if you are unsure of the formulae used.

Use the **Data ... Filters** option to answer the following questions.

(a) What components does supplier P888 supply?

(b) What components are used in product E?

(c) Which suppliers are due to deliver fresh supplies?

We look at a true database application (Microsoft Access) in Chapter 7.

4.3 Spreadsheets and data tables

Definition

The term **data table** is used by some spreadsheet packages (for example Excel) to refer to a group of cells that show the results of changing the value of variables.

Data tables can be most clearly explained using a simple example.

EXAMPLE: A ONE-INPUT DATA TABLE

Don't be put off by the terminology here. All this means is that **one** of the bits of the calculation changes and the other bits don't.

Suppose a company has production costs which it would expect to be in the region of £5m were it not for the effects of inflation. Economic forecasts for the inflation rate in the coming year range from 2% to 10%.

If this were part of a **scenario** that the company was trying to model on a spreadsheet a 'data table' could be produced showing the range of effects of these various possible levels of inflation simply by:

(a) Entering the basic data.

(b) Entering just one formula per item affected (production costs and profits in the example illustrated).

(c) Using the computer's data table tool.

Here is the problem set up on Microsoft Excel.

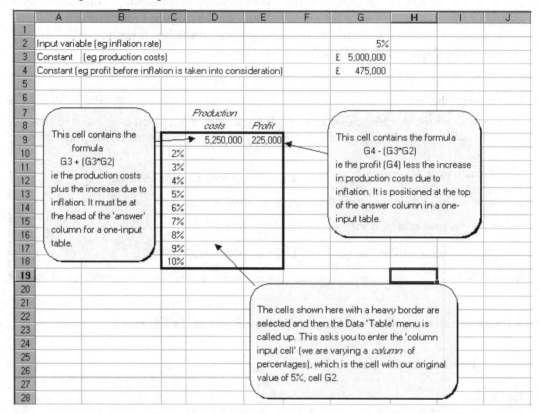

This is what happens after a single cell reference (G2) is entered, as prompted by the **data table menu.**

	A	B	C	D	E	F	G	H	I
1									
2	Input variable (eg inflation rate)						5%		
3	Constant (eg production costs)						£5,000,000		
4	Constant (eg profit before inflation is taken into consideration)						£ 475,000		
5									
6									
7				Production					
8				costs	Profit				
9				5,250,000	225,000				
10			2%	5,100,000	375,000				
11			3%	5,150,000	325,000				
12			4%	5,200,000	275,000	◄			
13			5%	5,250,000	225,000				
14			6%	5,300,000	175,000				
15			7%	5,350,000	125,000				
16			8%	5,400,000	75,000				
17			9%	5,450,000	25,000				
18			10%	5,500,000	(25,000)				
19									
20									

The shaded cells are automatically filled by the spreadsheet package to show the impact of inflation on production costs and profits.

4.4 Two-input data tables

It is also possible to use this facility if **two** of the numbers in the calculation are to be changed.

EXAMPLE: A TWO-INPUT DATA TABLE

Suppose the company is not sure that its production costs will be £5m - they could alternatively be only £4.5m or else they could be up to £5.5m. The problem is set up in a similar way on Excel. Study the diagram carefully.

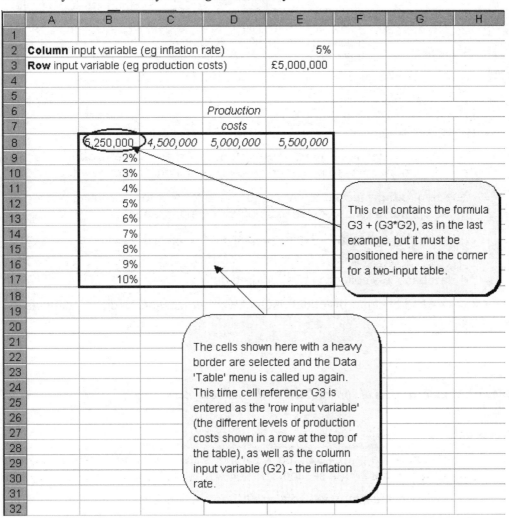

SOLUTION

Our solution is shown over the page.

	A	B	C	D	E	F	G	H
1								
2	**Column** input variable (eg inflation rate)				5%			
3	**Row** input variable (eg production costs)				£5,000,000			
4								
5								
6				*Production*				
7				*costs*				
8		*5,250,000*	*4,500,000*	*5,000,000*	*5,500,000*			
9		2%	4,590,000	5,100,000	5,610,000			
10		3%	4,635,000	5,150,000	5,665,000			
11		4%	4,680,000	5,200,000	5,720,000			
12		5%	4,725,000	5,250,000	5,775,000			
13		6%	4,770,000	5,300,000	5,830,000			
14		7%	4,815,000	5,350,000	5,885,000			
15		8%	4,860,000	5,400,000	5,940,000			
16		9%	4,905,000	5,450,000	5,995,000			
17		10%	4,950,000	5,500,000	6,050,000			
18								

Once more the cells shown here with shading are filled in automatically by the spreadsheet package

Chapter roundup

- The most widely used **operating system** is Windows. Certain features are common to all software produced for use in conjunction with Windows.

- The term **integrated software** can be used to refer to accounting packages made up of different modules or to 'office' type packages.

- A **spreadsheet** is an electronic piece of paper divided into rows and columns.

- A **database** is a collection of structured data.

- We looked at some **practical uses** of word processors and spreadsheets in this chapter.

We look at more aspects of spreadsheets in the next chapter.

Quick quiz

1   What is the purpose of the **X** symbol shown in the top right hand corner of a window? (See section 1)

2   What is the integrated software? (See section 2.1)

3   What is a spreadsheet? (See section 3.1)

4   What is the purpose of a database? (See section 4.1)

5   What is the purpose of a data table within a spreadsheet? (See section 4.3)

Answers to Activities

1   (a)   A spreadsheet is like an electronic piece of paper divided into rows and columns. It provides an easy way of performing numerical calculations. The principal feature of a spreadsheet is that, once it is set up, a change in any one of the values means that the others change automatically.

       (b)   Any five of the following (although you might have thought of other valid uses).

           (i)   Cash flow projections

           (ii)   Balance sheets

           (iii)   Profit forecasts

           (iv)   Sales forecasts

           (v)   General ledger

           (vi)   Inventory records

           (vii)   Job cost estimates

       (c)   Cell D5.

       (d)   The cell (or range of cells) that will be changed by keyboard or mouse input.

       (e)   (i)   'Text' means words or numerical data, such as a date, that cannot be used in computations.

           (ii)   A value is a number that can be used in a calculation.

           (iii)   A formula operates on other cells in the spreadsheet and performs calculations with them. For example, if cell B4 has to contain the total of the values in cells B2 and B3, a formula that could be entered in B4 is =B2+B3.

2   (a)   =SUM(B5:B6)

       (b)   =SUM(B6:D6)

       (c)   =SUM (E5:E6) *or* =SUM(B7:D7)

           or   (best   of   all)   =IF(SUM(E5:E6) =SUM(B7:D7),SUM(B7:D7),"ERROR")

3   (a)   (i)   =B6*0.175

           (ii)   =SUM(E6:E7)

       (b)   There should be a separate 'variables' section including (at least) the VAT rate and preferably also for input of six month sales.

	A	B	C	D	E	F	G	H
1	**Taxable Supplies plc**							
2	*Sales analysis - Branch C*							
3	*Six months ended 30 June 200X*							
4		Jan	Feb	Mar	Apr	May	Jun	Total
5		£	£	£	£	£	£	£
6	Net sales	=B12	=C12	=D12	=E12	=F12	=G12	=SUM(B6:G6)
7	VAT	=B6*$B$13	=C6*$B$13	=D6*$B$13	=E6*$B$13	=F6*$B$13	=G6*$B$13	=SUM(B7:G7)
8	Total	=SUM(B6:B7)	=SUM(C6:C7)	=SUM(D6:D7)	=SUM(E6:E7)	=SUM(F6:F7)	=SUM(G6:G7)	=SUM(H6:H7)
9								
10								
11	*Variables*							
12	Sales	2491.54	5876.75	3485.01	5927.7	6744.52	3021.28	
13	VAT rate	0.175						
14								

NOTES

4   (a)   Cell Formulae

C7   =SUM(B5:B6)

B12   =SUM(B9:B11)

B16   =SUM(B14:B15)

C17   =B12-B16

C18   =SUM (C4:C17)

C24   = C21+C22–C23

(b)   The finished spreadsheet appears below. You should be able to make further improvements eg formatting numbers, clearer layout.

	A	B	C	D	E	F
1	**Ed Sheet**					
2	*Balance sheet as at 31 Dec 200X*					
3		£	£			
4	*Fixed assets*					
5	Plant	20000				
6	Vehicles	10000				
7			30000			
8	*Current assets*					
9	Stock	2000				
10	Debtors	1000				
11	Cash	1500				
12		4500				
13	*Current liabilities*					
14	Creditors	2500				
15	Overdraft	1500				
16		4000				
17	Net current assets		500			
18	Net assets		30500			
19						
20	*Represented by*					
21	Opening capital		28000			
22	Profit for year		3500			
23	Drawings		1000			
24	Closing capital		30500			
25						

5   (a)   It can be used to call up a Go To window, to move quickly to a different part of a spreadsheet.

(b)   Select the cell and:

(i)   Overtype the existing data, or

(ii)   Click in the cell until a cursor appears and add, delete and retype as necessary, or

(iii) Click on the editing line at the top of the screen and add, delete and retype as necessary.

(iv) Press function key F2 and change the cell as necessary. Function key F2 is the best option.

(c)   The action just done is undone.

(d)   (i)   Position the mouse pointer over the first cell in the range to be selected, hold down the left mouse button, move the pointer to

BPP
PUBLISHING

the last cell in the range and release the mouse button. Every cell in the range except the one where you started will be highlighted. (*All* of these cells, including the first, are *selected.*)

(ii) Position the cursor in the first cell in the range to be selected, hold down the *shift* key and use the direction arrow keys to get to the last cell in the range. Release the shift key. Every cell in the range except the one where you started will be highlighted. (The starting cell is also *selected*, even though it is not highlighted.)

6 Click on cell D5 and then click the Σ button. Check that the 'moving' dotted line is circling cells A5 to C5 (if not, select this range of cells). Then click again on the Σ button.

Make E5 the active cell and repeat the procedure. Do likewise with cell C11 to get the sum of B8 to B10: you will have to select the range yourself after clicking on Σ.

7 (a) To do this you need to insert new rows and columns. Select the row *below* which, or the column to the *left* of which, you want the new row or column, click in the selected row or column with your *right* mouse button and choose Insert from the menu that appears.

(b) To do this position the mouse pointer on the line between the column headings A and B until it changes shape. Then double-click with your left mouse button.

(c) To do this select cells A1 and B1, then put the mouse pointer somewhere within the selected range, hold down the left mouse button and drag the selection to cells E12 and F12. Then release the left mouse button. Widen the columns as before.

8 Make sure you do this using the spreadsheet facilities rather than just by looking through the table. You'd have to use the spreadsheet facilities if you had 2,000 stock components to search through!

(a) A003, A009 and A017

(b) A005 and A009

(c) P036 and P227

Assignment 6 (30 minutes)

Tasks

(a) Here is a spreadsheet that has been prepared by someone who is new to your accounts department. (The comment about the formula was not on the original spreadsheet: it has been added by us.)

Required

Identify and explain **three** ways in which this spreadsheet could be improved.

	A	B	C	D	
1	6614	9790	8221.25		
2	5665	4966	4753		
3	7899	4462.5	4163		
4	7717	5212	9736		
5	12461	24430.5	26873.25		
6					
7					
8					
9					
10					
11					
12					
13					

The formula in this cell is =A1+A2+A3-A4

(b) Explain the steps in the construction and use of a spreadsheet **model**.

If you would like some help with your answer refer to the guidance provided over the page.

APPROACHING THE ANSWER

You may want to use this checklist and answer plan to help construct your answer.

(a)   Comment on the **presentation**

        Is it clear (from **headings and labels**) what the figures mean?

        Are the numbers **easy to read** (eg comma format, font, percentages shown as percentages and so on)

        Are **decimal places** consistent

        Are the numbers properly **aligned**?

        Are **totals** clearly distinguished?

    Comment on the **structure** and **logic**

        Could the data have been **laid out** in a different way

        Are there **rounding errors**?

        Are there better ways of doing the **formulae**?

        Have the **formulae** been **entered correctly**?

(b)   **Building a model**

        Variables in **input area**

        Formulae in **calculation area**

        Results in **output area** (not always necessary)

    Explain why this approach is preferred (eg 'what if?' analysis)

BPP
PUBLISHING

Chapter 7 :

USING SOFTWARE: MORE SPREADSHEETS, DATABASES AND E-MAIL

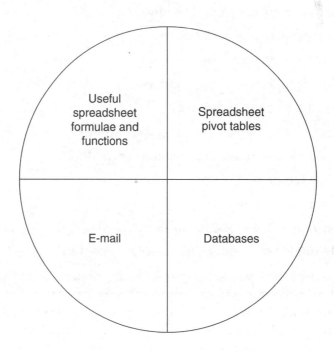

Introduction

In this chapter we explain the workings of some useful spreadsheet formulae and functions. It is important that you explore the many other features of a modern spreadsheet package for yourself. Remember, the on-line help facility provides an excellent source of information.

Later in the chapter we look at databases and what many people believe to be the most significant development of recent years – e-mail.

Your objective

After completing this chapter you should be aware of some common uses of spreadsheets, databases and e-mail.

1 USEFUL SPREADSHEET FORMULAE AND FUNCTIONS

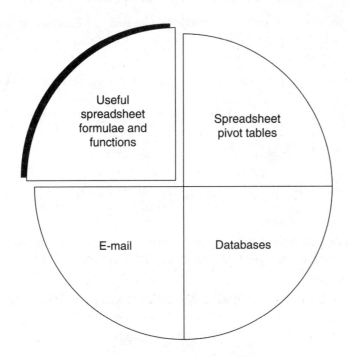

In this section we shall have a quick look at some functions that are useful when you are presented with pre-prepared data in a spreadsheet and you want to extract certain items.

1.1 Left, right and mid

You may need to extract only specific characters from the data entered in a cell. For instance, suppose a set of raw materials codes had been entered into a spreadsheet as follows.

	A	B
1	6589D	
2	5589B	
3	5074D	
4	8921B	
5	3827B	
6	1666D	
7	5062A	
8	7121D	
9	7457C	
10	9817D	
11	6390C	
12	1148A	
13	4103A	
14	8988A	
15	6547C	
16	5390A	
17	6189D	
18	8331C	
19	1992B	
20	7587A	

The four **digits** are, say, a number derived from the supplier's reference number, while the **letter** indicates that the material is used to make Product A, B, C or D.

If you wanted to sort this data in **alphabetical** order of **Product** you would have a problem, because it is only possible to arrange it in ascending or descending **numerical** order, using the standard Sort method.

To get round this you can extract the letter from each cell using the **RIGHT** function, as follows.

	A	B
1	6589D	=RIGHT(A1,1)
2	5589B	=RIGHT(A2,1)
3	5074D	=RIGHT(A3,1)
4	8921B	=RIGHT(A4,1)
5	3827B	=RIGHT(A5,1)
6	1666D	=RIGHT(A6,1)

The formula in cell B1 means 'Extract the last (or rightmost) one character from cell A1'. If we wanted to extract the last **two** characters the formula would be **=RIGHT(A1,2)**, and so on.

The formula can then be filled down and then the data can be sorted by column B, giving the following results.

	A	B
1	5062A	A
2	1148A	A
3	4103A	A
4	8988A	A
5	5390A	A
6	7587A	A
7	5589B	B
8	8921B	B
9	3827B	B
10	1992B	B
11	7457C	C
12	6390C	C
13	6547C	C
14	8331C	C
15	6589D	D
16	5074D	D
17	1666D	D
18	7121D	D
19	9817D	D
20	6189D	D

The function **LEFT** works in the same way, except that it extracts the **first** (or leftmost) character or characters.

The function **MID**, as you might expect, extracts a character or characters from the **middle** of the cell, starting at the **position** you specify, counting from left to right:

=MID([Cell],[Position],[Number of characters]).

In Excel the first character extracted is the one at the position specified, so if you want to extract the **third** character you specify position 3. In Lotus 1-2-3 it is the next character after the position specified, so if you want to extract the third character you specify position 2.

Activity 1   **(10 minutes)**

Cell A1 contains the data: **12-D-496**

(a)   What formula would you use to extract the **D** into a different cell?

(b)   What formula would you use to extract the **12** into a different cell?

1.2   Lookup

The LOOKUP function allows you to enter data that corresponds to a value in one cell in a column and return the data in the corresponding row in a different column. A simple example will make this clearer.

	A	B	C	D	E	F	G
1	1	Red					
2	2	Green					
3	3	Blue					
4	4	Yellow					
5							
6					1	Red	
7							
8							

Here the user enters a figure between 1 and 4 in cell E6 and the spreadsheet returns the corresponding colour from the range A1:B4. If the user had entered **3** then cell F6 would say **Blue**.

Here is the formula that is used to do this.

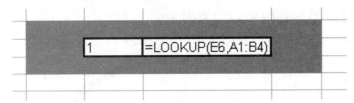

1   =LOOKUP(E6,A1:B4)

1.3   Merging the contents of cells

The next formula that is only available in Excel 97 and above.

Suppose data had been entered into a spreadsheet as follows.

What if you wanted the data in cells A1, B1 and C1 in a single cell: 21A64? To do this in Excel 97 you can simply join the contents of individual cells together using the **&** symbol, as follows. The formula could be filled down to give the same results for the rest of the list.

	A	B	C	D
1	21	A	64	=A1&B1&C1
2	62	P	14	
3	87	T	26	
4				

1.4 Paste special

Sometimes you may wish to convert a formula into an absolute value, for example you may want the contents of cell D1 in the above example to be '21A64', not a formula that gives this result.

To convert a formula to an absolute value, copy the relevant cell or cells in the normal way, then highlight another cell (say, E1 in the above example) and **right click**. From the menu that appears, choose **Paste Special.** The following dialogue box will appear.

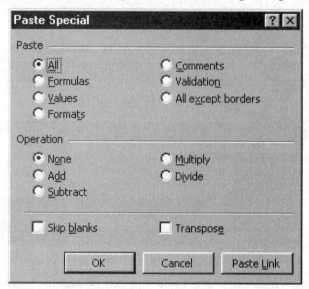

Here, if you choose **Values** then what will be pasted into cell E1 is the value '21A64', not the formula in cell D1.

2 SPREADSHEET PIVOT TABLES

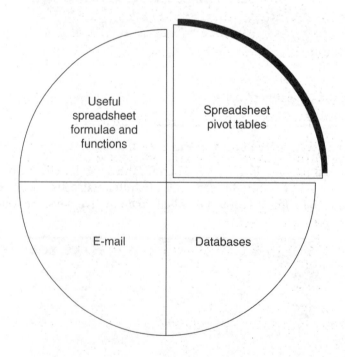

2.1 What is a pivot table?

Definition

> A **pivot table** is an interactive table that summarises and analyses data from lists and tables.

To understand pivot tables we first need to get a little bit more understanding of records and fields.

2.2 Records and fields

A typical database is made up of **records** and each record is made up of a number of **fields**. Here's an example of five records, each with four fields.

Surname	First name	Title	Age
Foreman	Susan	Miss	42
McDonald	David	Dr	56
McDonald	Dana	Mrs	15
Sanjay	Rachana	Ms	24
Talco	Giovanni	Mr	32

(a) Each **Row** is one **Record**. (Notice that both Row and Record begin with the letter R.)

(b) Each **Column** is one **Field**. (If you can remember that Rows are Records, this shouldn't be too hard to work out!)

The example above has records for five people, and each record contains fields for the person's surname, first name, title and age.

2.3 Analysing and interpreting data

There are lots of ways of analysing this data.

(a) We could find the **total number** of occurrences of each surname to see which was the most and least common. Likewise first names.

(b) We could find the **total number** of each title, as an indication of the most and least common marital status of the people.

(c) We could find the **average** age of the people

(d) We could find the **maximum** and **minimum** ages.

These simple statistics - **totals, averages, and highest and lowest** - are the most common way of finding some meaning amongst a mass of figures. We are also often interested in **unusual** information (for instance an age of minus seven), because it tends to highlight areas where there could be errors in our information.

2.4 Pivot tables

To extract information quickly and easily from a table in Excel we can simply highlight it and click on **Data** and then **Pivot Table Report**. This starts up a Wizard which first

NOTES

Core Unit 7: Management Information Systems

asks you to confirm the location of the data you want to analyse and then offers you the following options.

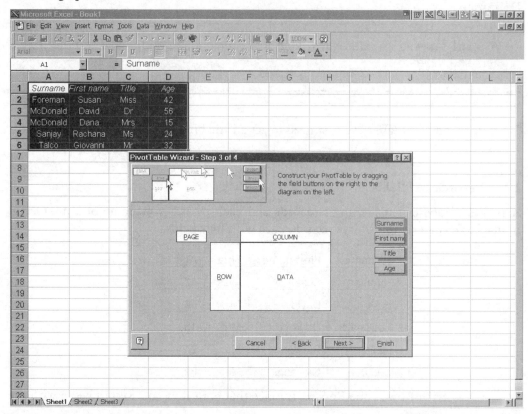

All you have to do to analyse the data is drag any of the labelled buttons on the right into the appropriate part of the white area. For instance, if we wanted to know the total number of surnames of each type we could drag the Surname label into the row area and then drag another instance of the surname label into the Data area. This is what you would see.

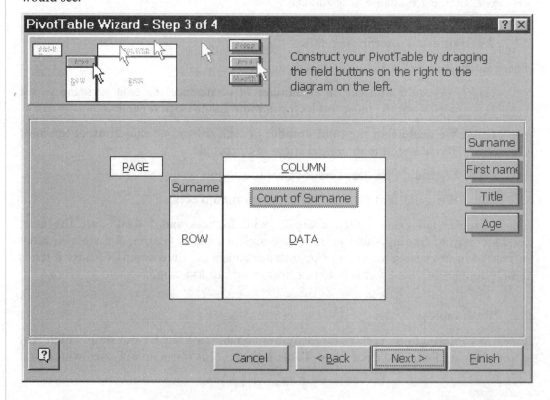

Note that in the Data area the name of the Surname label changes to Count of Surname but we do not have to accept this if it is not what we want. If we double-click on Count of Surname we are offered other options such as Sum, Average, Max, Min.

For now we will accept the Count option. Clicking on Next and Finish gives the following results.

	A	B
1	Count of Surname	
2	Surname	Total
3	Foreman	1
4	McDonald	2
5	Sanjay	1
6	Talco	1
7	Grand Total	5

More elaborate analyses than this can be produced. For instance, you could try setting up a pivot table like this.

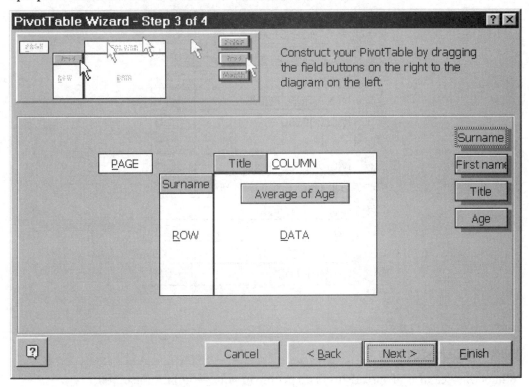

The result is as follows, showing that the average age of people called McDonald is 35.5 and the average age overall is 33.8.

	A	B	C	D	E	F	G
1	Average of Age	Title					
2	Surname	Dr	Miss	Mr	Mrs	Ms	Grand Total
3	Foreman		42				42
4	McDonald	56			15		35.5
5	Sanjay					24	24
6	Talco			32			32
7	Grand Total	56	42	32	15	24	33.8

This arrangement of the data also draws attention to the fact that the data includes a 'Mrs' who is only 15 years old. This is not impossible, but it is quite unusual and should be checked because it could be an inputting error.

If we don't happen to like the way Excel arranges the data it can be changed in a flash, simply by dragging the labels in the results to another part of the table. For instance if Title is dragged down until it is over cell B3 the data is automatically rearranged as follows.

	A	B	C
1	Average of Age		
2	Surname	Title	Total
3	Foreman	Miss	42
4	Foreman Total		42
5	McDonald	Dr	56
6		Mrs	15
7	McDonald Total		35.5
8	Sanjay	Ms	24
9	Sanjay Total		24
10	Talco	Mr	32
11	Talco Total		32
12	Grand Total		33.8

FOR DISCUSSION

What other features of spreadsheets do people in your group find useful?

3   DATABASES

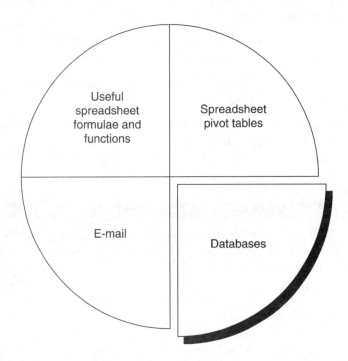

We are going to take a look at the use of a proper database package to analyse data. This is only an **introduction** to a topic that quickly becomes rather complex. We will concentrate on **Microsoft Access**. Other database packages follow the same principles.

As explained in the previous chapter, a database is an organised collection of data.

3.1   What distinguishes a database from a spreadsheet?

Spreadsheets do have some database capabilities such as sorting and filters. However, spreadsheets are designed more for flexibility in manipulation and presentation of information. Generally, mathematical manipulation of data is more easily achieved in a spreadsheet.

Databases are designed to store **greater volumes of data**, and they enable data required for different purposes to be stored in a single location. Databases can manipulate data using **Queries**, which are particularly useful when dealing with large data volumes. In very simple terms, a spreadsheet is the electronic equivalent of a piece of graph paper, while a database could be likened to a filing cabinet.

3.2   Importing data

Databases store data in **tables**. Tables can be created within the database package, and data records manually added to the table. This is time consuming, as data volumes handled by database packages are often large. The more common scenario is to **import** data from **a text file** (ASCII text), downloaded from an accounting software package. Or, the situation may arise where data held on a **spreadsheet** needs to be transferred into a database, perhaps to be held alongside other related data.

The **procedure for importing data** from either a text file or spreadsheet into a Microsoft Access table is outlined below.

Step 1. Make a note of the file name and location that contains the source data. If the data is held on a spreadsheet, also note the name of the particular sheet you want to import(eg 'Sheet 3').

Step 2. Save and Close the spreadsheet, or, if importing from a text file ensure the file is not being accessed by another application.

Step 3. Database packages are quite hungry for memory, so close all applications that you don't need.

Step 4. Open up Access, choose the option to create a new blank database, and give it a suitable file name. The elements of an Access database are arranged on a series of tabs as shown in the next illustration.

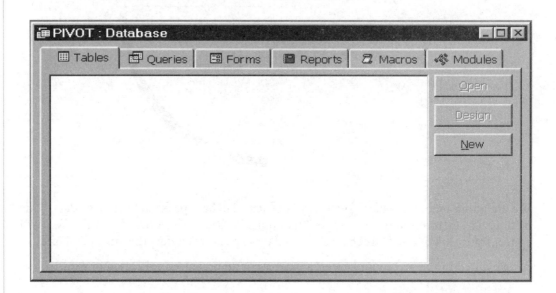

Step 5. Ensure the Table tab is active. Select the **File** menu, choose the **Get External Data** and then the **Import** option. Clicking on this produces a dialogue box identical to the familiar **Open file** dialogue. Change the **file type** to that required. For instance, if importing from an Excel spreadsheet change to Microsoft Excel; for a text file change to Text File. Then locate the file and click on **Import**.

Steps 6 and 7.

The options Access presents you with next will vary depending on the file type you selected in Step 5. In both cases, the 'Import Wizard' steps are straightforward.

Importing from a spreadsheet	*Importing from a text file*
You will get a list of all the **worksheets** in the spreadsheet file you specify. Choose the sheet that you want to import (you noted this down earlier) and click on **Next.**	You will be asked to identify how the text file is formatted to identify the positioning of column breaks. **Fixed width**, means the position of the characters within each line is consistent. **Delimited** means a character, such as a comma, identifies the division between columns. (You, or the person that created the file should know what format the file is. If in doubt, opening the file in Notepad or a similar text editor enables the contents to be viewed and the delimiter identified). Click on **Next.**
If the first row of your spreadsheet contains column headings, check the box that says **First Row Contains Column Headings,** then click on Next.	For fixed width files you are given the opportunity to identify the position of column breaks using the mouse. For delimited files you are asked to identify the delimiter (eg comma).

Step 8. As a rule you will want to store your data in a **New Table,** so this is the next option to choose. The ability to 'Append' (add to the bottom of an existing table), exists. This is useful when importing data into the same table, but from different source files.

Step 9. You are given the choice of specifying **further information** about the fields (columns) that you are importing, but there is no need to do this at this basic level, so click **Next.**

Step 10. You then have the choice of defining your own '**Primary Key**', which is the unique field in each line, or letting Access do it for you. It is usually acceptable to **let Access do it** for you, the default selection. Click **Next.**

Step 11. Finally **choose a name** for your table if you do not like the one that Access suggests, and click on **Finish.** You will then see an entry for your new database table.

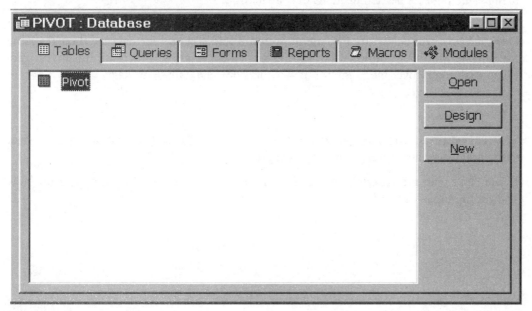

NOTES

If you **select your table and click Open** you will see how data is stored within the table. This view is known as the **datasheet**.

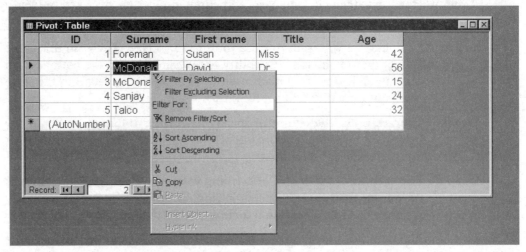

Within the datasheet you can select columns, right click then **sort** the data in them in ascending or descending order. You can apply and remove **filters** simply by right clicking on a record and including or excluding the item as you wish. In the illustration below, clicking on **Filter By Selection** would show you table including only the details for people called McDonald.

New records can be entered or existing ones edited, and there is a **Find** option in the edit menu to help locate particular items of information.

To see, or edit, the **table design** it is necessary to **open the datasheet**, then select the **Design View** icon below the File menu option. Field size and formats are then available for editing. Modifying table design should not be necessary at this level, but investigate if you wish to discover more about the workings of the database package.

3.3   Queries

The **real power** of a database, however, lies in its ability to **analyse and manipulate** data using practically any criteria you can dream up.

If you close your table, return to the set of index tabs, select **Queries** and click on **New** you get the following options.

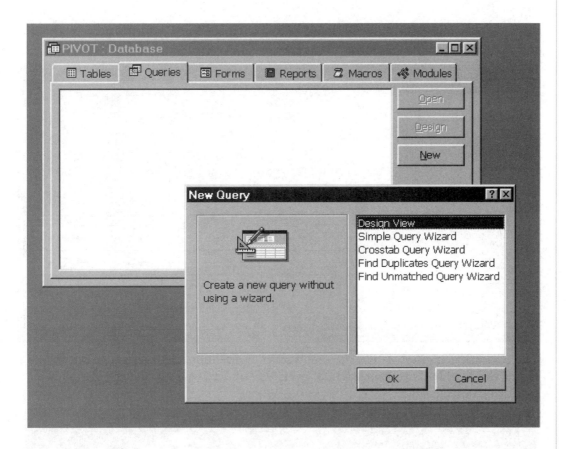

We shall not look at all of these options. The Simple Query Wizard takes you step by step through the process of building a query. The CrossTab Query Wizard performs a similar function to a Pivot Table. The functions of the other wizards speak for themselves. In this case, however, we are going to choose **Design View**.

If you click on this the first thing you are asked to do is to specify **which tables** the query will apply to. In our example we have only one table so we can simply select it and click on **Add** and then close the **Show Table** dialogue box. The screen will now look like this.

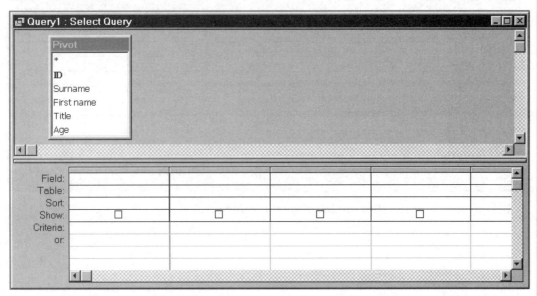

To design a query we click on the fields we wish to analyse in the list at the top to make them appear in the **design grid** below. For instance if we wish to perform an analysis of the **ages** in our table we would click on Surname (so we know which record is which) and Age to produce the following.

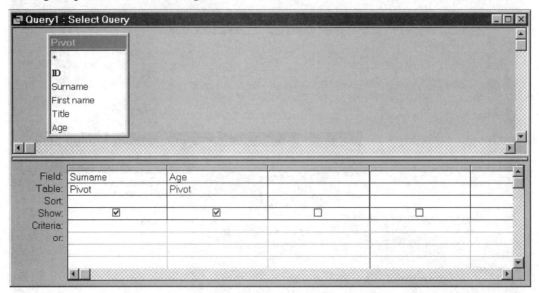

The cell entitled Criteria is the one that wants our attention. For instance, if we wanted to find the records of everyone who was over 40 or under 20 we could make the following entries for the Age field.

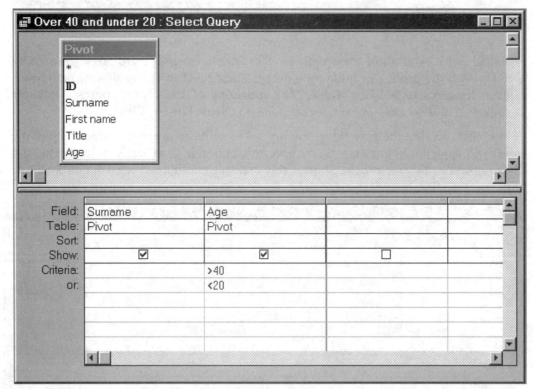

Clicking on Query and Run produces the following results.

If you are satisfied that you have the information you want you can **save** the query for future use (for instance to be run again when you have entered more records). If you are not satisfied you can switch back to design view (**View ... Design**), and alter it as you wish.

3.4 Queries using multiple tables

A query can pull together data from more than one Table.

For example we may have a Customer table containing customer codes and names, an Items table containing stock codes and descriptions, and a Transactions table. The three tables are shown below.

To write a query that combines data from multiple tables follow the following steps.

> *Step 1.* Before we are able to combine information from separate Tables, we need to tell Access how the information is related. To do this we form a **Relationship.** Ensure the Tables tab is active and select **Tools, Relationships**. Then select **Relationships, Show Table** and **Add** all three tables to the view. The window will now look like this.

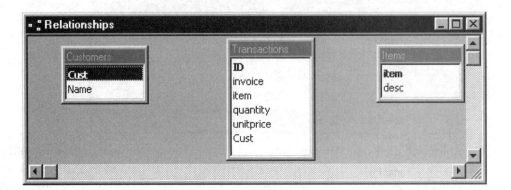

Step 2. Click and hold down the mouse while dragging the **common field** over to the other table. In the example above you would click over **Cust** in Customers, hold the left mouse button down, and drag over to the **Cust** in Transactions. Release the mouse button, click on **Create** and the **link** will show. The same procedure would be followed to link Item between the Transactions and Items tables.

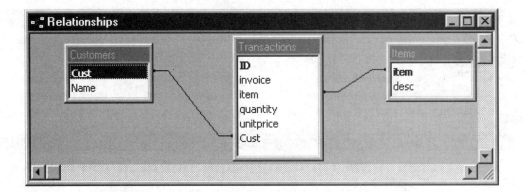

Step 3. Close the Relationship window, saving your changes.

Step 4. Activate the **Query tab** and click **New**. The options are as shown earlier under 5.12. If we chose the **Design View** option, the same principles explained in 5.13 to 5.15 can be applied to build this Query. Alternately, select the **Simple Query Wizard** option and click OK.

Step 5. Select each of the three tables in turn under the Tables/Queries option. For each Table select which fields you wish to appear in the Query using the **>** or **>>** buttons. After you have completed this procedure for all three tables, Click Next.

Step 6. Accept the default of Detail for the next option by clicking Next.

Step 7. Give your Query a title that will enable you to remember its purpose, and click **Finish**.

A sample of the resulting datasheet is shown.

Cust	Name	invoice	item	desc	quantity	unitprice
CABD	Cable Darlington	AK5	PLUE	Electric plug	6	1.99
CABD	Cable Darlington	AK5	SACB	Black sacks	5	1.99
CABD	Cable Darlington	AK5	PMBS	Paint - matt black 200ml	3	5.49
DESF	Desire Fencing	AK3	BUCL	Bucket - large	6	3.49
DESF	Desire Fencing	AK3	HAMD	Demolition hammer	1	6.99
FORF	Forfar Four Limited	AK6	SAH2	Hacksaw - medium	1	6.99
FULD	Fulham Drainage	AK8	PLIE	Pliers	1	6.49
HANS	Hansens	AK7	SPAF	Sandpaper - fine	4	2.49

Record: 1 of 19

3.5 Exporting data

The situation may arise where you wish to **extract data from a database** using a query, then export this sub-set of data into a spreadsheet, to perform further manipulations and formatting. The procedure for exporting data from Microsoft Access into a spreadsheet is explained below.

> ***Step 1.*** Design, run and save the query following the instructions above.

> ***Step 2.*** Select the Query tab, then click the name of the table or query you want to export. Select the **File** menu, and click **Save As/Export**.

> ***Step 3.*** In the Save As box, select **To An External File Or Database**, and then click OK.

> ***Step 4.*** In the Save As Type box, change the **file type** to that required, for example Microsoft Excel.

> ***Step 5.*** Within the Save In box, change the **location** to where you wish the spreadsheet to be saved. Enter the **name** you wish to give the spreadsheet in the File Name box.

> ***Step 6.*** Click **Export**. Microsoft Access creates the spreadsheet file containing the data from your query.

> ***Step 7.*** Close Microsoft Access (to free up memory), start your spreadsheet application and open the new file from the location you specified in Step 5.

Note that the same procedure can be followed to export the contents of a complete Table. Simply select the Table itself in step 2 rather than a query.

3.6 Expressions

When building queries a very wide variety of '**expressions**' can be used to define how the data in the table is displayed. Expressions are entered either in the **Criteria** cell or in the **Field** cell. Here are a couple of examples.

(a) **Extracting parts of fields only**. For instance you can enter the expression **Left([First name],1)** in the first Field cell and set Surname as the second field to display in the normal way, as follows.

Field:	Expr1: Left([First name],1)	Surname
Table:		Pivot
Sort:		
Show:	☑	☑
Criteria:		
or:		

(Access itself inserts the **Expr1:** part).

You will get the following results when you run the query.

	Expr1	Surname
▶	S	Foreman
	D	McDonald
	D	McDonald
	R	Sanjay
	G	Talco
*		

(b) **Performing calculations**. For instance the following query would extract records of people who will have reached retirement age in 10 years time.

Field:	Surname	Expr1: [Age]+10	
Table:	Pivot		
Sort:			
Show:	☑	☑	
Criteria:		>65	
or:			

3.7 Reports

Microsoft Access includes a powerful report writer. This enables professional presentation of meaningful data drawn from the database.

Report writing in databases is not as simple as formatting a spreadsheet. For this reason, always consider the possibility of exporting the data to a spreadsheet, and using the manipulation and formatting functions available within the spreadsheet to produce your report.

The steps involved in producing a report within Access are outlined below.

Step 1. **Design a query** that will extract the data you wish the report to contain. Run and save the query following the instructions given earlier.

Step 2. Close your query, return to the set of index tabs, select **Reports** and click on **New.** The following options are now available.

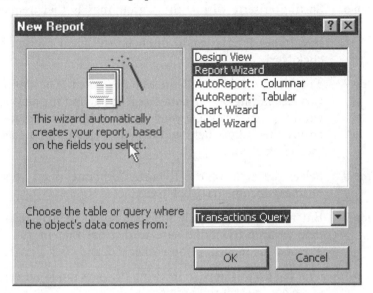

Step 3. Highlight Report Wizard, and in the lower box select the Query you wrote in Step 1. Click OK.

Step 4. You are now asked to select the fields you wish to report on. As we designed a query specifically for this report (in step1), we can simply ensure the name of this query is displayed in the Tables/Query box, and click on the double arrow (>>)box to select all fields. Click Next.

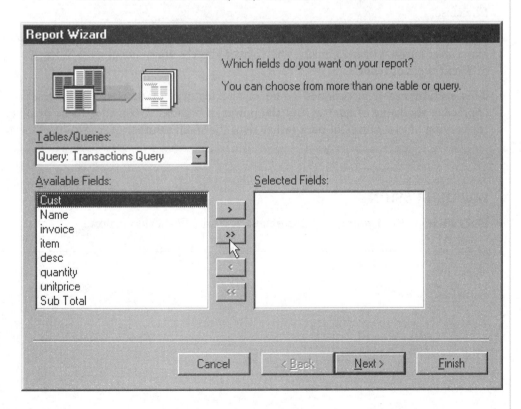

Step 5. You are then asked how would you like to view your data. This relates to grouping, and the criteria selected will depend on the purpose of the Report. Highlight the item you wish the report to be grouped by, such as Customers and click Next.

Step 6. Sorting criteria within these groupings is then requested. Up to four criteria can be selected by using the down arrows on the right of each box. (One criteria would often be sufficient.) Select your criteria and click Next.

Step 7. The layout options will then be presented. The options presented will vary depending on the data reported on, and the answers to the previous wizard questions. Make your layout and page orientation selections, and ensure the 'Adjust field width so all fields fit on a page' box is checked, then click Next.

Step 8. Select the style of the Report. Corporate is an appropriate style for business documents. Click Next.

Step 9. Enter a meaningful title for your report. If data relates to a particular date or time frame, be sure to disclose that in your title. Ensure the 'Preview the report' option is checked, and click Finish.

Step 10. The report will appear in Print Preview mode on screen. Print it out, and close the report window.

As a learning exercise, don't be afraid to **repeat the report producing process** a number of times, taking different options along the way. Unwanted reports can be deleted from the Reports index tab by highlighting the title to be deleted, right mouse clicking and selecting delete.

Reports can be **renamed** through right mouse clicking and selecting rename. To change the **heading** within the report highlight the report, click on the Design button, then double click in the Report Header text box. Overtype the title, select File save, and then File close.

As mentioned earlier, report writing in databases is not simple. **Experience** and **experimentation** will help ensure the correct choices are made at each Wizard stage for different types of reports.

This section has demonstrated some of the features of database packages. To fully appreciate the value of queries and the power of databases, consider these principles in the context of **vast stores of data** rather than the small number of records used here.

FOR DISCUSSION

Does anybody from your group use Access at work? For what purpose?

4   E-MAIL

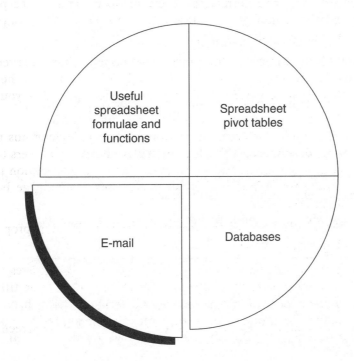

Useful spreadsheet formulae and functions

Spreadsheet pivot tables

E-mail

Databases

4.1   Electronic mail (E-mail)

Definition

> The term 'electronic mail', or **e-mail**, is used to describe various systems of sending data or messages electronically via a telephone or data network and a central computer.

E-mail has the following **advantages** over paper-based mail.

(a)   **Speed** (transmission, being electronic, is almost instantaneous). E-mail is far faster than post. It is a particular time-saver when communicating with people overseas.

(b)   **Economy** (no need for stamps etc). E-mail is reckoned to be 20 times cheaper than fax.

(c)   **Efficiency** (a message is prepared once but can be sent to thousands of employees at the touch of a button).

(d)   **Security** (access can be restricted by the use of passwords).

(e)   Documents can be retrieved from **word-processing** and graphics packages.

(f)   Electronic **delivery and read receipts** can be requested.

(g)   E-mail can be used to send **documents and reports** as well as short memos, for instance by **attaching** a file.

Typically information is 'posted' by the sender to a central computer which allocates disk storage as a **mailbox** for each user. The information is subsequently collected by the receiver from the mailbox.

(a) Senders of information thus have **documentary evidence** that they have given a piece of information to the recipient and that the recipient has picked up the message.

(b) Receivers are **not disturbed** by the information when it is sent (as they would be by face-to-face meetings or phone calls), but collect it later at their convenience.

Each user will typically have **password protected access** to his own inbox, outbox and filing system. He can prepare and edit text and other documents using a **word processing** function, and send mail using **standard headers and identifiers** to an individual or a group of people on a prepared **distribution list**.

E-mail systems may serve one department or the whole organisation. It is also possible to connect an e-mail system to outside organisations.

E-mail use is now widespread both **within organisations** and **between** them – via the Internet.

Activity 2   **(15 minutes)**

There are many types of e-mail software. Perhaps the most common is Microsoft Outlook. Ensure you can send a message using the e-mail system at your work or college. Find out how to attach a file (such as a spreadsheet) to your message.

We look at some of the drawbacks of e-mail in Chapter 9. In the next chapter we discuss the security and privacy implications of holding information.

Chapter roundup

- In this chapter we looked at some useful **spreadsheet formulae** and **functions** including:

  ° Left, right and mid
  ° Lookup
  ° Pivot tables

- **Databases** generally store greater volumes of data than spreadsheets. We looked at the workings of Microsoft Access including:

  ° Importing/exporting
  ° Tables
  ° Queries
  ° Expressions
  ° Reports

- **E-mail** is a system of electronic messaging. Advantages over paper-based mail include speed, cost and efficiency.

Quick quiz

1   When would you use the left, right or mid function provided in Excel? (See section 1.1)

2   What does the lookup function do? (See section 1.2)

3   What is a pivot table? (See section 1.2)

4   A field is made up of many records – TRUE or FALSE? (See section 2.2)

5   What is the difference between a database and a spreadsheet? (See section 3.1)

6   List five advantages of e-mail over paper-based mail. (See section 4.1)

Answers to Activities

1   (a)   =MID(A1,4,1). The starting position is position 4 because the hyphen between the 2 and the D counts as position 3.

     (b)   =LEFT(A1,2).

Assignment 7   **(30 minutes)**

Task

Explain how electronic mail works and what advantages it has over paper-based internal and external postal services.

Approaching the question

1   Give step-by-step details of how email works: our answer describes a typical menu-driven system. It also talks about mail boxes and mentions the role of the network administrator.

2   Think of as many advantages as you can. Our answer includes five, but you may be able to think of more.

Chapter 8 :
SECURITY AND PRIVACY

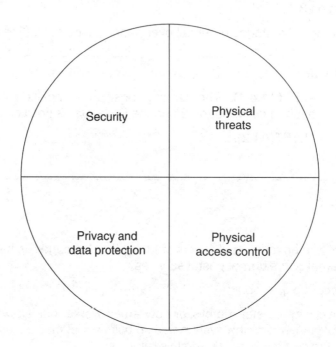

Introduction

This chapter deals with the **security** of information systems. We also look at how information systems may **threaten** personal **privacy** rights - and at legislation to prevent this.

Your objectives

After completing this chapter you should understand:

(a) The threats to computer systems.

(b) Common methods that aim to ensure the security of the MIS.

(c) Issues of confidentiality and compliance with statutes.

We looked at the security issues surrounding the Internet in Chapter 5.

NOTES

1 SECURITY

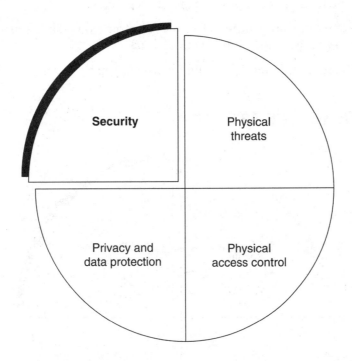

1.1 The responsibilities of ownership

If you own **something that you value** – you **look after it**. You keep it somewhere safe, you regularly check to see that it is in good condition and you **don't allow it to upset others**.

Information is a valuable possession and it deserves similar care.

Definition

> **Security**, in information management terms, means the protection of data from accidental or deliberate threats which might cause unauthorised modification, disclosure or destruction of data, and the protection of the information system from the degradation or non-availability of services.

Security refers to **technical** issues related to the computer system, psychological and **behavioural** factors in the organisation and its employees, and protection against the unpredictable occurrences of the **natural world**.

Security can be subdivided into a number of aspects.

(a) **Prevention**. It is in practice impossible to prevent all threats cost-effectively.

(b) **Detection**. Detection techniques are often combined with prevention techniques: a log can be maintained of unauthorised attempts to gain access to a computer system.

(c) **Deterrence**. As an example, computer misuse by personnel can be made grounds for dismissal.

(d)   **Recovery procedures**. If the threat occurs, its consequences can be contained (for example checkpoint programs).

(e)   **Correction procedures**. These ensure the vulnerability is dealt with (for example, by instituting stricter controls).

(f)   **Threat avoidance**. This might mean changing the design of the system.

2   PHYSICAL THREATS

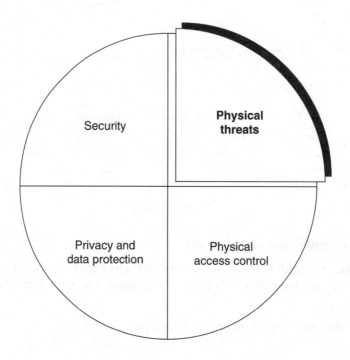

The **physical environment** quite obviously has a major effect on information system security, and so planning it properly is an important precondition of an adequate security plan.

2.1   Fire

Fire is the **most serious hazard** to computer systems. Destruction of data can be even more costly than the destruction of hardware.

A proper fire safety plan is an essential feature of security procedures, in order to prevent fire, detect fire and put out the fire. Fire safety includes:

(a)   **Site preparation** (for example, appropriate building **materials**, fire doors).

(b)   **Detection** (for example, **smoke detectors**).

(c)   **Extinguishing** (for example, **sprinklers**).

(d)   Training for staff in observing **fire safety procedures** (for example, **no smoking** in computer room).

2.2   Water

Water is a serious hazard. **Flooding** and water damage are often encountered following **firefighting** activities elsewhere in a building.

This problem can be countered by the use of **waterproof ceilings and floors** together with the provision of **adequate drainage**.

In some areas **flooding** is a natural risk, for example in parts of central London and many other towns and cities near rivers or coasts. **Basements** are therefore generally not regarded as appropriate sites for computer installation!

2.3 Weather

Wind, rain and storms can all cause substantial **damage to buildings**. In certain areas the risks are greater, for example the risk of typhoons in parts of the Far East. Many organisations make heavy use of **prefabricated** and portable offices, which are particularly vulnerable.

Cutbacks in maintenance expenditure may lead to leaking roofs or dripping pipes, which can invite problems of this type, and maintenance should be kept up if at all possible.

2.4 Lightning

Lightning and electrical storms can play havoc with **power supplies**, causing power **failures** coupled with power **surges** as services are restored.

One way of combating this is by the use of **uninterrupted (protected) power supplies**. This will protect equipment from fluctuations in the supply. Power failure can be protected against by the use of a **separate generator**.

2.5 Terrorist activity

The threat of bombs planted by **political terrorists** has beset UK organisations for many years. Other parts of the world such as the Middle East, central Europe and the US have been equally or worse afflicted. Political terrorism is the main risk, but there are also threats from individuals with **grudges.**

In some cases there is very little that an organisation can do: its buildings may just happen to **be in the wrong place** and bear the brunt of an attack aimed at another organisation or intended to cause general disruption.

There are some avoidance measures that should be taken, however.

    (a)   **Physical access** to buildings should be controlled (see the next section).

    (b)   Activities likely to give rise to terrorism such as **exploitation** of workers or **cruelty** to animals should be stopped.

    (c)   The organisation should consult with police and fire authorities about potential risks, and **co-operate** with their efforts to avoid them.

2.6 Accidental damage

People are a physical threat to computer installations because they can be **careless and clumsy**: there can be few of us who have not at some time spilt a cup of coffee over a desk covered with papers, or tripped and fallen doing some damage to ourselves or to an item of office equipment.

Combating accidental damage is a matter of:

    (a)   Sensible **attitudes** to office behaviour.
    (b)   Good office **layout**.

Activity 1

Your company is in the process of installing a mainframe computer. You have been co-opted onto the project team with responsibility for systems installation. What issues should be considered in relation to the risks of fire or flooding in the discussions about site selection?

3 PHYSICAL ACCESS CONTROL

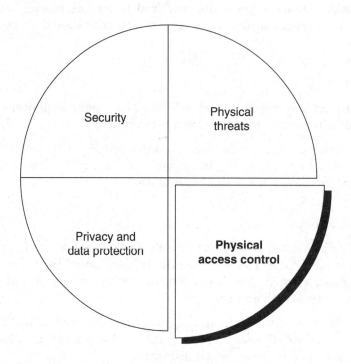

3.1 Controlling access

Access control aims to prevent intruders getting near the computer equipment or storage media. Methods of controlling human access range from:

(a) **Personnel** (security guards).

(b) **Mechanical devices** (eg keys, whose issue is recorded).

(c) **Electronic identification devices** (eg card-swipe systems).

Obviously, the best form of access control would be one which **recognised** individuals immediately, without the need for personnel, who can be assaulted, or cards, which can be stolen. However, machines which can identify a person's fingerprints or scan the pattern of a retina are too **expensive** for many organisations.

It may not be cost effective or convenient to have the same type of access controls around the whole building all of the time. Instead, the various **security requirements of different departments** should be estimated, and appropriate boundaries drawn. Some areas will be very restricted, whereas others will be relatively open.

Guidelines for security against physical threats which should be applied **within the office** include:

(a)   **Fireproof cabinets** should be used to store files, or **lockable metal boxes** for floppy disks. If files contain confidential data, they should be kept in a safe.

(b)   Computers with **lockable keyboards** are sometimes used. Computer terminals should be **sited carefully,** to minimise the risk of unauthorised use.

(c)   If computer printout is likely to include confidential data, it should be **shredded** before it is eventually thrown away after use.

(d)   **Disks** should not be left lying around an office. They can get lost or stolen. More likely still, they can get damaged, by spilling **tea or coffee** over them, or allowing the disks to gather **dust,** which can make them unreadable.

(e)   The computer's **environment** (humidity, temperature, dust) should be properly controlled. This is not so important with PC systems as for mainframes. Even so, the computer's environment, and the environment of the files, should **not be excessively hot**.

PINs

In some systems, the user might have an individual **personal identification number,** or PIN, which identifies him or her to the system. Based on the security privileges allocated, the user will be **allowed** access and editing rights to certain parts of the system, but **forbidden** access or editing rights to other parts.

Door locks

Conventional door locks are of value in certain circumstances, particularly where users are only required to pass through the door a **couple of times a day**. If the number of people using the door increases and the frequency of use is high, it will be difficult to persuade staff to lock a door every time they pass through it.

If this approach is adopted, a 'good' lock must be accompanied by a **strong door,** otherwise an intruder may simply bypass the lock. Similarly, other points of entry into the room/complex must be as well protected, otherwise the intruder will simply use a **window** to gain access.

One difficulty with conventional locks is the matter of **key control**. Inevitably, each person authorised to use the door will have a key and there will also be a master key maintained by security. Cleaners and other contractors might be issued with keys. Practices such as lending out keys or taking duplicate keys may be difficult to prevent.

One approach to this is the installation of **combination locks,** where a numbered keypad is located outside the door and access allowed only after the correct 'code', or sequence of digits has been entered. This will only be fully effective if users ensure the combination is kept confidential, and the combination is **changed** frequently.

Card entry systems

There is a range of card entry systems available. This is a more sophisticated means of control than the use of locks, as **cards can be programmed** to allow access to certain parts of a building only, between certain times.

These allow a high degree of monitoring of staff movements; they can for example be used instead of clock cards to record details of time spent on site. Such cards can be incorporated into **identity cards,** which also carry the photograph and signature of the user and which must be 'displayed' at all times.

Computer theft

A problem which is related to the problem of physical access control is that of equipment theft. As computer equipment becomes **smaller** and **more portable**, it can be 'smuggled' out of buildings with greater ease. Indeed much equipment is specifically **designed for use off-site** (for example laptops, notebooks, handhelds, bubblejet printers) and so control is not simply a question of ensuring that all equipment stays on site.

A **log of all equipment** should be maintained. This may already exist in basic form as a part of the fixed asset register. The log should include the **make, model** and **serial number** of each item, together with some other organisation-generated code which identifies the **department** which owns the item, the **individual** responsible for the item and its **location**. Anyone taking any equipment off-site should book it out and book it back in.

Computer theft may be carried out by persons who have official access to equipment. It may equally be carried out by those who do not. **Burglar alarms** should be installed.

Smaller items of equipment, such as laptop computers and floppy disks, should always be **locked securely away**. Larger items cannot be moved with ease and one approach adopted is the use of **bolts** to secure them to desks. This discourages 'opportunity' thieves. Larger organisations may also employ site security guards and install closed circuit camera systems.

Activity 2

Your department, located in an open-plan office, has five networked desktop PCs, a laser printer and a dot matrix printer.

You have just read an article suggesting that the best form of security is to lock hardware away in fireproof cabinets, but you feel that this is impracticable. Make a note of any alternative security measures which you could adopt to protect the hardware.

FOR DISCUSSION

What methods are used to control access to the premises of your place of work?

4 PRIVACY AND DATA PROTECTION

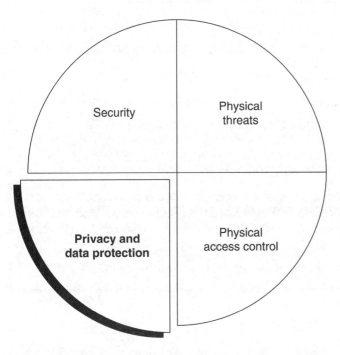

Definition

> **Privacy** is the right of the individual to control the user of information about him or her, including information on financial status, health and lifestyle (ie prevent unauthorised disclosure).

4.1 Why is privacy an important issue?

In recent years, there has been a growing popular fear that **information** about individuals which was stored on computer files and processed by computer could be **misused**.

In particular, it was felt that an individual could easily be harmed by the existence of computerised data about him or her which was inaccurate or misleading and which could be **transferred to unauthorised third parties** at high speed and little cost.

In the UK the current legislation is the **Data Protection Act 1998**. This Act replaced the Data Protection Act 1984.

In July 1995 the European Parliament adopted a new **Directive on Data Protection**, with two main purposes.

(a) To protect **individual privacy**. Previous UK law only applied to **computer-based** information. The directive applies to **all personal data, in any form.**

(b) To **harmonise data protection legislation** so that, in the interests of improving the operation of the single European market, there can be a **free flow of personal data** between the member states of the EU.

This directive **led to the introduction of the new Data Protection Act in 1998.**

BPP
PUBLISHING

4.2 The Data Protection Act 1998

The Data Protection Act 1998 is an attempt to protect the **individual**.

Definitions of terms used in the Act

In order to understand the Act it is necessary to know some of the technical terms used in it.

Definitions

Personal data is information about a living individual, including expressions of opinion about him or her. Data about other organisations (eg supplier or customer companies) is not personal data, unless it contains data about individuals who belong to those other organisations.

Data users are organisations or individuals who control the contents of files of personal data and the use of personal data which is processed (or intended to be processed) automatically - ie who use personal data which is covered by the terms of the Act.

A **data subject** is an individual who is the subject of personal data.

The data protection principles

There are certain Data Protection Principles which registered data users must comply with.

DATA PROTECTION PRINCIPLES

Schedule 1 of the 1998 Act contains the revised data protection principles.

1   Personal data shall be processed fairly and lawfully and, in particular, shall not be processed unless:

    (a)   At least one of the conditions in Schedule 2 is met (explained later in this chapter).

    (b)   In the case of sensitive personal data, at least one of the conditions in Schedule 3 is also met (explained later in this chapter).

2   Personal data shall be obtained only for one or more specified and lawful purposes, and shall not be further processed in any manner incompatible with that purpose or those purposes.

3   Personal data shall be adequate, relevant and not excessive in relation to the purpose or purposes for which they are processed.

4   Personal data shall be accurate and, where necessary, kept up to date.

5   Personal data processed for any purpose or purposes shall not be kept for longer than is necessary for that purpose or those purposes.

6   Personal data shall be processed in accordance with the rights of data subjects under this Act.

7   Appropriate technical and organisational measures shall be taken against unauthorised or unlawful processing of personal data and against accidental loss or destruction of, or damage to, personal data.

8   Personal data shall not be transferred to a country or territory outside the European Economic Area unless that country or territory ensures an adequate level of protection for the rights and freedoms of data subjects in relation to the processing of personal data.

The coverage of the Act

Key points of the Act can be summarised as follows.

(a) With certain exceptions, all **data users** have had to **register** under the Act with the **Data Protection Registrar**.

(b) **Individuals** (data subjects) are awarded certain **legal rights**.

(c) Data holders must adhere to the data protection principles.

Registration under the Act

The Data Protection Registrar keeps a Register of all data users. Each entry in the Register relates to a data user. Unless a data user has an entry in the Register he may not hold personal data. Even if the data user is registered, he must only hold data and use data for the **purposes** which are registered. A data user must apply to be registered.

The rights of data subjects

The Act establishes the following rights for data subjects.

(a) A data subject may seek **compensation** through the courts for damage and any associated distress caused by the **loss, destruction** or **unauthorised disclosure** of data about himself or herself or by **inaccurate data** about himself or herself.

(b) A data subject may apply to the courts for **inaccurate data** to be **put right** or even **wiped off** the data user's files altogether. Such applications may also be made to the Registrar.

(c) A data subject may obtain **access** to personal data of which he is the subject. (This is known as the 'subject access' provision.) In other words, a data subject can ask to see his or her personal data that the data user is holding.

(d) A data subject can **sue** a data user (or bureau) for any **damage or distress** caused to him by personal data about him which is **incorrect** or **misleading** as to matter of **fact** (rather than opinion).

Features of the 1998 legislation are:

(a) Everyone has the right to go to court to seek redress for **any breach** of data protection law.

(b) Filing systems that are structured so as to facilitate access to information about a particular person now fall within the legislation. This includes systems that are **paper-based** or on **microfilm** or **microfiche**. Personnel records meet this classification.

(c) Processing of personal data is **forbidden** except in the following circumstances.

(i) With the **consent** of the subject. Consent cannot be implied: it must be by freely given, specific and informed agreement.

(ii) As a result of a **contractual arrangement**.

(iii) Because of a **legal obligation**.

(iv) To **protect the vital interests** of the subject.

(v) Where processing is in the **public interest**.

(vi) Where processing is required to exercise **official authority**.

(d) The processing of '**sensitive data**' is forbidden, unless express consent has been obtained or there are conflicting obligations under employment law.

Sensitive data includes data relating to **racial origin, political opinions, religious beliefs,** physical or mental **health, sexual proclivities** and **trade union** membership.

(e)   If data about a data subject is **obtained from a third party** the data subject must be given.

(i)   The identity of the **controller** of the data.

(ii)   The **purposes** for which the data are being processed.

(iii)   **What data** will be disclosed and **to whom.**

(iv)   The existence of a right of subject **access** to the data.

(f)   Data subjects have a right not only to have a **copy of data** held about them but also the right to know **why** the data are being processed and **what is the logic** behind the processing.

Activity 3

Your Managing Director has asked you to recommend measures that your company, which is based in the UK, could take to ensure compliance with data protection legislation. Suggest what measures should be taken.

4.3   The Computer Misuse Act

The Computer Misuse Act 1990 was enacted to respond to the growing threat of hacking to computer systems and data. Hacking means obtaining unauthorised access, usually through telecommunications links (see Chapter 5). The Act can not prevent hacking, but by setting out offences and punishments it may deter some potential hackers.

Crime	Explanation
Unauthorised access	This means that a hacker, who, knowing he or she is unauthorised, tries to gain access to another computer system. It is the **attempt** which is the crime: the hacker's success or failure is irrelevant.
Unauthorised access with the **intention** of committing another offence	This results in **stricter penalties** than unauthorised access alone. However, it might be a suitable charge if a hacker had been caught in the early stages of a fraud.
Unauthorised **modification** of data or programs	In effect this makes the deliberate introduction of computer **viruses** into a system a criminal offence. However, this does not apply to the simple addition of data, just its corruption or destruction. Guilt is based on the **intention to impair** the operation of a computer or program, or prevent or **hinder access** to data.

Hackers were identified as one of the security issues associated with the Internet in Chapter 5.

Chapter roundup

- **Security** is the protection of data from accidental or deliberate threats and the protection of an information system from such threats.

- **Physical threats** to security may be natural or man made. They include fire,

- flooding, weather, lightning, terrorist activity and accidental damage.

- **Physical access control** attempts to stop **intruders** or other unauthorised persons getting near to computer equipment or storage media.

- Important aspects of physical access of control are **door locks** and **card entry systems**. Computer theft is becoming more prevalent as equipment becomes smaller and more portable. All computer equipment should be tagged and registered, and portable items should be logged in and out.

- **Privacy** is the right of the individual not to have information about him or her disclosed in an unauthorised manner.

- The **Data Protection Act 1998** is a piece of UK legislation which protects individuals about whom data is held. Both manual and computerised information must comply with the Act.

   ° Data users must register with the Data Protection Registrar and announce the uses to which the data will be put.

   ° The Act contains eight data protection principles, to which all data users must adhere.

- The **Computer Misuse Act 1990** was enacted in the UK to respond to the growing threat to computer systems and data from hacking. While it cannot *prevent* hacking, it recognises a number of offences and provides certain punishments.

Quick quiz

1 List six aspects of security. (See section 1.1)

2 How can fire be guarded against? (See section 2.1)

3 Should a mainframe computer be based in the basement? (See section 2.2)

4 How can problems caused by lightning be combated? (See section 2.4)

5 How can the risk of accidental damage be minimised? (See section 2.6)

6 List three methods of controlling access. (See section 3.1)

7 Define privacy. (See section 4)

8 What is a data user? (See section 4.2)

9 Summarise the eight data protection principles? (See section 4.2)

NOTES

Answers to Activities

1   (a)   **Fire**. Fire security measures can usefully be categorised as preventative, detective and corrective. Preventative measures include siting of the computer in a building constructed of suitable materials and the use of a site which is not affected by the storage of inflammable materials (eg chemicals). Detective measures involve the use of smoke detectors. Corrective measures may include installation of a sprinkler system, training of fire officers and good siting of exit signs and fire extinguishers.

    (b)   **Flooding**. Water damage may result from flooding or from fire recovery procedures. The main rule is to avoid siting the computer in a basement.

2   (a)   'Postcode' all pieces of hardware. Invisible ink postcoding is popular, but visible marking is a better deterrent. Soldering irons are ideal for writing on plastic casing.

    (b)   Mark the equipment in other ways. Some organisations spray their hardware with permanent paint, perhaps in a particular colour (bright red is popular) or using stencilled shapes.

    (c)   Hardware can be bolted to desks. If bolts are passed through the desk and through the bottom of the hardware casing, the equipment can be rendered immobile.

    (d)   Ensure that the organisation's standard security procedures (magnetic passes, keypad access to offices, signing in of visitors etc) are followed.

3   Measures could include the following.

    •   Obtain consent from individuals to hold any sensitive personal data you need.

    •   Supply individuals with a copy of any manual files you have about them if so requested.

    •   Consider if you may need to obtain consent to process personal data, on computer, paper or microfiche.

    •   Consider how you will be able to meet the notification requirements of the Directive in situations where you obtain personal data about individuals from third parties.

BPP
PUBLISHING

Assignment 8   **(40 minutes)**

An Institute of Systems Analysts is currently computerising its membership details. The membership system will store personal details about each member. The Institute intends to offer an employment service to companies, providing career details of members who may be suitable for job vacancies.

The system will have to comply with the principles of the Data Protection Act 1998. Three important principles of this Act are given below:

- Personal data shall be accurate and, where necessary, kept up-to-date

- Personal data held for any purpose shall not be kept longer than is necessary for that purpose

- Appropriate security measures shall be taken against unauthorised access to, or alteration, or disclosure of, personal data and against accidental loss or destruction of personal data

Tasks

(a) Explain why each of the three principles are important in the context of the membership system and describe how each principle might be enforced.

(b) The Institute is also worried about computer viruses. What is a computer virus? Briefly explain what measures might be taken to prevent a computer virus entering the membership computer system.

Note: Some material from Chapter 5 may be relevant.

Chapter 9 :
THE IMPACT OF THE IT REVOLUTION

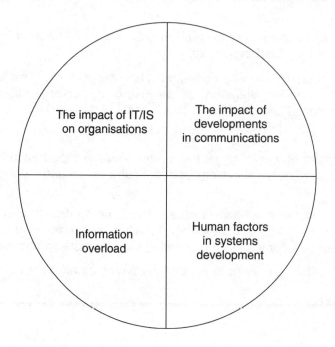

Introduction

The impact of technology on organisations and society in general over the last ten years has been dramatic.

This chapter explores some of the wider issues arising from this rapid change.

Your objectives

After completing this chapter you should be able to:

    (a)   Identify and evaluate the impact of developments in telecommunications.

    (b)   Recommend strategies for managing change in an IT context.

1 THE IMPACT OF INFORMATION TECHNOLOGY/ INFORMATION SYSTEMS ON ORGANISATIONS

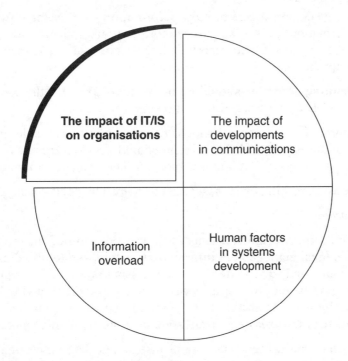

1.1 The organisational implications of office automation

Office automation in a variety of ways. Many of these are discussed at greater length elsewhere in this book; further points are outlined below.

Routine processing

The processing of routine data can be done in **bigger volumes,** at **greater speed** and with **greater accuracy** than with non-automated, manual systems.

The paperless office

There might be less paper in the office (but not necessarily so) with more data-processing done by keyboard. Data transmission is likely to shift from moving paper to moving data electronically. Files are more likely to be magnetic files or microform files rather than paper files.

Staff issues

Office staff will be affected by computerisation. The behavioural or 'human' aspects of installing a computer system are potentially fairly complex, but broadly speaking the following should be considered.

(a) Office staff must show a **greater computer awareness,** especially in areas of the office where computerisation is most likely to occur first - typically the accounts department.

(b) Staff must **learn new habits,** such as the care of floppy disks and VDUs, how to use keyboards, and remembering to make back-up copies of files for data security purposes.

(c) Managers may have to **learn to work at a workstation,** otherwise they will be less skilled than their staff.

Management information

The **nature and quality of management information** changes.

(a) Managers have access to **more information** - for example from a database. Information is also likely to be more accurate, reliable and up-to-date. The range of management reports is likely to be wider and their content more comprehensive.

(b) **Planning activities should be more thorough**, with the use of models (eg spreadsheets for budgeting) and sensitivity analysis.

(c) Information for **control** should be more readily available. For example, a computerised sales ledger system should provide prompt reminder letters for late payers, and might incorporate other credit control routines.

(d) Decision making by managers can be helped by **decision support systems**.

Organisation structure

The organisation structure might change. PCs give local office managers a means of setting up a **good local management information system,** and localised data processing. Multi-user systems and distributed data processing systems also put more data processing and information processing 'power' into the local office, giving local managers access to centrally-held databases and programs. Office automation can therefore encourage a **tendency towards decentralisation** of authority within an organisation.

On the other hand, multi-user systems and distributed data processing systems help **head office to keep in touch** with what is going on in local offices. Head office can therefore readily **monitor and control** the activities of individual departments, and retain a co-ordinating influence. It can therefore be possible for a head office to retain a co-ordinating (centralising) role, and to manage an expanding organisation with reasonable efficiency. Arguably, mega-mergers between large companies are only possible with the computerisation of management information systems.

Technological change

Office automation commits an organisation to **continual change**. The pace of technological change is rapid, and computer systems - both hardware and software - are likely to be superseded after a few years by something even better. Computer maintenance engineers are anyway often unwilling to enter into maintenance contracts for hardware which is more than a few years old, and so organisations are forced to consider a policy of regular replacement of hardware systems.

Customer service

Office automation, in some organisations, results in **better customer service**. When an organisation receives large numbers of telephone enquiries from customers, the staff who take the calls should be able to provide a prompt and helpful service if they have on-line access to the organisation's data files.

Open systems

Organisations develop computerised systems over a period of time, perhaps focusing on different functions at different times, and a number of consequences are likely to become apparent.

(a) They may have networks or other equipment supplied by a **range of manufacturers**.

(b) **Data is duplicated** in different areas of the business.

(c) Software may have become **inefficient** and **out of date**.

Open systems aim to ensure compatibility between different makes of equipment, enabling users to choose on the basis of price and performance. An open systems approach has a number of characteristics. The first is **vendor independence**. Applications can be 'ported' from one system to another. An open systems infrastructure supports **organisation-wide functions** and allows interoperability of networks and systems. Authorised users would be able to access applications and data from any part of the system.

2   THE IMPACT OF DEVELOPMENTS IN COMMUNICATIONS

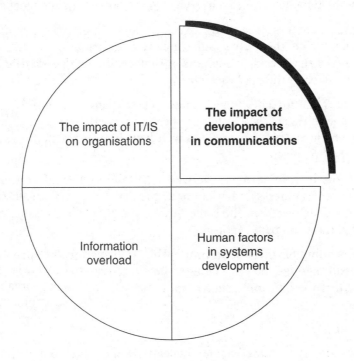

Communications technology is probably having a greater impact on organisational life than computers are at present. E-mail, videoconferencing and so on offer considerable benefits, but also have drawbacks.

We talked about the practical use and advantages of e-mail in Chapter 7. We will now explore some of the wider issues associated with the widespread use of e-mail.

2.1   The impact and possible drawbacks of e-mail

In spite of its advantages e-mail is not always the most suitable medium for communications. Possible shortcomings are as follows.

(a)   The nature of the **medium**. E-mail allows communication in the form of written words, numbers or graphics. Communication however entails more than just symbols of this type: it is estimated that perhaps 50% of the meaning that people are able to impart to each other in face-to-face conversation is non-verbal. Meaning is conveyed by body language and tone of voice to a much larger extent than is generally realised.

(b)   The nature of the **message**. People may wish to discuss detailed operational problems, whereas e-mail is best suited to short messages. Immediate two-way exchange of information is possible, but it will be hampered by the need to type in messages on a keyboard, especially if the users are not particularly competent typists.

(c) E-mail is a relatively **permanent** means of communication. It is likely that all exchanges are recorded and can be read by others. This may be undesirable from the point of view of users since some of their exchanges may be 'off the record', for example short-cuts that get round organisational bureaucracy, but solve operational difficulties.

(d) Senior managers may **value meetings** because they take place outside the main place of work, meaning that they are free of the usual daily pressures and better able to take an overview of the operations they manage.

(e) Large amounts of e-mail are likely to be received each day. Staff may quickly find themselves suffering from **information overload**. They will either spend excessive amounts of time dealing with e-mail or they will skip over much of the mail they receive and possibly miss important points.

(f) It is **uncomfortable to read** much more than a screen-full of information. Longer messages will either not be read properly or they will be printed out, in which case they may just as well have been circulated in hard copy form in the first place.

(g) **No distinction is made between different types of communication**. A short chatty message that might in the past have been scribbled on a Post-it note, is delivered in the same format and through the same medium as an important two page report.

(h) Depending on the system in use, the **facilities for data presentation** in an e-mail message may not be as sophisticated as they are in a spreadsheet or word processing application.

2.2 Voice mail

Voice mail (or v-mail) systems enable the **caller's message to be recorded at the recipient's voice mail box** similar to a mail box in an e-mail system. The main advantage of the system is that it only requires a telephone to be used. No typing or keying in is necessary. A voice mail message is basically a spoken memo: for the person sending the message it is much more convenient than typing it or having it typed and then faxing it.

Some companies allow their clients to use their voice mail network to leave messages for company representatives. The advantage of voice mail messages, compared to cellular radio or mobile communications, is that it is relatively cheap. However, it is not suitable for conversations. Voice mail can be used for different situations.

(a) To contact sales representatives 'in the field'.

(b) To leave messages in departments in **different time zones**.

(c) In organisations where employees might be **working away at a client's premises**.

2.3 Voice messaging

This is a kind of **switchboard answerphone** that takes the place of a human receptionist, or at least relieves the receptionist of the burden of dealing with common, straightforward calls. Typically, when a call is answered a recorded message tells the caller to dial the extension they want if they know it, or to hold if they want to speak to the operator. Sometimes other options are offered, such as 'press 2 if you want to know about X service and 3 if you want to know about Y'.

Such systems **work well if callers frequently have similar needs** and these can be accurately anticipated. They can be **frustrating** for callers with non-standard enquiries, however, and many people find the **impersonality** of responding to an answerphone unappealing. Badly set up systems can result in the caller being bounced about from one recorded message to another and never getting through to the person they want to deal with. Telecoms managers should regularly phone up their organisation from another location (or arrange for a 'mystery caller' to do so and give feedback) to see how well their call is dealt with.

FOR DISCUSSION

Most people have experienced the frustration of being stuck in what seems like an endless 'phone-loop'. What features should a well-designed automated call-managing system have?

EXAMPLE: INTERACTIVE VOICE RESPONSE (IVR)

Several pharmaceutical companies have installed sophisticated interactive voice response systems to deal with enquiries from doctors, chemists or patients. For example some allow the caller to press a number on their handset and have details of possible side effects sent back to them by fax.

2.4 Computer Telephony Integration (CTI)

Definition

> **Computer Telephony Integration (CTI)** systems gather information about callers such as their telephone number and customer account number or demographic information (age, income, interests etc).

The information is stored on a customer database and can be **called up and sent to the screen of the person dealing with the call**, perhaps before the call has even been put through.

Thus sales staff dealing with hundreds of calls every day might **appear to remember individual callers personally** and know in advance what they are likely to order. Order forms with key details entered already can be displayed on screen automatically, saving time for both the sales staff and the caller.

Alternatively a busy manager might note that an **unwelcome call** is coming in on the 'screen pop' that appears on her PC and choose to direct it to her voice mail box rather than dealing with it at once.

As another example, a bank might use CTI to prompt sales people with changes in share prices and with the details of the investors they should call to offer dealing advice.

3 HUMAN FACTORS IN SYSTEMS DEVELOPMENT

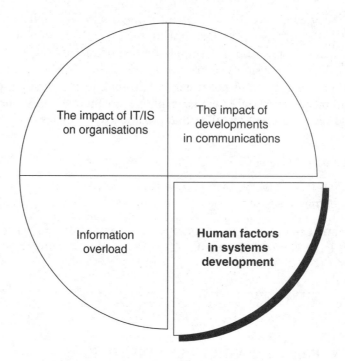

The impact of IT/IS on organisations

The impact of developments in communications

Information overload

Human factors in systems development

Information technology and information systems by their nature are areas that change constantly. This means that once automated (a big change in itself), a process is likely to undergo frequent changes in the future, as technology develops.

Whatever the scale of **systems development** – whether a manager who is not computer literate acquires a PC for departmental planning and ends up using it just to type memos, or whether a complex production planning and control system in a large manufacturing concern is computerised - there will inevitably be challenges.

3.1 Job security and status

Employees might think that a new system will **put them out of a job**, because the computer will perform routines that are currently done manually, and so reduce the need for human intervention. This threat to employment could unsettle the entire office staff.

Even when there is no threat of losing a job, a new system might make some staff, experienced in the existing system, feel that the value of their experience will be lost, causing a loss in their 'status' within the office.

In some cases, the resistance to a new system might stem from a fear that it will result in a loss in importance for a manager or even for a whole department. For example, the management of the department concerned might believe that the new system will increase access to information to others within the organisation.

Fear of change may in some cases lead to **disputes** and **disruptive behaviour**, such as:

(a) Interdepartmental disputes about access to information.
(b) A tendency to disregard the new sources of information.

3.2 Career prospects

In some instances, managers and staff might think that a new system will damage their career prospects by **reducing the opportunities for promotion**. When the effect of a system is to reduce the requirement for staff in **middle management and supervisory grades,** this could well be true.

On the other hand, today's successful manager should be able to adapt to information technology, and to develop a career means having to be flexible, accepting change rather than resisting it.

3.3 Social change in the office

New systems might **disrupt the established 'social system'** or 'team spirit' in the office. Individuals who are used to working together might be separated into different groups, and individuals used to working on their own might be expected to join a group.

Office staff used to moving around and mixing with other people in the course of their work might be faced with the prospect of having to work much **more in isolation** at a keyboard, unable to move around the office as much.

Where possible, therefore new systems should be designed so as to leave the 'social fabric' of the workplace undamaged. Group attitudes to change should then be positive rather than negative.

3.4 Bewilderment

It is easy for individuals to be confused and bewildered by change. The systems analyst must **explain the new system fully,** clearing up doubts, inviting and answering questions, etc from a very early stage in systems investigation onwards through the design stages to eventual implementation.

3.5 Fear of depersonalisation

Staff may be afraid that the computer will 'take over' and they will be **reduced to being operators** chained to the machine, losing the ability to introduce the 'human touch' to the work they do.

Dysfunctional behaviour might manifest itself in the **antagonism of operating staff towards computer specialists** who are employed to design and introduce a computer system. It might take the form of:

(a)   An **unwillingness to explain the details of the current system,** or to suggest weaknesses in it that the new system might eradicate. Since development staff need information from and participation by the operating staff to develop an efficient system, any such antagonism would impair the system design.

(b)   A **reluctance to be taught** the new system.

(c)   A **reluctance to help** with introducing the new system.

A new system will **reveal weaknesses** in the **previous system,** and so another fear of computerisation is that it will **show up exactly how poor and inefficient** previous methods of information gathering and information use had been.

If individuals feel that they are put under pressure by the revelation of any such deficiencies, they **might try to find fault with the new system** too. When fault-finding is not constructive - ie not aimed at improving the system - it will be dysfunctional in its consequences.

In extreme cases, dysfunctional behaviour might take a more drastic, aggressive form. Individuals might show a marked reluctance to learn how to handle the new equipment, they might be deliberately slow keying in data, or they might even damage the equipment in minor acts of vandalism.

3.6 Overcoming the human problems

Hostility to IT is as much an issue in management culture as it is in industrial relations. To overcome the human problems with systems design and implementation, management and systems analysts must recognise them, and do what they can to resolve them. The following checklist is suggested as a starting point.

(a) **Keeping staff informed.**

Employees should be kept fully informed about plans to install the new system, how events are progressing and how the new system will affect what people do.

(b) **Explanations.**

It should be explained to staff why 'change is for the better'.

(c) **Participation.**

User department employees should be encouraged to participate fully in the design of the system, when the system is a tailor-made one. Participation should be genuine.

(i) Their suggestions about problems with the existing system should be fully discussed.

(ii) The systems analyst's ideas for a new system should be discussed with them.

(ii) Their suggestions for features in the new system should be welcomed.

(d) **Nature of the work.**

Staff should be informed that they will be spared boring, mundane work because of the possibility of automating such work and so will be able to take on more interesting, demanding and challenging work.

(e) **Skills.**

Employees should be told that they will be able to learn new skills which will make them more attractive candidates either for internal promotion or on the external labour market. For example, experience with using databases or spreadsheet models could greatly enhance an office worker's experience.

(f) **Training.**

A training programme for staff should be planned in advance of the new systems being introduced. If there are to be job losses, or a redeployment of staff, these should be arranged in full consultation with the people concerned.

(g)   **Work patterns.**

Careful attention should be given to:

(i)   The design of work organisation.

(ii)   The developments or preservation of 'social work groups'.

(iii)   The inter-relationship between jobs and responsibilities in the new system.

(h)   **Planning.**

Change should be planned and managed. Reductions in jobs should be foreseen, and redundancies can be avoided if plans are made well in advance (eg staff can be moved to other job vacancies in the organisation). Training (and retraining) of staff should be organised.

(i)   **Help.**

Staff must have the option of contacting somebody who knows about the system to ask for help or advice.

(j)   **The analyst.**

When systems are designed in-house, the systems analyst should:

(i)   Ensure any proposed changes meet user requirements and are introduced following formal procedures.

(ii)   Build up a good working relationship with the people he or she has to work with.

(iii)   Work towards getting employees to accept change as a matter of course.

(iv)   Be willing to listen to and act on realistic user suggestions.

(k)   **Familiarisation.**

Users of the system must be given time to become familiar with it before it 'goes live'. Implementation by means of parallel running might be advisable.

4   INFORMATION OVERLOAD

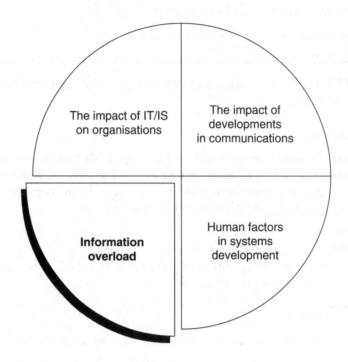

4.1   Too much information?

The volume of information a human being is required to process has increased dramatically over the last twenty years. Computing and communications developments have led to the capture and transmission of ever increasing amounts of information. However, only relevant information is useful. An excess of irrelevant information is harmful - a person is more likely to miss or miss-interpret vital information after being swamped with irrelevant material.

Technological developments such as e-mail adds to the problem. Now that everyone uses it, it often seems not much easier to get a reply to an e-mail message than to a phone message. In-boxes get stuffed with junk e-mails and are frequently ignored by their owners.

As a reaction to information overload new forms of software which carry out the extraction, organisation and selection of information for the **needs of the individual user** have been developed. A principal aim of the research and development going on in this area is to develop personalised information and message services, so that people receive the material which they require and nothing else.

There are two main approaches to avoiding information overload. Firstly, the **characteristics of the information passed to a human information processor** need to be considered. Secondly the **number of information sources** feeding an individual can be managed.

The qualities of information

The qualities of information were covered in Chapter 1. Refer to Chapter 1, Section 2.3.

4.2   Limiting the number of information sources

The approach taken to limiting the sources of information will depend on the situation. In some instances it may be sufficient to implement temporary measures to **delay** non-urgent information reaching a person at a particularly busy time. Other situations may require a **permanent change** to information flows. Some examples are shown in the following table.

Limiting tool	Comment
Delegate to colleagues	Communications regarding certain issues may be dealt with by others within the organisation. For example, routine client contact could be delegated to junior staff, and only strategic issues referred 'up the chain'.
Review reports received for duplication	Regular reviews of information received should be made. If information is duplicated one source should be deleted. The review should also consider what information would best be received together to aid interpretation.
Re-route incoming telephone calls	A secretary could be allocated to take telephone messages, putting through only calls of significance that require immediate attention. To be effective, the instructions concerning calls that should be put through, and how messages should be relayed must be specific.
Voice-mail	While voice-mail can be frustrating when trying to reach someone, it may be useful to temporarily divert calls to voice-mail when work pressures require no interruptions - and no other staff are available to divert calls to.
Filter incoming e-mail	E-mail programs have the ability to review and re-direct messages based on the message content, priority, sender and/or intended recipients. Non-selected messages may be copied to a selected person, or redirected to a non-urgent inbox to be dealt with later.
Use an Internet news-clipping service	A person may face a constant stream of industry related journals. These should be reviewed for relevant information - a time-consuming process. However, a news-clipping service could review relevant journals and newspapers on the Internet, and forward via e-mail copies of articles that meet user-defined criteria.
Use intelligent agents	These are programs that the user can set-up to perform tasks such as retrieving and delivering relevant information and automating repetitive tasks.

Activity 1

Think about the information you receive and the information you produce in your work or study. Could the volume of information or the number of information sources be reduced without reducing the quality of information?

Chapter roundup

- The world has changed rapidly over the past thirty years. The **communications age** has arrived, and is still developing at a rapid rate.

- The Internet has the potential to bring about significant **changes in society** as a whole.

- Technology has also had a significant impact **on the way organisations are structured**, and on the roles of staff.

- Communications developments are making **geographically dispersed structures** increasingly viable.

- The almost **constant change** prevalent in organisations and society as a whole is placing greater **demands on people**.

- People are now exposed to greater volumes and sources of information than ever before. If information flows aren't managed efficiently, **information overload** may occur.

Quick quiz

1   Why are automated systems more efficient in the processing of routine data? (See section 1.1)

2   What staff issues need to be considered in an office being computerised? (See section 1.1)

3   List five possible disadvantages of e-mail. (See section 2.1)

4   Distinguish between voice mail and voice messaging. (See sections 2.2-2.3)

5   What does CTI stand for? (See section 2.4)

6   Outline the concerns staff may have when a new system is proposed. (See section 3.1-3.5)

7   How may those fears be overcome? (See section 3.6)

8   Can too much information hinder understanding? (See section 4.1)

9   List five methods that could reduce the number of information flows reaching an individual. (See section 4.2)

Answers to Activities

1   You may be able to use some of the techniques explained in section 4.2 to combat information overload. Be careful not to 'cut' information that is needed immediately and is not provided from another source.

Assignment 9 (40 minutes)

The JB Company provides specialist information services to organisations which do not have either the staff expertise or financial resources to maintain an information services department. Information provided ranges from weather forecasts (both regional and national) to railways and airlines, stock market information to stockbrockers and general news bulletins to major TV and radio stations.

Information is collected by the JB Company through a variety of systems including Internet monitoring, reports from employees from any of the 129 offices worldwide, on-line links to stock markets, reviews of newspapers from around the world and monitoring of news reports on TV and radio. Most information is reviewed and summarised by a team of specialist information analysts, so only the appropriate highlights are sent to clients.

Mr A is one of the senior account managers in the JB Company. It is his responsibility to ensure that his clients receive appropriate information, and that he is up-to-date with information supplied to those clients should queries arise. Mr A therefore receives information through a variety of sources including:

- E-mail messages from staff and clients. Between 30 and 40 e-mails are received on a typical day.

- Telephone calls from information analysts and clients. The information analysts require strategic decisions regarding the information to provide to clients, while clients may telephone to request clarification on information received.

- Detailed information from the company's databases and Intranet connections.

- Detailed information from Internet sites which Mr A reviews every hour or so during the day.

- Verbal reports from staff who prefer to see Mr A face-to-face rather than use the telephone or e-mail systems.

Mr A believes that he is suffering from information overload.

Tasks

(a) Explain what is meant by information overload, and how this could affect the working efficiency of Mr A.

(b) Describe the IT and manual procedures that could be used to reduce the information overload on Mr A.

ANSWERS TO ASSIGNMENTS

Assignment 1

(a)   Data is a collection of raw facts, whereas information is data that has been processed into a form that is both usable and **meaningful** to the end user.

The case study describes the planned introduction of a customer loyalty card by a supermarket chain. Clearly a retail operation of this type would wish to collect, as a minimum, data in the following categories: customer name, customer's address, purchases made, quantities bought, times and dates that the purchases were made. By suitable **processing of this data** it is possible for the supermarket chain to be able to **produce information** that will allow it to predict:

(i)   The purchasing patterns of individual customers

(ii)   The purchasing patterns of a given store's customers

(iii) The purchasing patterns of the chain's customers on a national and regional basis, identifying purchasing trends such as, say, a shift to low-sugar foodstuffs

(iv)   The level of demand for a given product on a daily basis for individual stores, regions and nationally

(v)   The identity of regular, occasional and lapsed customers

It may also be desirable for the chain to collect further data such as customer's income level, age, marital status, number of children and so on. Processing this data appropriately would allow the store to gather information that could be used to target in-store offers to a particular group of customers who have a common lifestyle.

From personal experience the difference between data and information can be illustrated by the following example. A set of accounts for a company could be given as list of data items such as: postage, 0.50, 19/11/2000, chair, 75, 6/7/2000 and so forth. Such lists of data items are unrelated and convey little or no meaning to the reader. Is the postage fifty pounds, fifty pence, fifty dollars or fifty cents? Is it an item of expenditure or income? Was it the only amount spent on postage during the year? What relation, if any, does 'postage' hold to 'chair'?

However, if the data items are processed and presented as total amounts within categories such as assets, liabilities, income and expenditure the result is a report that provides meaningful information for a particular type of user such as, say, a company secretary.

(b)   In most, if not all organisations, **information is used to control operations** and responses to the current business climate and as an aid to future planning. It should be noted that these activities are usually highly inter-dependent. For example, a response to a given scenario often impacts upon future plans for the organisation, while long-term planning has implications both for operational control issues and the responses made by the organisation.

Anthony has produced a hierarchical model of decision making based upon three elements: strategic planning, management control and operational control. We can use **Anthony's model** to demonstrate how the information produced can be used to aid decision making in this case. Before doing so it is necessary to make the point that all information must be timely, accurate, complete and relevant to the user. Information that does not fulfil any of these criteria cannot be considered to be good information and will, at best, hinder the decision-making process and, at worst, cause the wrong decisions to be taken. Provided that the data is collected by Cheap 'n' Cheerful in a systematic and thorough manner (with suitable checks and controls used) we may assume that the **data** will be current, accurate and complete. In consequence we can assume that that the **information** derived from the collected data will also be current, accurate and complete, with the proviso that it must also be relevant and useful to the user.

Strategic planning is concerned with formulating long-term aims and objectives for Cheap 'n' Cheerful. The case study mentions that the chain is attempting to diversify into non-food goods such as clothing and electrical goods. This is an example of a strategic decision taken by the organisation. One way that the information gathered could be used to aid decision making at this level is by the identification of the customer base and, hence, suitability of new lines as saleable goods within the chain of shops. Such information can also be used as an aid to marketing new product lines on both global or niche levels.

Decisions made at the level of **management control** are concerned with providing and allocating resources within the organisation to meet the aims and objectives of the organisation. The information gathered by the chain can be used to identify the needs and wants of customers at a particular store or in a region. Levels of customer satisfaction or dissatisfaction can be also measured and management can take the appropriate action to increase customer satisfaction and, hopefully, sales.

At an **operational level** shopping patterns of customers can be identified. The store manager can then use this information to schedule the number of staff required to serve the expected number of shoppers. Similarly, the demand for a product on a daily, weekly or seasonal basis can be predicted thus allowing the correct quantity to be ordered and storage and shelf space to be allocated.

Assignment 2

An intranet uses software and other technology originally developed for the Internet on internal company networks. An intranet comprises an organisation-wide web of internal documents that is familiar, easy to use and comparatively inexpensive. Each employee has a browser enabling him or her to view information held on a server computer and may offer access to the Internet.

The main objective of an intranet is to provide easy access to information that helps people perform their jobs more efficiently. Many roles require increased access to knowledge and information. An intranet is a way of making this knowledge readily available.

Other objectives are outlined below.

To encourage the use of reference documents. Documents on-line are more likely to be used than those stored on shelves, especially if the document is bulky (for instance procedure manuals).

To create a sense of organisational unity. An intranet 'pulls together' in a co-ordinated fashion information from disparate parts of an organisation. It may be the only visible way some parts of a large organisation are linked.

The provision of an Intranet within CC plc should result in better provision of information by:

- Ensuring consistency in information held and provided to clients. The intranet will enable one set of data to be held and accessed by all 10 offices.

- Providing easy access to a larger pool of data. Information that managers previously 'kept to themselves' will be available to others.

- The intranet-Internet link will ensure the most up-to-date planning information is available. It would be useful to develop an intranet page complied from appropriate websites. (This must be kept up to date.)

Assignment 3

(a) A computer feasibility study is intended to evaluate the appropriateness of computerising an application which had been accomplished manually or by using another system. It is intended to accomplish three things.

    (i) Assess the information processing requirements found in an application.

    (ii) Identify and investigate various alternatives which could satisfy the requirements identified.

    (iii) Inform management about the options and the costs, benefits, technology, risks, labour implications etc of each.

(b) **Each of the three sections or stages in a feasibility study may be justified.**

The assessment of needs provides the foundation for all other analysis. Here one identifies what tasks are to be computerised and quantifies the requirements in terms of volume, speed, accuracy, security etc. Without this understanding of what the system will need to do it is most unlikely that an effective or economical system will be obtained. This phase looks primarily at the **functions to be performed** and the required performance standards.

Given the required tasks and performance standards a **variety of alternatives** may be reviewed and compared. The objective here is to keep an open mind and consider a full range of options. Several options might satisfy all performance criteria and then be referred to management for a final decision, perhaps with a recommendation for one.

The information provided to management on costs, benefits, etc allows them to consider any systems acquisition, development or upgrade. This information allows systems to be **compared more effectively**.

(c) The study would normally be carried out by a **feasibility study team**. This team would include:

    (i) Someone from the software house having a detailed knowledge of computers and systems design

    (ii) One or two senior managers having a detailed knowledge of the workings and staff of the departments affected

    (iii) An **accountant** to carry out cost-benefit analyses of the proposed system, and prepare a detailed budget for installing it

(d) The best solution for the organisation is best identified through a thorough **investigation**, as would be provided by the feasibility study. The understanding gained by studying an existing system and formalising its operation **will aid in designing** a new system, or in **developing a specification** for one. Any purchase of a package without first developing **a sound specification** is likely to leave the company with a system unsuited to their needs.

(e) Four factors which would justify **introducing a new computer system** for production planning and scheduling would be these.

    (i) **Better control over the handling of customer orders** so that these are dealt with more expeditiously.

(ii) **Improved production planning** to allow the company to fill orders more effectively and deliver production in a more timely fashion.

(iii) **Inventories will be more closely monitored** and improved production planning will reduce the amount of work in progress. These reductions will reduce the company's need for working capital to yield a direct improvement in cash flow.

(iv) By improving its production scheduling it will find that **better use of both equipment and labour will result**. This will improve profits, perhaps significantly.

Assignment 4

(a) Three reasons why an analyst should **investigate and document** the current business system are outlined below.

To obtain user input

It is important that users are involved in the systems project because they will be able to provide valuable information concerning how the system works. In any systems project, it is easy for users to be 'left out' of the systems development; this may lead to rejection of any final system as well as providing lack of confidence in the systems analysts and their team. Involving users in data collection will involve them in the project as well as helping to ensure that the systems documentation is as complete as possible.

To understand the problems with the current system

Any new system will be designed, not only to meet new design specifications, but also to **alleviate problems with the current system**. If information about the current system is not obtained, then any problems in the systems will not be identified and so the new system will not be written to remove those problems. Areas that may be improved by this analysis include introducing better controls, easier to follow work methods and clearer systems design and documentation.

Decrease new development work

Many of the features that are in the current system will be used in the new system. Providing documentation of the system will **help the analyst to understand** how the old system works. Having obtained this information, the analyst can decide whether or not to use the functionality of the current system or to write new software. If the current system information is not obtained then this decision cannot be made and software development work for the new system may take longer.

(b) Methods and models that can be used in investigating and documenting the current business system will include:

Questionnaires

Using a questionnaire means that the same set of questions can be sent to a large number of staff **quickly and cheaply**. The questionnaire can be tested prior to distribution to ensure that the questions are complete and accurate, while the large sample size can attempt to obtain a good representation of the target audience. However, the response rate from questionnaires can be quite low (typically 30%), and it is not always possible to remove ambiguity in the questions asked or ask additional questions to expand on the comments made.

Interviews

Interviews tend to provide better information than questionnaires because the interview is an **interactive** process. The interviewer can asked additional questions to check the understanding of the interviewee, while the interviewee can check understanding of questions being asked to avoid any ambiguity. The interviewee may also be able to provide additional insights into the current system, which will not have been provided in a questionnaire. However, interviews can take a long time to organise and carry out which may limit their use.

Flowcharting

A flowchart is a **pictorial representation** of the document flows in a system. This can be very useful for checking the accuracy of information collected about the current system because the user will be able to see document and the departments that the documents move through on the flowchart itself. Flowcharts do, however, take a long time to produce and can be difficult to modify should they be incorrect. Also, although they show document flows clearly, they may not show exactly what information is needed to complete a document or where pure data flows (as opposed to document flows) are in the system. Other techniques may therefore be required to provide a complete picture of the current system.

Decision tables

A decision table will help the analyst show in **tabular format**, all the different outputs that can be obtained from a set of inputs. For example, customers may be awarded discounts based on the product purchased, the value of transactions made during the year and even the day of the week that the product is purchased on. A decision table can be constructed to show the **different combinations of factors** ('conditions' in the table) that will result in specific discount amounts ('actions'). This table can be validated by discussions with users to provide the analyst with confidence that all appropriate discount rates have been accounted for. The decision table assists programming work by making potentially difficult decisions easier to understand.

Assignment 5

REPORT

To: The Directors, AB plc

From: A Consultancy

Date: 30 March 20X1

Subject: Configuration options for the new computer systems

Terms of reference and executive summary

Further to your letter of instruction of 28 January 20X1, we were asked to produce a report for the half year board meeting specifying the reasons for and against using different computer systems. The current manual system was documented, and a number of options discussed with management. This report summarises the results.

The two options being actively considered are the following.

(a)   A central mainframe with terminals at each depot (the 'centralised system').

(b)   Minicomputers such as IBM AS/400s at each regional depot connected together over a network (the 'distributed system').

255

The second option, using a network of minicomputers, is better suited to the organisation's requirements. We recommend that this option be actively considered.

Centralised system

This will involve setting up a room at head office or a central location in which to run the mainframe-based system. This room will have to have good environmental control, together with security. In addition you should consider establishing a back-up computer facility which could be used in the advent of a breakdown on the main machine.

The centralised system will be linked to the depots by leased telephone lines. These will be expensive to run, but in the case of the larger depots will provide voice facilities, allowing you to save on the current voice phone charges.

The system will require specialised staff to run it. This will impose a new department on the organisation, and will result in an additional headcount of approximately fifteen. There will be a small loss of jobs at the regional level.

Advantages of the centralised system

(a) Having a central up-to-date set of data which will be accessible by all depots.

(b) Maintaining a single set of data, which will eliminate inconsistencies in data used for different purposes.

(c) Providing the head office with the centralised control which the current system lacks, as freight can be tracked from one depot to another.

(d) Setting up of a centralised and specialised DP team with expert knowledge focused in one department.

Disadvantages of a centralised system

(a) Capital costs. The back-up system and the high cost of the main computer are both major factors.

(b) Operating costs, for example, high telecommunications costs.

(c) The problem of being entirely dependent on one machine. Computers do fail, and the impact on the business of the central machine failing would be great.

Distributed system

This would involve installing a minicomputer at each region, and another at the head office. Although space would have to be found for each, they can be installed in standard office environments. Staff would have to be trained at each site, and these staff could provide back up in the event of others being on leave or sick.

Advantages

(a) Keeping the responsibility for the system with the regions. This would encourage the regions to 'own the system' and would also encourage them to keep the data accurate.

(b) In the event of any single machine failing it would be reasonably easy to acquire another on a short-term basis.

(c) Lower communication costs, as most line usage will be within individual regions.

(d) Speed of processing is improved and local priorities can be better satisfied.

Disadvantages

(a) Control would require on-going monitoring and effort. A supervisor at each region would have to be designated as the person responsible for ensuring procedures were adhered to.

(b) Installation of, and training on, new versions of software would take more time and cost more. In addition, the logistics of installing later releases of software would require careful monitoring.

(c) Capital costs, involving acquisition of six minicomputers, will be high, although with phased regional implementation this can be spread more easily than a single mainframe purchase.

(d) Operating costs, particularly staff costs, will be high as it will be necessary to maintain a certain level of expertise at each regional office, resulting in some duplication.

Assignment 6

(a) There are many ways in which the spreadsheet could be improved, including (*three of*) the following.

 (i) Headings should be added to the columns and labels to the rows. An overall title would also be useful, if it is not clear from the title of the file itself or of this worksheet.

 (ii) A consistent size and type of font should be used, For instance the figures in cells A2 and C1 to C5 are in a different font size and type to the other figures.

 (iii) The figures should be given to a consistent number of decimal places. Some are stated to nil decimal places, others to one decimal place and others to two. If one figure has to be stated to two decimal places, then all of them should be.

 (iv) It may be easier to read the figures if they are presented in comma format.

 (v) The totals in cells A5 to C5 should be given top and bottom borders to make it clear that they are totals.

 (vi) The formula in cell A1 is badly constructed. A better approach would be to enter the figure in cell A4 as a negative number and use the formula =SUM(A1:A4) in cell A5. This avoids the need to type in all the cell references individually and minimises the risk of entering the wrong sign(s) in the formula.

 (vii) The totals in cells B5 and C5 are simply the sum of the four figures above them. In other words, unlike in column A, the figures in row 4 are not treated as negative. This may be what was intended, but there is some doubt because the approach is not consistent.

(b) A spreadsheet model should be built as follows.

 (i) All the variables in the problem should be identified and entered in separate cells in one part of the spreadsheet with clear labels. This is the input area.

 (ii) In a different part of the spreadsheet the formulae that act upon the variables should be entered. This is the calculation area. It may also be necessary to use functions such as 'IF' functions.

 (iii) The results of the calculations may be displayed in a third output section of the spreadsheet. In less complicated cases this may be combined with the calculation area.

Once built in this way the model could be used to carry out 'what if' analysis. The values of the input variables could be altered as appropriate and the impact of such changes could be instantly evaluated.

Assignment 7

The term electronic mail or email is used to describe various systems of sending data or messages electronically over networks.

Network users who are registered as e-mail users will be given a user identity and allocated a password allowing them to enter the e-mail system. On selecting the relevant menu option, a user will be presented with a series of basic facilities such as:

- Create a new message
- Edit an existing message
- Read a new message
- Send a message
- File a message
- Move or refile a message
- Retrieve a message
- Delete a message

If the user wishes to send a memo to a user in another office they choose the New Message option. He or she will be presented with a screen that resembles a word processor. Using this a message can be created. Basic word processing functions (edit, wraparound, manipulation of blocks etc) are standard. Once the message is prepared it can be saved. If the user wishes to send it immediately, the recipients e-mail address must be entered in the correct field. Here, details of addressee and other people to whom copies should be sent are entered. There may be options for requesting a delivery receipt and/or a read receipt. The message can then be sent and at the same time given a name and filed.

The filing system consists of a number of folders; each can be used for messages relating to a different customer or subject.

Once a message has been sent, it is received by a central computer which allocates disk storage as a 'mailbox' for each user and signals the arrival of messages to recipients. Clearly the successful working of the system depends on regular checking of 'in-trays' by all users. Systems may offer a two-tier mailbox for each user, one private and one public, accessible by all users or by users in a particular grade/department.

Housekeeping controls may exist, for example, to ensure that any letter 'binned' can be retrieved for a certain period before being irretrievably lost, and that any letters not filed in a folder are binned after a certain period. The network administrator will monitor users who fail to use the system or to clear their in-trays, so that they can be 'retrained' or taken off the system. If mail is to be sent or copied to non-users, hard copy can be printed at a network printer.

Advantages

Electronic mail has the following advantages over paper-based postal services.

(a)   Speed. A message reaches its recipient within fifteen minutes of being sent.

(b)   Reliability. Receipts can be generated to confirm delivery and that the addressee has read the message.

(c)   Economy. There is an IT cost to email, but stationery, photocopying postage and courier costs and time can be saved.

(d)   Security. Each user's filing system, inbox and outbox is password protected.

(e)   Flexibility. Existing documents can be 'attached' to memos and transmitted with them (eg spreadsheets, reports etc).

Assignment 8

(a) *Personal data shall be accurate and, where necessary, kept up-to-date.*

This principle means that data on the membership system must be correct at all times; the implication is therefore that as members details change, so the data on the membership system must be amended to reflect those changes. If the data is not correct, then the Institute could provide prospective employers with incorrect information, which may prejudice a member's chances of obtaining a job. This action would reflect badly on the Institute and could result in legal action by the member in some situations.

The Institute can try ensure that the membership information is correct, firstly by recording where the original information came from. If members provide inaccurate information concerning their qualifications or salary then the Institute can hardly be found liable for any inaccuracies in this information. To check the accuracy of the current information on the system, a printout of the record for each member can be made and that member asked to confirm that the details are correct. Again, if the member signs the form then it is good evidence that membership information is accurate.

Personal data shall not be kept longer than is necessary for its purpose.

Personal data can only be collected and stored for specific purposes. When the reason for collecting that information has been expired, then there is no longer any need to maintain that information. If the data is maintained on the membership system then there is a danger that the data will be disclosed accidentally with other valid information. To avoid this situation occurring, data that is no longer required should be deleted from the membership system.

In this situation, it is likely that salary information will only be required where members are applying for jobs via the Institutes job vacancy service. When a member has found a suitable job, then the salary information is no longer required and should be deleted from the membership system.

The other situation where data should be deleted is where a person ceases to be a member of the Institute, possibly due to non-payment of subscription or resignation. If either of these situations occurs, then the details of that member should be removed. This action may be under manual control or by the computer system itself. After a specified amount of time, such as three months, if the subscription has not been paid, then the member's information can be automatically deleted from the system.

Appropriate security measures shall be taken against unauthorised access to, or alternation, or disclosure of, personal data and against accidental loss or destruction of personal data.

This principle means that the personal data must be kept secure, and that the data can only be accessed and disclosed in accordance with the reasons for which it is being held. To ensure that this principle is maintained, then adequate security must be placed around the membership system. The security system must be sufficient to stop not only removal of the data, but also access and amendment of that data on the company's system.

The following controls will be needed to meet these requirements.

Security over access to the membership system including door locks and security passes to enter buildings.

Access controls on computer systems such as passwords.

Appropriate backup of the data to guard against accidental or even deliberate destruction of the data at the Institute.

(b)   A computer virus is a computer program that has been written to cause deliberate damage to a computer's software, hardware or both. Various measures can be taken to stop a virus entering the computer system.

Running appropriate anti-virus software. The anti-virus software will automatically scan any programs and data files being transferred onto the computer and provide an alert to the user if a virus is detected. Steps can then be taken to disinfect the file before any damage is done to the computer receiving that file.

Ensuring that staff are aware of the need to ensure viruses are not transferred onto the computer. This can be carried out by having all staff signing conditions of employment which include the clause that only authorised software may be used on company computers. This will help to eliminate the spread of viruses via e-mail attachments or other unauthorised programmes.

Ensuring that the computer maintaining the membership system is not attached to a network. This control will be effective where only a limited number of people are required to access the system, and they are located in one office. Providing network or intranet access increases the risk of viruses being spread because they can easily be transferred from other computers on the network.

Assignment 9

(a)   **Information overload**

Information overload occurs when a person receives more information than they can efficiently process. There are two main causes of information overload. An individual may simply receive too much information, or the number of information sources may be too numerous.

Mr A at JB Company suffers from both of these causes. He receives so much information from a variety of sources (e-mail, telephone, face to face, reports) that he is swamped.

The efficiency of Mr A

Information overload reduces Mr A's efficiency as he has to sift through all this information to find what is relevant. There is so much information that some vital information may be missed.

Too much of his time is spent gathering and deciphering information. Between 30 and 40 e-mails are received from staff and clients each day. Some of these may contain vital information requiring urgent action, others could be classified as low priority and others could be 'junk' mail. Widely circulated messages from both within and outside the organisation may be of little interest or value to Mr A, but identifying these messages is time consuming.

Mr A will also receive telephone queries from information analysts and clients. In many cases, queries will have to be answered at once, and therefore he should be in a position to give quick and accurate replies. He also receives information from Internet sites every hour or so. Dealing with queries and digesting further information is time-consuming. It also seems that Mr A will have very few periods of uninterrupted work, which is likely to lead to inefficient work practices.

Mr A needs to delegate query handling to a suitably able colleague, as the potentially large number of clients are taking up too much of his time. (His workload needs to be reduced, as discussed in part (b) of this answer).

(b) To tackle the problem of information overload affecting Mr A the following areas need to be considered:

- Mr A's role and responsibilities

- The information he needs to fulfil his role and responsibilities

- The possible use IT and other measures to manage information

Manual procedures

The number of clients that Mr A is responsible for will be a driver of the amount of information he needs to do his job. If Mr A is able to delegate client queries his workload and the amount of information flowing to him would reduce.

Mr A seems to be involved in many operational tasks. A personal assistant could be appointed to him, who would have the responsibility of handling incoming telephone calls and e-mail. There is a risk here that, unless this assistant is suitably qualified in this respect, there may be times when information required by Mr A does not get through to him.

Depending on the number of clients Mr A deals with, it may not be realistic to receive so may telephone calls, requiring him to retain the information mentally, as is also the case where face-to face discussions are held. It would seem that he simply has too many queries to deal with, hence the need to re-organise his responsibilities, so that he deals only with those decisions that it is necessary for him to make.

IT procedures

Mr A reviews Internet sites every hour or so. This alone could be more than enough work for one person, depending on the number of sites visited. This may already be being done by the analysts. Alternately, an Internet monitoring agent could do this job and automatically advise Mr A when particular events occur, such as information being updated.

The JB Intranet could enable information to be retrieved and searched on using client name or client code. This would make information retrieval more efficient.

E-mail messages could be prioritised so that Mr A is aware primarily of only the urgent ones. Defining 'urgent', however, could be a problem; if left to the sender, there is the danger that all messages could be classed as urgent, and hence the effectiveness of the system would be compromised.

Clients could also be given access to the Intranet where they could access the information or also be re-directed to other sites containing additional information. There may also be areas where support systems such as Expert Systems (ES) or Executive Information System (EIS) may be employed.

The EIS could present Mr A with summarised high level information so he does not have to sift through low level data. If Mr A required lower-level detail he could 'drill down' to view it.

GLOSSARY AND INDEX

Acceptance testing: testing of a system by the user department, after the system has passed its systems test.

Adaptive maintenance: taking account of anticipated changes in the processing environment.

Bespoke software: designed and written for a specific situation or task. The package may be written 'in-house' or by an external software house.

Business system: collection of people, machines and methods organised to accomplish a set of specific functions.

Centralised architecture: involves all computer processing being carried out on a single central processor. The central computer is usually a mainframe or minicomputer designed to be accessed by more than one user.

Client: machine which requests a service from the server.

Closed system: system which is isolated from its environment and independent of it.

Computer supported co-operative: term which combines the understanding of the way people work in groups with the enabling technologies of computer networking and associated hardware, software, services and techniques.

Computer Telephony Integration (CTI): system which gathers information about callers such as their telephone number and customer account number of demographic information (age, income, interests etc).

Corrective maintenance: carried out in reaction to a system failure, for example in processing or in an implementation procedure, its objective is to ensure that systems remain operational.

Critical success factors: a few key areas of the job where things must go right for the organisation to flourish.

Data: raw material for data processing.

Datamining: software looks for hidden patterns and relationships in large pools of data.

Datawarehouse: consists of a database, containing data from various operational systems, and reporting and query tools.

Data dictionary: an index of data held in a database, used to assist in maintenance and any other access to the data.

Data redundancy: duplication of data items.

Data subject: an individual who is the subject of personal data.

Data table: used by some spreadsheet packages (for example Excel) to refer to a group of cells that show the results of changing the value of variables.

Data users: organisations or individuals who control the contents of files of personal data and the use of personal data which is processed automatically.

BPP PUBLISHING

NOTES

Database: a collection of structured data which may be manipulated to select or sort some or all of the data held.

Decision support system: combine data and analytical models or data analysis tools to support semi-structured and unstructured decision making.

Distributed architectures: spread the processing power throughout the organisation at several different locations. With modern distributed systems, the majority of processing power is held on numerous personal computers (PCs) spread throughout the organisation.

Documentation: this includes a wide range of technical and non-technical books, manuals, descriptions and diagrams relating to the use and operation of a computer system.

Dynamic testing: is testing that is performed by executing a program. It involves running the program and checking the results are as expected.

Electronic commerce: is the process of trading on the Internet.

Electronic mail (E-mail): used to describe various systems of sending data or messages electronically via a telephone or data network and a central computer.

Encryption: this involves scrambling the data at one end of the line, transmitting the scrambled data, and unscrambling it at the receiver's end of the line.

Environmental scanning: this is used to describe the process of gathering external information.

Executive support system: pools data from internal and external sources and makes information available to senior managers in an easy-to-use form. ESS help senior managers make strategic, unstructured decisions.

Extranet: this is an intranet that is accessible to authorised outsiders.

Feasibility: a formal study to decide what type of system can be developed which meets the needs of the organisation.

Feedback: this is defined as modification or control of a process or system by its results or effects, by measuring differences between desired and actual results.

File conversion: this means converting existing files into a format suitable for the new system.

Filtering: this means removing 'impurities' such as excessive detail from data as it is passed up the organisation hierarchy.

Fourth generation language (4GL): this loosely denotes software which enables systems designers to 'write' a program with little programming knowledge.

Groupware: is a term used to describe a collection of IT tools designed for the use of co-operative or collaborative work groups.

Information: is data that has been processed in such a way as to be meaningful to the person who receives it.

Information technology: this is used to describe the coming together of computer technology with data transmission technology, to revolutionise information systems.

Integrated software: this refers to programs, or packages of programs that perform a variety of different processing operations.

Integration testing: involves testing two or more software units to ensure they work together as intended. The output from unit integration testing is a debugged module.

Internet: is a global network connecting millions of computers.

Intranet: is an internal network used to share information.

Knowledge: this is information within people's minds.

Knowledge management: this describes the process of collecting, storing and using the knowledge held within an organisation.

Management information system (MIS): this converts data from internal and external sources into information, and communicates that information in an appropriate form to managers at all levels.

Methodology: procedures, techniques, tools and documentation aids which help systems developers in their efforts to implement a new information system.

Network: an interconnected collection of autonomous processors.

Office automation system: are computer systems designed to increase the productivity of data and information workers.

Off-line testing: this describes the testing of a software program carried out on machines not controlled by the central processor.

Off-the-shelf package: this is one like Microsoft Word or Sage Line 50, that is sold to a wide range of users and intended to handle the most common user requirements.

On-line testing: this is carried out under the control of the principal central processor.

Open system: is a system connected to an interacting with its environment.

Perfective maintenance: is carried out in order to perfect the software, or to improve software so that the processing inefficiencies are eliminated and performance is enhanced.

Performance testing: is conducted to evaluate the compliance of a system or component with specified performance requirements.

Personal data: is information about a living individual.

Pivot table: this is an interactive table that summaries and analyses data from lists and tables.

Privacy: this is the right of the individual to control the use of information about him or her.

Prototype: is a model of all or part of a system, built to show users early in the design process how it will appear.

Remote access: this describes access to a central computer installation from a terminal which is physically 'distant'.

Security: this means the protection of data from accidental or deliberate threats.

Server: is a machine which is dedicated to providing a particular function or service requested by a client.

Spreadsheet: is an electronic piece of paper divided into rows and columns. It provides an automated way of performing calculations.

Static testing: describes the process of evaluating a system or component based on its form, structure and content. The program or process is not executed or performed during static testing.

Structured data: this is a collection of data, any item of which can be used as a subject of enquiry.

System: this is a set of interacting components that operate together to accomplish a purpose.

Transaction processing system: performs and records routine transactions.

Unit testing: means testing one function or part of a program to ensure it operates as intended.

Usability testing: is conducted to establish the relative ease with which users are able to learn and use a system.

User acceptance testing: is carried out by those who will use the system to determine whether the system meets their needs. These needs should have previously been stated as acceptance criteria. The aim is for the customer to determine whether or not to accept the system.

Virus: is a piece of software which infects programs and data and possibly damages them and which replicates itself.

Word processing: is a program used primarily to produce text based documents.

Workflow: is a term used to describe the defined series of tasks within an organisation to produce a final outcome.

Absolute cell references, 175
Access control, 224
Accessibility, 114
Accidental damage, 223
Accounting records, 22
Active cell, 165
Adaptive maintenance, 98
Analysing data, 201
Application Service Providers (ASP), 142
Areas of feasibility, 58
Artificial intelligence (AI), 40

Batch processing, 19
Benchmark tests, 133
Bespoke development risks, 135
Bespoke software, 124, 130, 134
Beta version, 88
BIOS, 118
Bit, 117
Bugs, 99
Bulletin boards, 146
Business system, 4
Byte, 117

Cache, 118
CAD, 35
Call-back buttons, 146
Card entry systems, 225
CASE tools, 63
CAST, 87
CD-R, 123
Cell, 160
Central processing unit (CPU), 116
Central server, 127
Centralised architecture, 125
Chip, 117
Class, 65
Client applications, 128
Client workstation, 127
Client-server architecture, 127
Closed system, 6
Computer Aided Software Testing, 87
Computer Output on Microfilm (COM), 121
Computer Telephony Integration (CTI), 239
Computer theft, 226
Consultancies, 24
Control systems, 6
Controlling, 8
Corporate applications, 128
Corporate server, 127

Corrective maintenance, 98
Cost-benefit review, 102
Costs, 59
Critical success factors, 76
    building, 76
    data sources, 77
    monitoring, 76
Ctrl + Z, 166
Cursor, 160
Customer Relationship Management (CRM), 46
Customer service, 236
Cut, Copy and Paste, 156

Data, 8
    unauthorised modification of, 230
Data capture, 22
Data dictionary, 70
Data dictionary, 138
Data mart, 44
Data processing, 139
Data Protection Act 1984
    registration under, 229
Data Protection Act 1998, 228
Data protection principles, 228
Data subject, 228
    rights of, 229
Data tables, 187
    one-input, 187
    two-input, 189
Data users, 228
Data warehouse, 43
Data warehousing, 43
Database, 68, 69, 71, 205
    data dictionary, 70
Database administrator (DBA), 70
Database and sorting facilities, 138, 179
Database systems, 68
Datamining, 47
Decentralised architecture, 126
Decision making
    information for, 9
Decision support systems (DSS), 17, 21
Departmental server, 127
Depersonalisation, 241
Diagnostic software, 139
Digital Versatile Disk (DVD), 123
Direct changeover, 96
Distributed architecture, 126
Document image processing, 36, 37
Documentation, 93, 99
Door locks, 225
Downsizing, 115
DVD, 123

Dynamic testing, 86

E-commerce, 145
Economic feasibility, 59
Effectiveness, 103
Efficiency, 103
EFTPOS, 120
Electronic commerce, 145
Electronic data interchange (EDI), 24
Electronic mail, 217, 244
Electronic office communication, 237
E-mail, 217, 244
Encryption, 147
Entering data, 165
Enterprise Resource Planning (ERP), 46
Enterprise servers, 115
Environment, 6
Environmental scanning, 24
EPOS, 120
Executive Support System (ESS), 16
Expert systems, 35, 40
Explicit knowledge, 33
External data sources, 23
External information, 23
Extranet, 38

F2 (edit), 166
Facilities Management (FM), 141
Feasibility study, 55, 57, 58
Feasibility study report, 61
Feedback, 7
File conversion, 94
Filtering, 7
Find and Replace, 157
Fire, 222
Firewall, 147
Floppy disks, 122, 226
Formatting, 157
Formflow, 37
Formulae, 173
Fourth generation language (4GL), 64
Frequently-Asked Questions (FAQs), 146
Function key F2 (edit), 166
Function key F4, 175
Fuzzy logic, 35, 42

Gigabytes, 117
GigaHertz, 117
Go To (F5), 165
Groupware, 35, 36

Handheld, 116
Hard disks, 122
Hardware, 136
Hardware monitors, 104
Headings and layout, 172
Help desk, 139
Heuristics, 40
Hoax, 147
Hyperlinks, 37

Impact analysis, 71
Incremental approach, 142
Information
    benefits, 32
    value of, 30
Information
    qualities of, 8
Information as a commodity, 30
information bureaux, 24
Information centre (IC), 75, 139
Information services, 24
Information society, 30
Information superhighway, 145
Informix-4GL, 66
Inkjet printers, 122
Input devices, 118
Inputs, 5
Insourcing, 144
Integrated circuit, 117
Integrated software, 153
Integration, 20
Intel, 117
Intelligent agents, 35, 245
Interactive voice response (IVR), 239
Internal data sources, 22
Internal information, 23
Internet, 24, 76
Interpreting data, 201
Intranets, 35, 38
Investment workstation, 35, 39

Java, 64
Joint applications development, 75
Joint venture sourcing, 142

Keyboard, 119
Keyword search, 146
Kilobytes, 117
Knowledge, 32
Knowledge management, 32
Knowledge Work Systems (KWS), 18, 39

Knowledge Workers, 18
KWS, 18, 39

Laptop, 116, 226
Laser printers, 122
LEFT function, 198
Libraries, 24
Local applications, 128
Local area network (LAN), 125
Local server, 127
Locks, 225
LOOKUP function, 199
Lotus Notes, 36
Magnetic Ink Character Recognition (MICR), 119
Maintenance
  causes of, 99
  types of, 98
Management information, 236
Management information system, 15, 16
Manual systems, 114
Megabytes, 117
Megahertz (MHz), 117
Membership functions, 43
Memory, 117, 118
Methodologies
  evaluating, 62
Methodology, 61
  advantages and disadvantages, 62
Metrics, 104
Microfilm, 121
Microsoft Access, 205
MID function, 198
Motherboard, 117
Mouse, 119
Multiple sourcing, 142
Mutidimensinal data analysis, 43

National Computing Centre, 55
Natural language, 40
Neural networks, 42
Notebook, 226

OAS, 18
Object-oriented Programming, 64
OCR, 120
Office Automation System (OAS), 18, 36
Off-line testing, 85
Off-the shelf packages, 124, 130, 135
On line analytical processing (OLAP), 44, 45
On-line processing, 19

On-line testing, 85
Open system, 6, 237
Operating systems, 124
Operational feasibility, 58
Operational information, 10
Optical character recognition, 120
Optical mouse, 119
Organisation structure, 236
Organisational learning, 33
Output devices, 121
Outputs, 5, 101
Outsourcing, 141

Paperless office, 235
Parallel running, 96
Paste special, 200
Peer-to-peer architecture, 129
Perceptive systems, 40
Perfect information, 11
Perfective maintenance, 98
Performance indicators, 77
Performance measurement, 9
Performance testing, 86
Personal data, 228
Personal identification number (PIN), 225
Phased changeover, 97
Physical access control, 224
Pilot operation, 97
PIN, 225
Pivot tables, 201
Planning, 8
Portables, 116, 226
Post-implementation review, 105
Post-implementation review report, 105
Prestel, 24
Primary cache, 118
Print option, 156
Printers, 122
Privacy, 227
Problems
  identification of, 55
Processes, 5
Processor, 116
Productivity, 114
Program testing, 84
Programming tools, 124
Project managers, 106
Prototype, 66
Prototyping, 66

Quality of output, 115
Queries, 208

NOTES

Query languages, 73
QWERTY, 119

RAM, 117
Random Access Memory (RAM), 117
Rapid applications development (RAD), 75
Ratios, 77
Read-Only Memory (ROM), 118
Recording transactions, 9
Reference works, 24
Relative cell references, 175
Remote diagnostic software, 139
Report production, 73
Responsibilities of ownership, 221
Review and maintenance, 56
RIGHT function, 198
Robotics, 40
Rockart, 76
ROM, 118

Scanners, 120
Security, 221
    physical threats, 222
Selecting
    non-adjacent data, 180
Server types, 127
Service bureaux, 141
Social change, 241
Software
    integrated software, 153
Software choice, 131
Software monitors, 104
Sorting facilities, 184
Speed of processing, 114
Spell-checking, 157
Spreadsheets, 158
Static analysis, 86
Static testing, 86
Status checking, 146
Steering committee, 138
Strategic information, 9
Strategic level information system, 16
Stress testing, 87
Structured data, 68
Structured walkthroughs, 74
Sum function, 160
Support centre, 139
System
    boundary, 5
    component parts, 5
    environment, 6
System changeover, 96

System logs, 104
System requirements
    changes in, 99
System testing, 84, 85, 88
Systems analysis, 55
Systems design, 56
Systems development lifecycle
    drawbacks, 56
Systems development life-cycle, 55
Systems development staff, 139
Systems implementation, 56
Systems integration, 141
Systems investigation, 55
Systems theory, 4

Tacit knowledge, 33
Tactical information, 9
Tape storage, 123
Tape streamers, 123
Technical feasibility, 58
Technical manual, 93
Technological change, 236
Terms of reference, 57
Testing, 84
Testing plan, 88
Testing strategy, 88
Time share, 141
Title bar, 151
Topic, 24
Touch screens, 120
Touch sensitive pads, 119
Trackball, 119
Training, 91
Training plan, 91
Transaction Processing System (TPS), 18
Transactions, 8

Unauthorised modification of data, 230
Undoing actions (Ctrl + Z), 166
Unit integration testing, 85
Unit testing, 85
Usability testing, 87
User acceptance testing, 86
User groups, 76
User involvement, 74
User manual, 93
User validation, 74
Users of information, 29
Utilities, 124

VDU, 119, 122
Virtual Reality, 35

PUBLISHING

NOTES

Virtual reality systems, 39
Virus, 146
Visual Display Unit (VDU), 119
Voice mail, 238
Voice messaging, 238

Water, 222
Website, 145
Weighted rankings, 133
Windows, 119
Wizards (interview style interface) and
  intelligent algorithms, 146
Word, 153
Word processing, 152
Workflow, 37
World Wide Web (www), 145

X axis and Y axis, 182

Zip disk, 122
Zip drive, 122

ORDER FORM

Any books from our HNC/HND range can be ordered in one of the following ways:

- Telephone us on **020 8740 2211**

- Send this page to our **Freepost** address

- Fax this page on **020 8740 1184**

- Email us at **publishing@bpp.com**

- Go to our website: **www.bpp.com**

We aim to deliver to all UK addresses inside 5 working days. Orders to all EU addresses should be delivered within 6 working days. All other orders to overseas addresses should be delivered within 8 working days.

BPP Publishing Ltd
Aldine House
Aldine Place
London W12 8AW
Tel: 020 8740 2211
Fax: 020 8740 1184
Email: publishing@bpp.com

Full name: _____

Day-time delivery address: _____

_____

_____ Postcode _____

Day-time telephone (for queries only): _____

Please send me the following quantities of books:

Core

		No. of copies	Price	Total
Unit 1	Marketing (8/00)		£7.95	
Unit 2	Managing Financial Resources (8/02)		£7.95	
Unit 3	Organisations and Behaviour (8/00)		£7.95	
Unit 4	Organisations, Competition and Environment (8/02)		£7.5	
Unit 5	Quantitative Techniques for Business (8/02)		£7.95	
Unit 6	Legal and Regulatory Framework (8/02)		£7.95	
Unit 7	Management Information Systems (8/02)		£7.95	
Unit 8	Business Strategy (8/00)		£7.95	

Option

Units 9-12	Business & Finance (8/02)		£10.95	
Units 13-16	Business & Management (1/01)		£10.95	
Units 17-20	Business & Marketing (1/01)		£10.95	
Unit 21-24	Business & Personnel (1/01)		£10.95	

	Sub Total	£

Postage & Packaging

UK : Course book £3.00 for first plus £2.00 for each extra	£
Europe : (inc. ROI) Course book £5.00 for first plus £4.00 for each extra	£
Rest of the world : Course book £20.00 for first plus £10.00 for each extra	£

	Grand Total	£

I enclose a cheque for £_____ (cheque to BPP Publishing Ltd) or charge to Access/VISA/Switch

Card number: ☐☐☐☐☐☐☐☐☐☐☐☐☐☐☐☐☐☐☐☐☐☐

Issues number (Switch only): _____

Start date: _____ Expiry date: _____

Signature _____

REVIEW FORM & FREE PRIZE DRAW

We are constantly reviewing, updating and improving our Course Books. We would be grateful for any comments or thoughts you have on this Course Book. All original review forms from the entire BPP range, completed with genuine comments, will be entered into a draw on 31 January 2003 and 31 July 2003. The names on the first four forms picked out will each be sent a cheque for £50.

Pippa Riley
HNC/HND Range Manager
BPP Publishing Ltd, FREEPOST, London W12 8BR

Full name: _____

Address: _____

_____

_____ Postcode _____

Where are you studying?

Where did you find out about BPP range books?

Why did you decide to buy this Course Book?

Have you used our texts for the other units in your HNC/HND studies?

What thoughts do you have on our:

- Introductory pages

- Topic coverage

- Summary diagrams, icons, chapter roundups and quick quizzes

- Discussion topics, activities and assignments

The other side of this form is left blank for any further comments you wish to make.

Please give any further comments and suggestions (with page number if necessary) below.

FREE PRIZE DRAW RULES

1　　Closing date for 31 January 2003 draw is 31 December 2002. Closing date for 31 July 2003 draw is 30 June 2003.

2　　Restricted to entries with UK and Eire addresses only. BPP employees, their families and business associates are excluded.

3　　No purchase necessary. Entry forms are available upon request from BPP Publishing. No more than one entry per title, per person. Draw restricted to persons aged 16 and over.

4　　Winners will be notified by post and receive their cheques not later than 6 weeks after the relevant draw date.

5　　The decision of the promoter in all matters is final and binding. No correspondence will be entered into.